MW01041848

Paul J. J. Welfens

Market-oriented Systemic Transformations in Eastern Europe

Problems, Theoretical Issues, and
Policy Options

With 20 Figures and 29 Tables

Springer-Verlag

Berlin Heidelberg New York
London Paris Tokyo
Hong Kong Barcelona
Budapest

PD Dr. Paul J. J. Welfens
University of Münster
Department of Economics
Universitätsstr. 14-16
W-4400 Münster, FRG

ISBN 3-540-55793-8 Springer-Verlag Berlin Heidelberg New York Tokyo
ISBN 0-387-55793-8 Springer-Verlag New York Berlin Heidelberg Tokyo

This work is subject to copyright. All rights are reserved, whether the whole or part of the material is concerned, specifically the rights of translation, reprinting, reuse of illustration, recitation, broadcasting, reproduction on microfilms or in other ways, and storage in data banks. Duplication of this publication or parts thereof is only permitted under the provisions of the German Copyright Law of September 9, 1965, in its version of June 24, 1985, and a copyright fee must always be paid. Violations fall under the prosecution act of the German Copyright Law.

© Springer-Verlag Berlin · Heidelberg 1992
Printed in Germany

The use of registered names, trademarks, etc. in this publication does not imply, even in the absence of a specific statement, that such names are exempt from the relevant protective laws and regulations and therefore free for general use.

2143/7130-543210 – Printed on acid-free paper

For Pusia and Jola

PREFACE

After more than four decades of a socialist command economy model countries in Eastern Europe have embarked upon a systemic transformation process to market economy systems. The former Council of Mutual Economic Assistance (CMEA) was dissolved in 1991 and in late 1991 the USSR's history ended with the reemergence of Russia and the creation of the Commonwealth of Independent States. The politico-economic upheavals in Eastern Europe that began in 1989 (in Poland: 1980) - 200 years after the French Revolution - have developed their own dynamics, including the semantic reorientation, namely as most observers rediscovered that what used to be dubbed Eastern Europe (in European parlance this included the USSR) is really central and eastern Europe.

The socialist system collapsed for many reasons, and certainly the announcements made in Moscow in the 1960s to surpass Western Europe in terms of per capita output look strange today. In the East as in the West it had been overlooked that income growth was achieved in Eastern Europe at the expense of wealth destruction or neglect of wealth building: natural resources were increasingly exhausted and reinvestments not made (implying a "consumption" of the capital stock).

The social costs of producing goods in socialism were not correctly perceived by planners and the society. Indeed there were intertemporal external effects of production meaning that part of the social cost of production would become visible only many years after the date of production. If producing more steel today causes rising toxic waste, sludge and emissions that reduce the value of buildings today and the possibility of future production, the social costs are much higher than indicated by the momentary use of production factors. The Stalinist command economy model was an anarchy of cost accounting in which nobody really knew what the social costs (the opportunity costs for society) really were. The cost of environmental clean-up in Eastern Germany is at least $ 150 bill. which is more than its gross national product in 1989, the German Democratic Republic's last year of 40 years of existence. If one assumes a capital-output ratio of 4:1 and that 50 % of the capital stock in the former GDR is obsolete (often because buildings are physically decrepit or because of relative price shocks) one gets an impression about the enormous loss of wealth that was programmed by socialist production, but for decades did not become visible.

Socialism deemphasized individualism, focussed on mass production in state-owned firms and relied on a monopolistic party system whose bureaucrats were expected to organize production in accordance with central planning. In the end the USSR was the biggest producer of steel, tractors and energy worldwide, but its citizens enjoyed a very modest standard of living; moreover, with the state-restricted access to news and the outside world there was very limited information about the situation of their socialist islands and their position relative to the capitalist islands. In Eastern Europe life expectancy was shorter, weekly working hours much longer and holidays (a "time income") much shorter than in Western Europe so that the East-West income gap is much greater than suggested by a pure comparison of per capita incomes. Stock variables, namely wealth and money, have been neglected in socialist theory and by economic policy. Only in the Western world did the 1970s bring a theoretical shift towards conducting economic analysis less in terms of flow variables than in terms of stock variables (monetarism was influential in this). However, it seems that both in the West and in the East there is still a lack of political emphasis on preserving and increasing the value of assets: Wealth is more important than income in the long term.

Eastern Europe is now returning to market-oriented systems, and certainly - as shown by West European economies - life in a market economy is not without problems and pitfalls. However, for individuals, firms and society learning is easier, at least in an open society with a functional political and economic system.

Before a market economy is established one has to go through a difficult transition stage in which income and wealth positions of many could reduce. In most cases this should not be considered as indicating insufficient achievements and performance because the qualifications nurtured under socialism are of such limited use in a market economy. If one has trained for and successfully participated in the Winter Olympics one should not be disappointed if a sudden invitation to participate in the Summer Olympics does not bring too many medals.

The last time that Eastern Europe, excluding the USSR was a market economy as a whole was neither prosperous nor stable. In the interwar years there were many national and international economic problems in Eastern Europe, later compounded by the World Depression of 1929-1936. Turning back to market-oriented models of production and distribution raises many questions not only for Eastern Europe, but for the Old World in general.

With the advent of the Asian NICs and the Japanese model of capitalism, the world of industrialized market economies and the spread of international organizations, the capitalist world economy had changed in a different way than MARX and other socialist protagonists had anticipated. Eastern Europe's reintegration into the network of market economies takes place under conditions that are different from the time when Russia and later smaller East European countries left the market system. There are many theoretical issues that are associated with systemic transformation in Eastern Europe. This book can offer only some modest element of analysis, but we hope to demonstrate that Western economics can usefully be applied to the problems of transformation. Elements of a spontaneous economic order may emerge in Eastern Europe; however, lack of constructivism and deliberate system design could mean in certain countries falling back into the historical tracks and problem settings of the interwar years.

With the opening up to the Western world Eastern European economies are experiencing a series of economic shocks: price shocks, interest rate shocks, technology shocks and, in the case of the smaller ex-CMEA countries, an energy price shock - these countries face the problem of strongly reduced energy supplies from the ex-USSR and all countries have to live with the switch to much higher energy prices. For Eastern Europe the series of adjustment impulses certainly is stronger than the OPEC price shocks were for the rich OECD countries in the 1970s; then industrial output declined by 5-12 percent in major countries in one or two years, and the import price increase itself implied a resource transfer abroad of 2-3 percent of GNP. Adjustment problems and distribution conflicts were serious enough in Western Europe.

In the East European transition the magnitude of adverse macroeconomic developments in terms of the fall of industrial output and the degree of obsolescence of the capital stock is at least two or three times as much; the external environment, characterized by high West European real interest rates and moderate growth prospects for the OECD countries in the early 1990s is not very favorable either. Limited external support is available for a tremendous historical experiment, namely for transforming socialist systems into functional market economies. Despite these challenges Eastern Europe could become a new European growth pole if one could assume that it catches up with its own historical economic potential that was so poorly used and developed by the command economy model.

Eastern Europe could be a new growth pole in Europe and could - in an optimistic scenario - even catch up with the dynamics of Asian newly industrializing countries whose economic development has been so impressive since the 1970s and the 1980s (in 1991 Hong Kong's exports exceeded those of the USSR and Taiwan as well as Korea came close to the Soviet figures). However, a less optimistic scenario would be that East European economies rather follow Latin American disaster settings of the 1980s when sharply rising foreign debt, falling real income and wages as well as rising unemployment brought economic hardship and political instability for a whole region - finally spilling over into the OECD countries where banks, firms and governments faced adjustment needs, too.

When the market economy model has to be (re-)introduced one rediscovers some old advantages of this approach to organizing economic transactions in a decentralized way via private firms competing in contestable markets. A competitive market economy operates on the basis of the interplay of the invisible hand of anonymous markets and the visible handshake of innovative firms. With a well-defined framework of institutions, property rights and rules the market system generates enormous per capita output, sustaining growth and a never-ending creative development with many structural changes facing millions of individuals. From the perspective of socialist systems these changes mean facing the chilly wind of capitalist uncertainties to which not too many people in Eastern Europe are used.

It will take much time to change institutions, attitudes and organization modes in an evolutionary process; it also took decades to channel the dynamics of the capitalist industrial revolution in Western Europe 150 years ago. Only individual achievement was honored in early capitalism, but modern market economies have developed at least some ethics and institutions - in Europe state social policies as well - that are supposed to mitigate social and economic hardship; and finally, competition policies have been enacted in market economies that prevent excessive market power and generate competitive pressure that brings prices down and encourages innovative producers. Eastern European economies have to take many steps at the same time, and an adequate sequence, timing and consistency of reforms will be difficult to achieve.

This book is a contribution to the theory of systemic transformation and comparative economic systems analysis. We will consider the major impulses for the collapse of the socialist economies in Eastern Europe (chapter A), raise the question which challenges systemic transformation will pose (chapter B), which issues arise in the context of the prime tasks of organizing privatization and stimulating foreign investment (chapter C), what foreign economic liberalization could mean for Eastern Europe (chapter D) and finally what some of the global dimensions of the East European transition could be (chapter E). We can, of course, only touch upon some selected areas and issues; however, we hope to focus on some of the most important ones. As regards major issues I do not claim that my analysis is perfectly right or ideal in any way; however, the purpose is to make a contribution to the ongoing discussion in the economics profession about the problems and options in the transformation in Eastern Europe. Moreover, one may expect that the economics profession as such will correctly identify and analyze all major problems of the East European transition.

My interest in Eastern Europe dates back to two projects at the University of Duisburg where in the 1980s young economists as well as established professors developed a series of joint Polish-German research projects. I owe a sustaining professional interest in the East European developments to these projects and the personal contacts that emerged within this framework. In a strict sense, however, this book is based on several papers that have influenced various chapters. My paper "Allocation, Pricing and the Socialist Equilibrium Shadow Economy" presented in Pavia in 1988 (annual conference of the ASSOCIAZIONE ITALIANA PER LO STUDIO DEI SISTEMI ECONOMICI COMPARATI) is in part the basis of chapter A, whereas other elements have been developed in the following two years. Chapter B dates back to a paper whose first draft I wrote in Washington DC in 1990/91, when I enjoyed the hospitality of the AICGS/The Johns Hopkins University. Chapter C is a revised draft of a paper presented at the conference Eastern European Economies in Transition, organized by the Society of Government Economists in Washington D.C. in March 1991. Chapter D is based on a paper presented at the German Studies Association's annual conference in Los Angeles in 1991 as well as a paper (Some New Aspects of Foreign Economic Liberalization in the East European Transition) which I presented at a World Bank seminar in March 1992. The final chapter is from a presentation to a group of NATO reserve officers in Bonn in early 1992.

I am immensely indebted to all the people with whom I could discuss my views, approaches and ideas. Special thanks go to Piotr Jasinski, Oxford University, to Peter Murrell (comments on C) at the University of Maryland, to Martin Schrenk at the World Bank and to Helga Hessenius, UC Berkeley, who offered comments on certain chapters or the papers mentioned or supported my project with controversial discussions. The University of Münster where I held a professorship in Economics/Eastern European Economies in 1991/92 offered a stimulating environment for my research. However, this book would not have been completed without the assistance of Cornelius Graack, University of Münster, and the reliable and strong editing support of Tim Yarling, George Washington University. Finally, I am most grateful to my wife who encouraged my project with endless patience, tolerance and a good sense of humor.

Münster, May 1992

Paul J.J. Welfens

Table of Contents

A: Characteristics of the Centrally Planned Economy and Systemic Collapse

1. The Rise and Fall of Marxist Theory and Socialism

Eastern Europe is facing a complex transformation process after the collapse of socialism in the last quarter of this century. This collapse is the result of an intellectual legacy and ideology which initially came from the West. The West, however, was prudent enough not to follow the ideas of MARX and ENGELS, but developed different answers to the obvious misery of the Industrial Revolution and the dynamics of market economies with their contradictions of fast, volatile and sometimes unstable financial markets on the one hand, and, slow factor markets and goods markets on the other hand. After a brief analysis of the crisis of socialism, we will turn in chapters B-E to theoretical and practical questions of systemic transformation.

The idea of this book is to describe and analyze the crisis of socialist economies in Eastern Europe and explore the requirements, problems and success-promising options for a market-based reform in Eastern Europe which is meant to include the (ex-)USSR. For economists there are numerous theoretical challenges as there are many urgent practical problems to be solved in the unique systemic transformation of socialist economies. Certainly, this book can address only some major issues and topics, but it is intended to integrate some recent research, to apply economic theory to selected transformation problems and to stimulate further research on the economics of the East European transformation process. There is much disillusion in Eastern Europe with the socialist system, but at the same time there is no firmly rooted conviction that transformation to a market economy will be sustainable and economically successful. The accumulated distortions are enormous, the problems in integrating Eastern European economies into the international market economies with their sharp global competition are huge and the patience of people limited, while the experiences upon which to draw for transformation are certainly limited. In this book no broad attempt will be made to describe the socialist economic model and its numerous variants, including those of market socialism;[1] this has been extensively done by many authors. Marxist theory and the theory of MARX and ENGELS is also well covered in the literature. A brief summary of some basic ideas seems sufficient for our analysis.

High hopes to achieve high and stable economic growth, to obtain a relatively equitable income distribution - while avoiding "exploitation" of labor - and to realize a more effective

---

[1] An excellent presentation of the Soviet economic system is NOVE, A. (1986), The Soviet Economic System, 3rd ed., Boston: Unwin. See on market socialism especially BRUS, W. and LASKI, K. (1989), From Marx to the Market, Oxford: Clarendon Press. A very readable book describing the failure of socialism (without taking into account the crucial role of the shadow economy) is WINIECKI, J. (1988), The Distorted Type of Soviet-Type Economies: London: Macmillan. Some basic problems of socialist systems are analyzed in GEY, P., KOSTA, J. and QUAISSER, W., eds. (1987), Crisis and Reform in Socialist Economies, Boulder: Westview; DEMBINSKI, P. (1991), The Logic of the Planned Economy, Oxford: Clarendon. HARTWIG, K.H. and THIEME, J., eds. (1992), Transformationsprozesse in sozialistischen Wirtschaftssystemen, Heidelberg: Springer.

and efficient system than capitalism were the basis for the socialist command economy. The "anarchy of spontaneous market coordination" and cyclical economic development was to be overcome by the Bolshevik revolution in Russia in 1917. Central planning on the basis of quantitative output targets for state industry was expected to lead to economic success. Since every worker would understand that the whole value-added originating from his/her work would either benefit him/her directly in the form of wages (or future wages in the case that his firm retained some profits for investment) or the supply of public services, the motivation of the labor force should be higher than in capitalism where the private owners of industrial assets have the right to appropriate any residual income - sales revenues minus wage expenditures and capital costs. It took more than seven decades of centrally planned economies to understand that individual motivation of the labor force was systematically eroding in socialist economies and, worse, that motivation could neither be effectively focussed on productivity increasing coordination of millions of individuals nor be used to encourage individual creativity. Indeed, socialism had always emphasized the needs of the mass society in which each individual would recognize his/her value and position as derived from belonging to a mass society and the institutions controlled by the state and the party. This idea of collectivism is in sharp contrast to the idea of individualism according to which each adult and each child is a personality himself and rightfully can claim protection against an obviously powerful state; the protection of minorities against any tyranny of the majority in a mass society is part of the individualistic view of human beings and modern societies. Individual rights have to be strongly anchored in a constitution that somehow represents a fundamental consensus of the members of a society, and these are additionally protected against the tyranny of state power by a systemic division of powers (executive, legislative and judicative - if one is to follow the American or French Revolution).

After World War II the Soviet socialist command economy was imposed in other Eastern European countries, too. The Stalinist model of the command economy certainly brought a rapid industrialization of East European countries - except for the CSSR which already had been an industrialized country before World War II. The GDR clearly was also an exception in the sense that it was already highly industrialized before World War II and actually represented a major part of Germany's heavy industry in the 1930s. An open question is whether catching-up would have been faster in a market economy framework.

In socialist Eastern Europe there was some apparent success in catching up with the West, namely in the sense that East European economies played a growing international role in heavy industry production in the 1950s and the 1960s. However, when the core fields of innovation and production moved to electronics, software development and the service industry, the centrally planned economy showed a growing weakness. While avoiding sharp cyclical output developments they could not achieve the rate of technological progress and the type of innovations that were realized in Western market economies and Japan. Moreover, one must take into account that before Lenin's revolution Russia was No. 5 worldwide in terms of industrial output.

The catching up process that was later achieved was based largely on a dictatorial industrialization strategy in which 30-40 million people became the sacrifices of the socialist development model. In the PR China Mao's "Big Leap" brought the death of another 15 million people on the road of socialism. Historical observers probably would not strongly emphasize the sacrifices of socialist development if it had really brought a decent economic life for the whole population in the long term. Instead it increasingly became clear that socialism is unable to generate mass prosperity which became at least widespread in North America, Western Europe, some Newly Industrializing Countries and Japan. That capitalism developed a variety of successful market economy models was another point in favor of capitalism in the rivalry against socialism. Japan Inc. and the various East Asian NICs with their respective models could all inspire the search for modern capitalist development; even the EC countries were able to overcome the Eurosclerosis of the 1970s and thereby proved that politico-economic reforms in Western market economies are possible. Eastern European economies went through a series of reforms in the late 1950s, the 1960s and the 1970s, but nothing changed the general perception that no sustainable economic dynamics could be mobilized by the socialist model. Where history offered a real test of comparative systemic performance - in Germany and in Korea - there was a visible victory of the capitalist variant.

Marxist theory claims that socialism is superior to capitalism in terms of economic rationality and that it is also more just in the sense that it avoids exploitation of labor by an ever more concentrating capitalist class (owner of industrial assets) which tries to prevent the - unavoidable - fall of profit rates by mergers & acquisitions and ultimately, by forming monopolies. Aggressive international competition also implies that capitalist countries become increasingly sharp rivals, and this leads to capitalist wars. Imperialism is - in the view of LENIN - the last stage of capitalism whose firms increasingly penetrate foreign territories (today's developing countries) and exploit natural resources and the population in their attempt to maximize profits and build industrial empires. In this view the capitalist international system is conflict-prone and bound to lead to international wars in which the system-internal contradictions accentuate such that more and more capitalist countries will enter a revolutionary stage - finally, becoming socialist economies, too. The dictatorship of the working class as represented by the Communist party will be necessary to avoid counter-revolutions and to ultimately make sure that the superior economic rationality of socialism can prevail.

Paradoxically, the protagonist of the command economy model expected to realize in the socialist system an "almost-neoclassical world" in which firms are understood mainly as representing the implementation of production functions, in which money would play no role (and inflation not be relevant) for the real sphere and in which structural change could be centrally planned and organized in a world with insignificant transaction costs. Certainly, inflation was not expected to be a problem, nor economic stagnation or cyclical instability; however, in the 1980s all three phenomena could be observed in the socialist economies of Eastern Europe. Central planners were willing to concede systemic problems and envisage partial reforms; e.g. in the USSR, where the whole economy had been organized along branch ministries which had little communication among each other, the year 1958 brought reforms that organized planning according to regional entities, and in 1962 LIBERMAN proposed reform ideas that were partly realized in 1965. Premiums and hence monetary incentives played a major role in this reform, but pricing problems and the efficiency of investment selection were not addressed. Hungary presented a different example of systemic reforms, especially in the period 1968 to 1981, where the latter year represents an important change in the foreign trade organization that used to be based on foreign trade monopolies in all branches. Hungary decided to award more than 100 firms the right to engage in now often parallel exports, and by end-1986 about 300 firms had established rights for foreign trade. There were periodic reforms in Poland and most other CMEA countries, too. However, reforms never managed to solve the fundamental systemic problems of socialism, especially the problem of motivation of people, the efficient organization of firms and industries, the optimum selection of investment projects and hence the promotion of sustaining economic growth, and, finally, maximizing the value of assets (or at least maintaining their value over time).

Yugoslavia adopted a special variant of the socialist system in which workers of the respective firms influenced the selection of managers and shared with the management basic rights of some enterprise autonomy. Critics in the West often argued that Yugoslavian self-management would lead to resistance to hiring additional workers since new workers' productivity would have to be high enough to match average labor productivity so that per capita wages and premiums would not have to be cut; in capitalism the marginal product rule would - by contrast - imply that a firm would hire workers as long as the marginal product of labor (not the higher average product) was above the real wage rate. While this criticism was valid in many cases, the alleged tendency of underinvestment in the Yugoslavian system did not materialize. Workers were not so myopic on the one hand, and, on the other hand, not so influential to systematically prefer high present wages - and hence less investment - over higher future wages associated with high investment. As a matter of fact, the Yugoslav system brought about record investment-GNP ratios in Europe (up to 40 %); given a very high investment output ratio economic growth was moderate. Therefore it seems clear that the problem was not underinvestment, but a poor selection process in investment decisions. Since a functional capital market did not exist, the natural tendency of a firm's employees to reinvest profits exclusively in their own firm reduced the macroeconomic prospects for a high marginal product of capital that would often have required channeling funds into an anonymous capital market from which firms with the most profitable projects could have absorbed most of the investment funds available in the economy at large. Without M&A opportunities across industries and facing no need to pay cash dividends (as a visible and credible signal of profitability) socialist firms were unable to realize those investments with the highest social return.

In Yugoslavia as in the CMEA countries reality was very different from the vision of MARX, LENIN and others. Socialist economies largely failed to establish viable economic systems at all. Capitalist economies were not without periods of crisis, and the Great Depression 1929-37 should not be forgotten. However, socialist economies were unable to live up to the expectations of the population and to fulfill the political promises of the ruling party.

1.1 The Crisis of the Socialist Systems in Eastern Europe

Based on a strategy of economic growth which relied on an increasing participation rate of the female population, massive exploitation of natural resources, the use of mass production and the promotion of heavy industries, the Eastern European countries increased output (static economies of scale) and productivity in the 1950s and 1960s. As long as there was an elastic labor supply - stemming from agricultural labor surplus or from rising participation ratios - economic growth could be maintained, especially since labor surplus was coupled with high investment output ratios of 30-38 percent in Eastern Europe. Even with declining marginal product of capital rising real incomes could be achieved.

1.2 Some Stylized Facts

In the 1960s the CMEA countries also embarked upon a more specializing - actually monopolistic - intra-CMEA division of labor. In this system barter trade and multi-tier exchange rates were barriers to trade that were never really overcome. The transferable ruble (TR) introduced in 1963 did not represent a convertible currency and thus did not overcome the problem of trade-reducing quotas implicitly derived from the need and incentive to balance bilateral trade flows. Intra-industry trade with competition-enhancing effects was an exception and generally the degree of economic openness remained low. World market impulses only played a role in those countries where the share of trade in manufacturing products with Western market economies was relatively high - Hungary and Poland were the countries most exposed to world market forces.

Import substitution strategies were emphasized in the other countries of the CMEA where monopolistic state trade organizations institutionally separated the world market from the socialist production sphere. High intra-CMEA trade shares of Bulgaria, the CSFR and Romania - with considerable "socialist trade" with China - therefore indicate the high role of politically determined and managed trade as opposed to Western trade on the basis of comparative advantages.

The ex-USSR suffers from the special problem of big countries for which trade opportunities are typically smaller than in smaller countries; at least these opportunities as well as the scope of prodigality are more difficult to recognize since it is more difficult to compare economic performance and product variety, especially if personal contacts with people abroad are limited. Moreover, smaller countries are more naturally inclined to actively search for prospects for international trade and to accept a free trade regime. Big countries sometimes can improve their terms of trade by means of restricting imports. Given the huge internal market potential there is also a greater incentive to adopt strategic trade policies which seek to establish a comparative advantage for domestic firms by promoting their exploitation of dynamic economies of scale (e.g. by public procurement rules that discriminate against foreign suppliers and reduce their opportunity to move down the learning curve) as well as by promoting R&D with state subsidies. However, in contrast to the U.S. where the export-GNP ratio was only four percentage points higher than in the USSR, the Soviet industry has no world market links via a network of foreign subsidiaries and foreign direct investment flows accruing from Japan, the U.K. and other countries. Only domestic sources of growth were available in Eastern Europe.

All CMEA countries faced slow economic growth and rising open (CPI) inflation as is obvious from Tab. A1. High growth rates of the 1960s were not sustainable, official inflation rates above 2 percent became common in the 1970s, and there was a clear acceleration after the 1980s (for obvious reasons - related to the incentive problem of official wages - governments could not allow prices in the unofficial economy to increase much faster than those in the official economy). Negative growth rates were recorded in all socialist economies in 1990 which indicates the cost of systemic reform in Poland, Hungary, Yugoslavia and the CSFR, but also points to the costs of non-reform in the slowly reforming countries USSR, Bulgaria and Romania.

Tab. A1: Developments in Real Output and Inflation (% changes, annual averages)

	Bulgaria		CSSR		GDR		Hungary		Poland		Romania		USSR		Yugoslavia	
	g_Y	g_P	g_Y	g_P	g_Y	g_P	g_Y	g_P	g_Y	g_P	g_Y	g_P	g_Y	g_P	g_Y	g_P
1960 -70	7.7	–	4.2	–	4.1	–	5.5	–	6.1	–	8.6	–	7.2	–	6.7	–
1970 -80	7.1	2.0	4.7	1.2	4.8	0.0	5.0	4.6	5.4	4.6	9.4	1.0	5.1	0.3	5.8	17.5
1980 -85	3.7	1.0	1.8	2.0	4.5	0.0	1.8	6.7	-0.8	32.5	3.0	5.0	3.2	1.0	0.7	47.5
1989	-0.5	6.2	1.3	1.5	2.0	8.2	-0.2	19.0	-0.2	260.0	-7.9	0.9	2.5	1.9	0.6	1240.0
1990	-13.5	19.3	-3.1	10.0	-19.5	-4.0	-4.5	29.0	-12.0	585.0	-10.0	5.7	-4.0	5.3	-7.5	585.0

Source: BIS (1991), 61st Annual Report, Basle.

Tab. A2: Income Disparities and Share of the Service Industry in Selected Countries

	Year	Lowest 20 %	Second Quintile	Highest 40%/20%	Service Share, 1988 % of GNP
Poland	*1987*	*9.7*	*14.2*	*58.1/35.2*	*35*
Hungary	*1983*	*10.9*	*15.3*	*55.2/32.4*	*49*
Italy	1986	6.8	12.0	64.5/41.0	56
Germany (W)	1984	6.8	12.7	62.8/38.7	47
France	1979	6.3	12.1	64.3/40.8	60*
U.S.	1985	4.7	11.0	65.9/41.9	65
Taiwan	1978	8.9	13.7	59.3/37.2	–

* share of employment in total employment (1987).

Source: World Bank (1990), World Development Report; OECD (1991), Services in Central and Eastern European Countries; Taiwan Statistical Yearbook; own calculations.

While new service industries and world market forces - such as the rise of the Newly Industrializing Countries (NICs), the oil price shocks of the 1970s and innovation dynamics - drove structural adjustment and growth in Western market economies the socialist economies maintained heavy industry as the dominating core of industry. The service industry which accounted in OECD countries for a share of 47-65 percent recorded shares of 35-49 percent in CMEA countries (Tab. A2). The service industry and the liberal professions in particular were therefore underrepresented in Eastern Europe, and this partly explains why the income share of the lowest quintile in socialist economies are typically higher and those in the highest income quintile are typically lower than in market economies (extremely high tax rates for those working in the crafts industry play a role, too). The socialist economies of Eastern Europe had relatively high shares of agriculture (see Tab. A3) - except for the CSSR and the GDR - and they neglected, compared to the OECD countries, the growth opportunities of the service industry.

Tab. A3: Sectoral Developments in Eastern Europe, the U.S.S.R., and Industrial Countries, 1961-88 (in %)

	Sectoral Growth Rates[1]				Employment Shares[2]					
	Agriculture		Industry[3]		Agriculture			Industry[3]		
	1961-80	1981-88	1961-80	1981-88	1960	1980	1988	1960	1980	1988
Eastern Europe	1.0	2.3	4.9	1.3	43.0	22.9	21.5	25.7	32.9	32.4
Czechoslovakia	1.3	1.3	3.5	1.2	23.8	12.5	12.1	36.3	37.2	36.6
Poland	–	2.2	5.2	0.5	49.6	29.5	28.2	22.4	29.1	25.9
Hungary	2.3	2.7	4.0	1.3	35.7	19.6	18.4	29.7	32.9	33.0
Bulgaria	0.6	-0.6	7.0	1.6	54.5	23.9	19.5	19.4	31.4	33.0
Romania	1.6	5.1	7.9	1.4	65.6	30.1	28.5	13.2	32.2	33.7
German Dem. Rep.	1.4	1.9	3.6	2.1	16.0	10.4	10.2	39.8	38.9	39.0
U.S.S.R.	1.0	0.6	5.0	2.5	41.3	23.6	21.7	20.5	25.0	24.6
Indust. countries[4]	1.4	2.6[5]	4.5	2.5[5]	18	6	5[6]	38	38	34[6]
Taiwan*					32.8	9.2	6.6	24.9	45.0	47.3

* share in output in net domestic product is indicated for Taiwan
[1] Real average annual growth rate.
[2] Percent of total labor force.
[3] Includes construction.
[4] Grouping based on World Bank, *World Development Report 1989.*
[5] 1981-87.
[6] 1987.

Source: IMF (1990), World Economic Outlook, Spring, Chapter V, based on the following publications: For sectoral growth in Eastern Europe: Thad P. Alton, "Economic Growth and Resource Allocation in Eastern Europe," in Reorientation and Commercial Relations of the Economies of Eastern Europe, Joint Economic Committee, 1974, pp. 251-98; and Thad P. Alton, "East European GNPs, Domestic Final Uses of Gross Product, Rates of Growth, and International Comparisons," in Pressures for Reform in the Eastern European Economies, Vol. 1, Joint Economic Committee, 1989, pp. 77-96; for sectoral growth in the Soviet Union and employment shares: National Foreign Assessment Center, Handbook of Economic Statistics, 1989; for industrial countries: World Bank, World Development Report, various issues; and Fund staff estimates. Taiwan Statistical Yearbook.

The official statistics show some decline in the growth of factor productivity for Eastern Europe in the 1970s and the 1980s. Taiwan, one of the Asian NICs, clearly outpaced all East European economies in its structural change in the four decades after World War II. Employment shares in Bulgaria, Poland and Romania were still higher than 50 % in 1960. In 1988 these countries recorded shares of 20-29 percent, while in the OECD countries the share of employment in agriculture was only about 5 percent in the 1980s. Taiwan's share of agriculture in net domestic output dropped from 32.2 percent in 1960 to 6.6 percent in 1988.

Not only were Taiwan, the Republic of Korea and some other developing countries effectively catching-up with the OECD countries, but they also recorded a growing share in OECD imports in the 1970s and the 1980s, whereas the market shares of East European countries reduced. While the Asian NICs had adopted outward oriented development strategies, the socialist systems had adopted inward-oriented strategies. As the following Table (Tab. A4) shows the Asian NICs were particularly successful in raising their market shares in product categories of technology intensive goods, and this testifies to the effective technological catching-up process and learning by doing (and exporting) in Asian NICs.

Tab. A4: Imports of OECD Countries by Goods Categories from CMEA Countries and Asian NICs (Hong Kong, Malaysia, Singapore, Korea,R., Taiwan), 1965 and 1986

	resource intensive	labor intensive	capital intensive	R&D intensive goods, easy to imitate	R&D intens. goods, diff. to imitate
CMEA (7)					
1965	55.1	16.6	18.3	4.7	5.3
1986	57.8	17.2	11.9	7.0	6.2
USSR					
1965	67.7	9.1	19.4	1.5	2.3
1986	78.1	6.0	8.2	5.1	2.6
Asian NICs					
1965	38.8	43.3	13.6	2.1	2.3
1986	8.8	50.4	5.8	17.5	17.5

Source: Kostrzewa, W. (1988), Verpaßt Osteuropa den Anschluß auf den Weltmärkten, Kieler Diskussionsbeiträge No. 144, Institut für Weltwirtschaft Kiel.

2. Distortions of Socialist Economies

Labor productivity reduced growth sharply after 1973, where one explanation could be the inability to sustain labor productivity growth once the elastic industrial labor supply from the agricultural sector and from a rising participation rate was no longer available. This would point to a systemic weakness in innovativeness, at least compared to the Western economies and the NICs. Technological progress/total factor productivity reduced in the USSR after 1973 - similar to the case of Latin America (see Tab. A5). Static inefficiencies were considerable in Eastern Europe.[2] In Eastern Europe the official growth rates of real national income were high relative to most OECD countries (Tab. A6) - but statistics did not reveal the destruction of wealth (including natural assets via emissions), the low quality of output and the wasteful use of intermediate products. Official statistics created the illusion of a successful economic catching-up process vis-à-vis the West. However, personal inspection always suggested a different story. With increasing openness for information and communication on the one hand,

Tab. A5: Growth of Labor, Total Factor Productivity, and the Capital Stock in the U.S.S.R. and Selected Countries, 1951-84, (annual percentage changes)

	Labor Productivity[1]		Capital Stock		TFP*	
	1951-73	1974-84	1951-73	1974-84	1951-73	'74-84
U.S.S.R.	3.6	1.0	8.6	6.7	0.5	-1.4
Indust. countries[2]	4.8	2.7	4.7	3.2	3.4	1.3
Latin America[3]	3.2	0.2	4.7	5.0	1.8	-1.3
Korea	4.2	4.8	5.9	10.8	2.8	1.4
Taiwan	4.9	4.1	7.7	10.0	3.5	1.2

* TFP = Total Factor Productivity
[1] GDP per hour worked (Latin America: GDP per employed person).
[2] Weighted average of 16 industrial countries.
[3] Weighted average of Argentina, Brazil, Chile, and Mexico.

Source: IMF (1990), World Economic Outlook, Spring, Chapter V, based on Angus Maddison, The World Economy in the 20th Century, Paris, 1989, pp. 81, 91.

---

[2] KEMME estimated that output losses due to static inefficiency reached 8-10 % in Poland. See KEMME, D.M. (1990), Losses in Polish Industry Due to Resource Misallocation, Yearbook of East-European Economics, Vol. 14, No. 2, 139-158. Static efficiency requires equalizing marginal rates of substitution of input factors across industries; otherwise the production frontier line is not reached. The KEMME estimate seems to be very conservative. In a comparative systems perspective one should also look for links between dynamic efficiency (innovativeness) and static efficiency. Relatively innovative market economies might show a greater variance in static output efficiency than noninnovative socialist systems. A fair test on static efficiency would ask how strong static efficiency conditions would be fulfilled if the degree of innovativeness - hence requirements for continuous adjustment on the supply side - in CPEs were as high as in market economies.

Tab. A6: Selected Macroeconomic Indicators, 1951-88

(Percentage changes at annual rates, unless otherwise noted)

	Gross Domestic Product (real)			Per Capita GDP (real)			External Trade	
	1951-73	1974-82	1983-88	1951-73	1974-82	1983-88	Total[1]	East Bloc Trade[2]
astern Europe[3]	4.7	1.9	2.7	4.0	1.3	2.3	37	60.9
(excluding Poland)		(2.5)	(2.0)		(1.9)	(1.8)		
Bulgaria	6.1	2.4	1.4	5.3	2.0	1.2	63	77.4
Czechoslovakia	3.8	1.8	1.8	3.1	1.1	1.4	41	72.8
GDR	4.6	2.6	2.1	4.9	2.8	2.2	36	61.8
Hungary	4.0	1.9	1.4	3.5	1.5	1.5	38	44.2
Poland	4.8	0.5	4.2	3.5	-0.4	3.3	27	40.7
Romania	5.9	3.7	2.9	4.8	2.7	2.5	43	45.1
.S.S.R.	5.0	2.1	1.9	3.6	1.2	1.0	13	51.5
ugoslavia	5.7	5.0	0.9	4.6	4.1	0.2	38	31.8
ndustr. countries[4]	4.9	2.1	3.1	3.7	1.4	2.5	28	2.6
Austria	5.3	2.4	2.3	4.9	2.5	2.3	55	7.8
Finland	4.9	2.7	3.4	4.3	2.4	3.0	62	15.4
France	5.1	2.6	1.8	4.1	2.1	1.3	39	2.3
FRG	5.9	1.6	2.4	4.9	1.7	2.5	41	3.7
Italy	5.5	2.3	2.7	4.8	1.9	2.5	48	4.0
Japan	9.3	3.6	4.2	8.1	2.6	3.5	25	1.7
U.S.	3.7	1.6	4.3	2.2	0.6	3.3	18	0.8
NICs								
Korea	7.5	6.9	9.9	5.2	5.2	8.4	66	...
Taiwan	9.3	8.2	8.4	6.2	5.4	7.0	97	...

[1] Sum of exports and imports in percent of GNP in 1980.

[2] External trade with Eastern Europe and the Soviet Union in percent of total trade in 1988.

[3] GDP weighted average. The weights in 1985 were (in percent) Bulgaria 7.0, Czechoslovakia 16.6, G.D.R. 21.7, Hungary 9.7, Poland 29.7, and Romania 15.3. The USSR economy is estimated to be about eight times as large as Poland's.

[4] Weighted average of 16 industrial countries; except for external trade: weighted average for the 7 countries in the table.

Source: IMF (1990), World Economic Outlook, Spring, Chapter V; data are based on the following publications: Gross domestic product and population growth from Angus Maddison, The World Economy in the 20th Century, Paris, 1989; The World Bank, The World Bank Atlas 1989, Washington, 1989; external trade/GNP from Paul Marer, Dollar GNPs of the U.S.S.R. and Eastern Europe, Baltimore, 1989, pp. 112-13; East Bloc trade shares from Economic Commission for Europe, Economic Survey of Europe in 1988-89, New York, 1989; and Fund staff estimates; Taiwan Statistical Yearbook.

and, on the other hand, with rising opportunities to travel (even one-way opportunities bringing expatriates on a visit to their East European homelands) the contradiction between official statistics and reality would become gradually apparent - at first only for the ruling elite, later also for important groups in society.

A very revealing case is the former GDR whose real economic performance became obvious after German unification in 1990. If one assumes that the GDR reached 50 percent of West German GNP in 1951, the fact that per capita GNP in 1990 - the year of unification - was 1/3 - as is obvious from recent statistics - of the West German figure, the annual real growth rate of the GDR cannot be even half as high as suggested by the official period averages of 4.9 % in 1951-73 (the same as in West Germany), 2.8 % and 2.2 % for 1974-82 and 1983-1988, respectively (West German growth rates: 2.1 and 1.3 % for 1974-82 and 1983-88, respectively). A major mistake in the GDR statistics is obviously related to not using world market prices or market determined (hypothetical equilibrium) exchange rates that would have reduced the real value of GDR output strongly as compared to official figures and officially used exchange rates. Not correctly deflating nominal figures might have been another problem in some socialist economies. A third problem is related to the fact that reinvestment was neglected in socialist economies; one may note that the ratio of reinvestment to net investment in West Germany - as an example from the West - is about 2:1. Since the investment-output ratio was 18 % in West Germany, the German output could be raised (once and for all) by 12 % simply by completely reducing output for reinvestment purposes; this, of course, can only be a transitory means to artificially increase disposable income. A similar caveat holds for the growth rates of all former CMEA countries, and with hindsight even the GDR's traditional claim that it enjoyed the highest standard of living and was the CMEA's leading economy in terms of per capita production is quite doubtful; Hungary probably held this position, and this despite the fact that it received no resource transfers. Such transfers were given in the 1960s, 1970s and 1980s to the GDR under various headings; e.g. for postal services and for road links between Western Germany and West Berlin, located in the midst of the GDR.

Since the 1970s the socialist CMEA countries have suffered from economic stagnation in the official economy, increasing inflationary pressures and a rapid growth of the shadow economy. More and more resources - physical inputs, time etc. - have been extracted from the official economy and contributed to the growth of a flexible-price shadow economy in which consumers obtain desired goods and services at relatively high prices, but without the problem of standing in line and facing uncertainty (plus side payments) as is typically the case in the official economy. The political and economic crisis resulted in the collapse of the command economy system in Eastern Europe in the late '80s and, in the case of the GDR, in a rapid integration into the West German market economy.[3] Furthermore, declining terms of trade - reflecting reduced international competitiveness - have contributed to the slowdown of economic growth, where many East-Asian NICs have overtaken the CMEA countries in terms of per capita income in the past two decades.[4] The system of state-administered trade within an inward-oriented command economy has turned out to be extremely inefficient. Not only static efficiency criteria are typically not fulfilled, but dynamic efficiency is not enhanced by a system in which multiple exchange rates and all kinds of import restrictions distorted trade and restricted the number of suppliers.[5]

Finally, politico-economic reforms have been launched in several CMEA countries, most notably in Hungary, Poland and the USSR, but also in a radical sense in the former GDR which became a part of the Federal Republic of Germany in 1990.[6] Parallel to the reduction of economic growth of the official net material product in the 1980s, the socialist shadow economy has expanded in the CMEA countries. The theoretical analysis conducted here argues that the unofficial system plays an important role as a catalyst for economic change and system transformation in the long term.

In the following analysis we focus on selected particularities of the allocation of capital, intermediary products, labor and foreign exchange as well as the pricing rules in socialist systems to explain the systemic tendencies bringing forth a considerable shadow economy; it is shown that direct or indirect preferential allocation of goods leads to a kinked demand curve in the shadow economy. We also raise the question how a price index for a socialist economy could reflect increasing shortages in a command system characterized by state-administered prices. A basic concept of quasi-inflation is developed which also takes into account the problem of mismatches in the product varieties desired and offered which are so typical for socialist systems. The analysis has some natural extensions to analyzing exchange rate movements after opening up a socialist system, where we emphasize that the marginal utility of money is determined both by the amount of goods and the variety of products obtainable.

---

[3] The increasing systemic problems of various CMEA countries were analyzed by various scholars. For the case of the USSR see OFER, B. (1987), Soviet Economic Growth: 1928-1985, Journal of Economic Literature, 25 (1987), 1767-1850; HEWETT, E.A. (1988), Reforming the Soviet Economy, Washington, D.C.: Brookings. See for the CMEA countries as a group BRADA, J. C. (1985), The Slowdown in Soviet and East-European Economic Growth, Osteuropa Wirtschaft, 30 (1982), 116-128. For further empirical evidence see: SLAMA, J. (1988), Verwendung technisch-ökonomischer Kennziffern zur Analyse des Wirtschaftswachstums und des technischen Fortschritts sozialistischer Länder, in: WELFENS, P.J.J; BALCEROWICZ, L., eds., Innovationsdynamik im Systemvergleich, Heidelberg: Physica, 300-321; UN COMMISSION FOR EUROPE (1990), Economic Reforms in the European Centrally Planned Economies, New York.

[4] See WELFENS, P.J.J. (1987), Growth, Innovation and International Competitiveness, Intereconomics, 22 (1987), 168-174.

[5] See on this WELFENS, P.J.J. (1990a), Economic Reforms in Eastern Europe: Problems, Options and Opportunities, testimony before United States Senate, Small Business Committee, March 23, 1990.

[6] See on the process and problems of German unification: WELFENS, P.J.J. (1992), Ed., Economic Aspects of German Unification, New York: Springer.

The problems faced by domestic firms after opening up can be tremendous as the case of German unification shows, where retail sales in the former GDR in August 1990 (and April 1992) were 45 % below the 1989 values.[7]

2.1 The Monopoly Problem

Opening-up the economies within the CMEA group brought no additional competition in Eastern Europe, but reinforced under the heading of international socialist specialization the fragile system-specific network of monopolistic firms which constitute the socialist official economy. As access to Western imports was tightly restricted, each firm faced high delivery risks with respect to the existing small range of specialized suppliers; even if input quantities were supplied in accordance with plans, there was the risk of quality problems whose occurrence shows a considerable variance. Consequently, all kinds of strategic behavior of socialist firms were observed.

The firms used their information advantage vis-à-vis the planning authorities to obtain generous input allocations that allowed them to cope with delivery risk and helped them to easily fulfill the quantitative targets of the state plans (problem of tautness of plans). Naturally, socialist managers were eager to overfulfill the plan, so that wage premiums could bc paid and career promotion be expected. If wage increases exceeded productivity gains, the rise in unit costs translated into higher prices, or, more often, into higher required subsidies that would cover the difference between costs incurred and prices obtained.

The socialist bias to supply the bulk of goods for basic needs at low or artificially lowered prices created (i) a sustaining excess demand in the goods markets, (ii) insufficient incentives to increase output, and (iii) continuing needs to allocate subsidies to firms producing mass consumer goods. Implicit excise taxes on certain goods were used by state planners who wanted to generate enough corresponding extra profits to cover the rising amount of subsidies for non-profitable firms. However, this mechanism for balancing the state budget did not work in the late 1970s and the 1980s, when increasing world market prices called for adjustments in the assortment of products produced, in the energy-intensity of technologies employed and in the location of industries. The USSR passed these oil price hikes with a lag to its major CMEA trading partners and enjoyed some windfall profits from the OPEC price surges; however, rising aspirations of the Soviet people could not be reduced, when world market prices for

---

[7] See Deutsche Bundesbank, Monthly Report, October 1990, where the Deutsche Bundesbank emphasizes that East German consumers, once facing unrestricted access to Western goods, strongly increased expenditures on West German and other Western consumer goods.

primary products and energy started to fall after 1981. The tremendous international relative price changes that occurred in the world markets in the 1970s and 1980s hardly led to major structural changes in the inward-oriented CMEA countries, where intra-bloc trade relied much on bilateralism and a myriad of exchange rates applied to different product groups. In the 1970s and 1980s the CMEA countries were facing increasing competition from the flexibly reacting Newly Industrializing Countries which relied on an outward-oriented development strategy, relative world market prices, a strategy of nurturing firms and markets, an efficiency-promoting trajectory of progressively reduced protectionism and a successful adoption-cum-dissipation of modern technologies.

2.2 Innovation Gap, Inefficient Investment and Stagnation

A major problem of socialist economies is their insufficient capability to generate and diffuse technological progress. The whole chain of innovation dynamics may be categorized as inspiration, invention, innovation, investment and imitation. Inspiration requires an open society in which competition of ideas, individuals and institutions as well as horizontal and vertical mobility generate a sustaining stream of new innovative ideas. Access to foreign countries and openness towards foreign influences are also important. Clearly, the iron curtain isolated East European societies for more than four decades from the West - with major exceptions in Poland, Hungary and Yugoslavia which also enjoyed the flow and exchange of ideas with a large expatriate community. The input into the invention process was high as measured by the number of scientists and engineers (relative to the population); however, the absence of competitive pressure from markets led to the problem that the innovation potential was not systematically geared towards marketable products and cost-reducing or quality-enhancing process innovations. Moreover, the dozens of branch ministries all used to focus on inventions in their respective industries and rarely were joint projects - cutting across industries - set up; nor would conglomerate firms (as Mitsubishi in Japan, Daimler Benz in Germany or United Technologies in the U.S.) provide a basis for the diffusion and exchange of innovative ideas and applications. Moreover, in Western countries most innovations are not applied in the industry which developed them, but in other industries. Hence the investment process and hence the rate of capital-embodied technological progress is non-optimal if there is a lack of "diagonal industrial relationships" which effectively constitute conglomerate information and communication networks.

Imitation was weak for various reason, the main one being the principle to organize planning, production and investment along industry lines and the general lack of internal and external competition. Innovative investment projects that contribute to a better quality of output produced or allow a greater product variety are financed in Western economies via a competitive capital market. Firms which have built a reputation as successful inventors - engineering firms and firms producing machinery and transport equipment - as well as successful users of new technologies can expect to raise equity capital and loans at more favorable rates than firms with a less favorable innovative record; hence they can finance larger investment projects and expand capacity faster than others which creates an incentive for all firms to strive for dynamic efficiency; i.e. to generate an efficient rate of innovation. In new technology fields where ιeputation, of course, can not already exist already, venture capital firms share the risk of invention and innovation in return for sharing high average returns on investment. It is well known that the small and medium-sized firms are relatively more innovative (relative to a currency unit spent on R&D) than big firms in Western market economies. New firms and hence smaller or medium-sized firms were almost completely lacking in Eastern Europe which is another element in explaining their weak innovation record. The following Tab. A7 clearly shows the weak innovativeness of socialist economies as measured by the number of patent applications made outside the country of origin. A small West European market economy such as Austria had more patent applications filed in the EC and outside Europe than the USSR in 1987/88 and the impressive domestic patenting record of the GDR also looks weak if applications abroad are considered.

Tab. A7: Innovations of Socialist Countries as Measured by Patent Applications 1987/88 (Inpadoc Statistics, 1990)

	total	of which application in		
		more than one country	EC-coun-tries	countries out-side Europe
country of origin				
USSR	51 013	395	360	357
Hungary	1 704	380	353	192
Poland	4 342	80	70	11
CSFR	7 201	201	188	43
Romania	58	1	0	1
Bulgaria	962	69	48	19
GDR	12 867	894	810	97
Yugoslavia	262	48	41	13
for comparison				
Austria:	2 003	1298	1250	443

Source: IFO-Institut, Das technologische Potential der RGW-Länder im Spiegel der Patentstatistik, Ifo-Schnelldienst, 12/90.

According to modern growth theory - as represented by ROMER (1983, 1990) and CANTWELL (1989) - capital, human capital, unskilled labor and ideas (proxied by patents) are the basic factors that explain economic growth.[8] Moreover, economies of scale, endogenous technological progress and imperfect competition play major roles for sustaining high economic growth in market economies. CANTWELL emphasizes that knowledge is essentially a stock phenomenon in the sense that one has to accumulate useful information, store it and continuously update it if a strong innovation record is to be developed by firms and industries, respectively. This view is important because it implies that high sustaining economic growth in Eastern Europe cannot be expected in the medium term - at least not until one has launched a successful technological catching-up process and developed experience in generating innovations within a framework of open international competition.

Lack of functional capital markets implied inefficient capital formation, and housing shortages restricted the mobility of human capital and the best use of skilled labor as well as of unskilled labor. Additionally, in socialist economies the development, application and diffusion of new knowledge is much slower and less comprehensive than in market economies which largely can explain the economic stagnation in Eastern Europe and the widening West-East European income gap as well as the rising gap between Asian NICs and socialist CMEA countries. While the NICs invested heavily in improving their R&D capabilities and at least partly relied on foreign direct investment to broaden and update their technological knowledge basis on the one hand, and, on the other hand, were eager to expose their industries to world market competition via export promotion (which also yielded static and dynamic economies of scale), the CMEA countries refused to accept foreign direct investment inflows and emphasized import-substitution strategies. Finally, while countries such as Korea and Taiwan were eager to promote advanced human capital formation by sending thousands of students abroad every year, no CMEA country would deliberately invest in human capital formation in the West. When the CMEA countries faced the NICs in the 1970s and the 1980s in the world market, the results were declining world market shares of the socialist economies, falling terms of trade and rising foreign indebtedness (relative to GNP). While Korea was able to modernize its economy while paying its foreign debt - with a peak of some $ 50 bill. in the mid-1980s - Poland built up a similar foreign indebtedness but was never able to translate imported know-how and capital goods into sustaining modernization of its industry, above all its export industries.[9] Once the resource basis of Eastern Europe had become exhausted such that the switch to a more innovative economy would become the key to sustaining growth, economic stagnation became inevitable. Aspiration levels were still increasing in the 1970s and the

---

[8] See on ROMER's approach ROMER, P. (1983), Dynamic Competitive Equilibria, Increasing Returns and Unbounded Growth, Chicago: University of Chicago; ROMER, P. (1990), Are Nonconvexities Important for Understanding Growth?, American Economic Review, Vol. 80.

[9] On the inefficiencies of technology imports in Poland see RAPACKI (1988).

1980s, but real per capita growth lost momentum, and it became more and more difficult for per capita consumption to increase from the domestic resource basis. Making only reduced capital allowances, ignoring negative value-added as exemplified by the destruction of nature,[10] and increasing foreign indebtedness become two ways to conceal the looming systemic crisis.

As a result of the growing mismatch between consumer demand and official output supply, the official economic system eroded. Increasing shortages in the official economic systems, the gap between the structure of output as provided by the socialist system and the preferences of people, and - in some countries (Hungary, Poland, Yugoslavia) - double digit inflation have stimulated activities in the shadow economy. Consumers in the official economy faced forced substitution - say, as an illustrative case, drinking alcohol instead of eating bread which was out of stock in the shops frequented. With rising shortages in the official economy and with narrow product varieties available in the official distribution system, many consumers turned to unofficial imports and goods produced by individuals in the shadow economy.

Inefficient Investment and Overinvestment

Although the CMEA countries were not homogeneous with respect to central planning models realized, they shared some common principles relevant for the allocation of resources in the official economy and the shadow economy. The shadow economy obviously satisfies needs with respect to the individuals' preferences for goods and services, income and the structure of wealth. Therefore we have to look for those tendencies in the socialist system that create either a global or a structural imbalance in official markets.

Since the means of production are state-owned, the state acts as a monopolistic producer of investment goods and of most consumption goods. Because government also controls imports and exports of both raw materials and intermediate goods it has rather comprehensive control with respect to the provision of factor inputs. Thus, the socialist system should, in principle be able to provide a socially optimal bundle of output goods, where the use of shadow prices is supposed to contribute to optimal resource planning.[11]

As most socialist countries were economically backwards initially or underindustrialized societies, there is a long tradition in spurring industrialization by heavy state investment - the latter leading in combination with monopolistic industry structures to relatively oversized firms

---

10 See WELFENS, M. (1992a), (1992b).
11 See KANTOROVICH, L.V. (1965), The Best Use of Economic Resources, Oxford: Clarendon.

and hence regional concentration of industries.[12] What evolved as an initial, historically understandable development strategy has, however, become a permanent feature of socialist countries. The reason that high investment output ratios (I/Y) - around 30 percent in most Comecon countries in the 1970s and the early 1980s - became a permanent phenomenon is obvious. As consumer interests are not effectively organized in socialist countries, while firms in the regionally and sectorally highly concentrated investment goods industry are well organized and have close links to the political center, there is a tendency for overinvestment; there was no competitive capital market. The marginal product of capital (MPC) of many investment projects was low or negative and since economic growth g_Y is I/Y times MPC g_Y was low - there was a waste of capital goods in Eastern Europe. Moreover, as control with respect to quality standards is low, the durability of investment goods is impaired so that depreciation is effectively higher than in market economies.

This amounts to saying that the "consumption capacity effect" of investment is low. Foregoing present consumption in order to invest therefore does not necessarily lead to higher future consumption. Private household's savings on which the state banking system pays interest, contribute to financing these investments; but to the extent that the "marginal consumption effect of investment" falls short of the real interest rate paid (which amounts to monetized extra household income), aggregate demand tends to exceed aggregate real consumption output, already depressed by excessive investment spending. The resulting excess demand in consumer goods markets typically cannot be eliminated because prices are government controlled and state-administered at levels below market-clearing.

2.3 State-administered Allocation of Goods and the Pricing Rules

Socialism, often adopted - viewed from a historical perspective - in underindustrialized countries with a very uneven income distribution and thus great differences in individual households' consumption levels, aimed to spread consumption goods in a relatively even way. Hence, price subsidies were often granted in order to assure that basic needs of all people could be satisfied. However, as production goals are fixed by the state at the same time and, in the case of price-subsidized products, output mostly falls short of the amount of goods desired at the fixed price, there is an additional excess demand factor. To the extent that price subsidies lead to a government deficit which is financed by the central bank, price

---

[12] Big firms were assumed to help realize static economies of scale; at the same time the very small number of firms existing in each industry - generally not being exposed to much internal or external competitive pressure - impeded dynamic economies of scale and the diffusion of innovations which often require the interaction of many firms from different industries. In all CMEA countries about 2/3 of the industrial labor force was working in firms with more than 500 employees, whereas in Western market economies firms with less than 500 employees account for the majority of jobs in the official economy.

subsidization transitorily creates an excess supply in the money market. This corresponds to an excess demand in the official consumer goods markets and leads via "forced substitution" on the demand side to a rising demand (cum increasing prices) in the shadow economy. To the extent that a higher demand for foreign exchange arises, either because transactions in the shadow economy require foreign exchange or because acquiring foreign exchange is part of individuals' savings and portfolio management decision, a devaluation of the domestic currency will occur in black exchange rate markets.

In socialist countries product prices in the official sector are determined on a cost basis in all firms and - disregarding price subsidies - prices equal average costs. These might be equal in some exceptional cases with marginal costs, namely when the firms produce an output, where the average cost curve has its minimum. But the decisive characteristic of the cost-based price rule is that in contrast to market economies, relative price increases do not stimulate the most efficient actual and potential producers to increase their output. If prices are raised by governments this might result in the case, where of n production sites the n-1 least efficient ones have increased their output. Prices in a market economy inform the existing and potential suppliers to which level their marginal costs and consequently output could be expanded for each individual firm that wants to be in this market.

The fundamental differences between average costs = prices in the socialist countries and the case of prices = average costs (=marginal costs k') in market economies is illustrated for the simple case of two firms A and B in Figure 1. In a market economy a demand-induced price increase (or a price increase in the world market) implies in the case of profit-maximizing price-taking firms that firm A with a relatively low cost increase in the case of output expansion will increase output more than its rival, firm B. Raising the price from p_1 to p_2 has led to an overall output expansion of q_{A2}-q_{A1} + q_{B2}-q_{B1}. In the context of a socialist country, the same output increase might be realized in a totally different way. Only firm B might increase its output, i.e. a quantity corresponding to q_{A2}-q_{A1} is additionally supplied by firm B whose production is now q_{B3}. Note that q_{A1}+q_{B3} (the socialist case) is equal to q_{A2} + q_{B2}. Average costs are the weighted sum of firm's individual average costs in socialist countries, where the non-optimal allocation of resources clearly implies strong price increases beyond p_2.

If planners raise the production goals only for firm B or if firm B is the only firm that can enforce an augmentation of its labor and capital inputs, the same output increase is obtained with a higher increase in aggregate average production costs. Consequently, the price increase is higher than in the case of a market economy.

Fig. A1: Cost-efficiency, Allocation and Prices

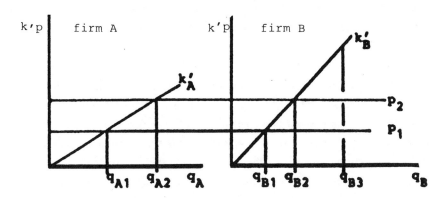

In view in the money excess supply resulting from price subsidies for "basic goods", these price increases might even be welcomed by the monetary authorities because an increase of the aggregate price level reduces inflation pressures in the system. An additional cost push factor might be taken into account. If firm B has increased its output by distracting labor from firm C which supplies with firm D the consumer goods market, this will increase average production costs for consumer goods if C was - relative to D - in a similar way more cost effective than was A vis-à-vis B in the first market considered.

2.4 Tendency to Build up Reserve Capacities

As regards the socialist shadow economy, an important question is, where the factor inputs for unofficial supply come from. The basic mechanisms for this supply to emerge are related to the planning and production process in the official economy.

Production goals are set by the government in quantitative terms. Defining production goals for final output goods requires in turn specifying corresponding production plans for capital and labor supply as well as for intermediate inputs. Since the socialist firms face a monopolistic supply of intermediate inputs, they always face the risk that their only supply source will fail to meet contract-specified or centrally planned production goals so that potential short-falls in the delivery of intermediate inputs are always likely. Due to their information advantage vis-à-vis the planning authorities, they have the means to obtain the consent of the authorities for such excessive input allocation. The well-known system-specific problem of the optimal "tautness" of plans emerges here. As the central authorities accept firms' exaggerated demand for factor inputs, they implicitly allow the producers of intermediate goods to be allocated a higher amount of factor inputs than are actually required for planned production of consumption and investment goods. Suppliers of the investment goods industry and the military-industrial complex enjoy a particularly strong position because of the already mentioned tendency of central planners to overinvest; the latter might partly be understood as a compensation for the lack of disembodied and embodied technological progress.[13]

No producer has an interest in revealing the excess stock of factor inputs available, namely for two reasons: (1) with excess factor supply it is - and this is a traditional argument - relatively easy to meet production goals which is in the interest of managers pursuing a career in the socialist industry with its ultimate "crowning options" in the state bureaucracy;[14] (2) it raises within the firm's competition for workers their ability to get the workforce they need, because workers can be offered either shorter effective working hours due to easily realizable production goals (absence from the working place is thus encouraged) or the workers receive an implicit extra income by enjoying the benefit of drawing upon some factor inputs for their own private use. Input hoarding thereby ultimately reinforces the tendency of an excess demand in the official labor market. Together with the soft budget constraint faced by socialist firms and guaranteed full-employment, excess demand conditions in labor markets contribute to a tendency of consistent wage pressure.

Since socialist firms which face a soft budget constraint cannot go bankrupt there is continuous pressure on the government to accommodate wage increases and excessive investment (excessive in the sense of those projects which yield marginal products of capital which are below real interest rates). The only countervailing factor is the budget constraint faced by the government itself. If wage pressures lead to higher government budget deficits which, in turn, are financed by an accommodative monetary policy, excess supply in the money market results. This excess supply is rapidly exhausted by rising prices in the price-flexible shadow economy and by an increasing domestic currency depreciation rate. As foreign currencies, mainly the US dollar and the Deutsche mark, partly serve as a means of transaction in the unofficial economy and constitute an important element of wealth holding, there is the phenomenon of currency substitution which tends to accelerate with the rise of the domestic monetary overhang and the expansion of the socialist shadow economy. From a theoretical point of view it is clear that the price of foreign exchange (in black markets) will rise until the marginal utility of domestic and foreign currency is equilibrated.[15]

---

[13] As regards the low innovativeness of socialist systems see BALCEROWICZ, L. (1988), Innovationsspezifika, Wirtschaftssystem und Innovationsleistung von Wirtschaftssystemen, in: WELFENS, P.J.J.; BALCEROWICZ, L., eds., Innovationsdynamik im Systemvergleich, Heidelberg: Physica, 28-59.

[14] This is in contrast to market economies, where businessmen rarely consider politics as the highest dimension of a successful business career.

[15] In periods of a real devaluation of the domestic currency redistributive wealth effects in favor of those who have or have access to foreign exchange is to be expected.

Currency depreciation and rising prices for assets as well as for goods in the flexible price shadow economy will eliminate an excess supply in the money market which in turn raises wages and incomes paid in the shadow economy and thus impairs work motivation in the official economy. Firms that face increasing absenteeism and reducing work efforts will react by pressing the government to allocate higher wage funds so that wages paid in the official economy can be raised in nominal terms and maintained in real terms - the latter requiring that rising prices for consumers expenditures in the shadow economy be matched either by higher nominal wages which increase the range of loss-making firms and thereby raises the public deficit that is covered by printing money; or, above all, as in the case of civil servants and socialist administrators ("managers"), by extra income from bribery and corruption which represents a kind of profit-sharing scheme among those earning high incomes in the shadow economy, whereby the legitimacy of the socialist command model is undermined; or real income positions are maintained by "quasi-income" from improved and relatively cheaper access to goods, services and foreign exchange supplied by the firm or the state at preferential conditions which contradicts the socialist emphasis on equality of incomes.

Competing and rising aspirations of various influential groups in the society lead in combination with a growing disorganization of the official sector and a stagnating output to serious disruptions: for social reasons rising price subsidies for mass staple goods cannot be avoided, for politico-economic reasons the growth of investment and military budgets can hardly be reduced and for lack of efficient modernization and use of imported technologies a growing transfer of resources is required as consequence of rising foreign indebtedness. Socialist governments then try to raise revenues by increasing "internal exports", that is selling domestic goods for foreign exchange in special shops such as INTERSHOP in the former GDR, PEWEX in Poland or BERIOSKA in the Soviet Union. Moreover, trying to raise revenue from printing money becomes increasingly important, where it is clear that inflationary impulses do not immediately show up in a rise of state-administered prices in the official economy.

2.5 Quasi-inflation in the Socialist Economy

The Monetary Sphere in the Socialist Economy
In socialist economies the monetary sphere is not as inactive as socialist economy models or planners have always suggested, and basic analytical tools developed for market economies - such as the demand for money and well-defined monetary aggregates - are indeed useful in

socialist countries, too.[16] The determinants of the money supply and the transmission
mechanism, however differ, distinctively from Western market economies.

In socialist economies many investment projects dubbed as strategic investment projects were
oversized and liquidity-creating due to the absence of functional capital markets and the system
specific soft budget constraint operating in a gradually deteriorating internal and external
framework.[17] Soft credit conditions and the absence of capital markets as a control device of
investment decisions created only one major link between the real sphere and the monetary
sphere. Moreover, there was direct currency substitution in the private sector whose preference
for convertible Western currencies has played a disturbing role in most CPEs. Systemic traits,
namely currency inconvertibility, multiple exchange rates and black markets for foreign
exchange largely represent sustaining impulses for inefficiency and distortions of the official
incentive system. This generates impulses for the growth of the shadow economy in which a
considerable part of transactions typically require foreign exchange so that a direct link exists
between the real shadow economy and the black currency market as the monetary shadow
economy. Analytically this implies that transaction technologies $T=t(k)$ C - with $k=(M/P)/C$
denoting the real money stock per consumption unit C; $t'<0$, $t''>0$ - are different in the
official and the unofficial economy.[18]

Moreover, in some socialist countries, such as Poland, Hungary and Yugoslavia, the officially
existing possibility for individuals to hold a foreign exchange account that offered
internationally competitive interest rates implied an additional side constraint for monetary

[16] See e.g. THIEME, H.J., ed. (1985), Geldtheorie. Entwicklung, Stand und systemvergleichende Anwendung,
Baden-Baden: Nomos 1985; HARTWIG, K.H. (1987), Monetäre Steuerungsprobleme in sozialistischen
Volkswirtschaften, Stuttgart: Fischer 1987; BOTH, M. and WELFENS, P.J.J. (1989), Internationale
Determinanten des Geldumlaufs, in: CASSEL, D. et al., eds., op. cit. 151-168; McKINNON, R. (1990),
Financial Control During the Transition from a Centrally Planned to a Market Economy, paper presented at the
AER annual meeting, Washington D.C., Dec. 28, 1990. Moreover, there are interesting parallels between the
external monetary control aspects of developing countries and socialist economies: See CLAASSEN, E.M., ed.
(1991), Exchange Rate Policies of Developing and Socialist Countries, San Francisco: ICS 1991.

[17] The role of investment behavior for macroeconomic disequilibria is stressed e.g. by GROSFELD, I (1987),
Modelling Planner's Investment Behavior: Poland, 1956-81, Journal of Comparative Economics, Vol. 11 (1987),
180-191.

[18] If per consumption unit shopping time is given by T and T*, respectively, the individual maximizes a utility
function with the arguments consumption in the official economy C, C* in the shadow economy and F leisure,
where maximization of U(C,C*,F) is subject to the constraints $T+T*+L+L*+F=1$ (with L, L* = labor in the
official and the unofficial economy) and the budget constraint. With currency substitution in the sense that
transactions in the shadow economy as well as in the official economy - say for bribe payments - require foreign
exchange the transaction functions are $T=t(m,f)C$ and $T*=t*(m,f)C$, where m denotes M/P and f the real stock of
foreign exchange, respectively. If, to stay as simple as possible, production technologies were the same in both
sectors and only labor inputs were required, total real output $Z=zL$ and the budget constraint would read with b_0
denoting nonmonetary real wealth: $b_0 + \Sigma a^t(1-T-T*-F) = \Sigma a^t [C+qC* + im + (j+\alpha)f]$, where a is the
discount factor $1/1+r$, i the nominal interest rate on domestic deposits and j the interest rate on foreign exchange
deposits. The right-hand side makes clear that output is reduced if T (or T*) is increasing, and it will increase
whenever the opportunity costs - say the nominal interest rate or the devaluation rate - of holding money rise so
that the desired m is reduced by a rising effective price level for the overall economy.

policy. In contrast to Western countries there is a one-tier banking system that is under the control of the central bank; however, the central bank itself is subject to the control of the finance ministry which in turn faces pressure from various influential groups.

A specific problem of currency substitution is related to the fact that the effective aggregate money supply consists of the domestic component M plus the foreign component eM* (e=black market exchange rate, M*=foreign exchange) such that a devaluation of the domestic currency raises via a higher e the effective money supply. This implies a double endogeneity of the aggregate money supply - for the foreign component via changes in e and for the domestic component via the soft budget constraint. For any desired transition to a market economy this implies a double monetary control problem. On the one hand, a unified and relatively stable exchange rate is needed which in turn requires a sharp nominal devaluation of the official exchange rate (raising eM). It often has been argued that socialist economies suffer from a monetary overhang which is equivalent to inflationary phenomena in market economies in some way. There has, however, never been a clear concept of how to develop a consistent system-independent analytical framework. Subsequently we will address the system-specific feature of preferential supply of goods and services in the command economy and then the question of what a basic approach to a system-independent framework for measuring and analyzing inflation could look like.

2.5.1 Administered Prices and Preferential Supply in the Official Economy

Relevance of Systemic Principles for the Shadow Economy
In socialist economies the means of production are state-owned and the state firms act as monopolistic producers of investment goods and of most consumption goods. Because government also controls imports and exports of both raw materials and intermediate goods it has a rather comprehensive control with respect to the provision of factor inputs; furthermore, the state controls the official foreign exchange market via its monopolistic state-banking system.[19] Thus, the socialist system should, in principle be able to provide an optimal bundle of output goods to all consumers - at least if planners' preferences would mirror those of the consumers and if "shadow prices" (in the sense of mathematical optimization theory) could be correctly derived from consistent models. Clearly, reality is very different. E.g. KALICKI (1989) finds that a rationing variable R is significant in the demand for money in Poland: $\ln m_t - \ln m_{t-1} = z(\ln m^d_t - \ln m_{t-1})$, with $\ln m^d_t = b_0 + b_1 Y + b_2 R + b_3 \pi^* + b^4 a$ (a=devaluation rate; π^*=unofficial inflation rate), where the adjustment coefficient z is relatively high.

---

[19] Cooperative banks play a relatively important role only in Hungary and Poland within the CMEA country group.

Certain goods and services are allocated by the government or the state firms in a preferential way to civil servants and the workers in core industries (firms in the export and military goods industry). Even the officially supplied, generally available goods contain an element of indirect preferential supply in the sense that any excess demand situation discriminates against those people who are less well informed and have high opportunity costs of standing in line.

Subsequently, we assume within a simple model that initial demand in the official economy is given by 26 consumers (consumer groups) A to Z. Furthermore, it is assumed that the marginal willingness to pay depends on income or wealth and that income may serve as a proxy for the opportunity cost of standing in line. Assume that total official production of goods is q_1, where, say, half of this quantity, q_0 is sold (preferentially) at a relatively low state-administered price to those groups whose marginal willingness to pay is given by the arc SX on the demand curve in Figure A2 (civil servants and military personnel indeed had preferential access to goods and services in CMEA markets).

Fig. A2: Interdependency Between the Official Economy and the Shadow Economy

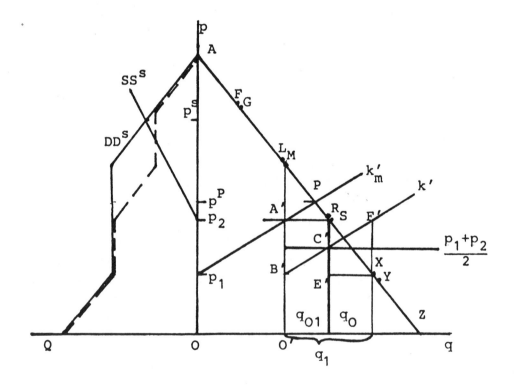

Furthermore, at the same time $q_1-q_0=q_{01}$ is sold in the official distribution system at the state-administered price p_2. Hence there will be a kinked excess demand curve which represents demand for the unofficial economy. Who will succeed in satisfying his/her needs in the official economy? If group G-L (see their corresponding willingness to pay as expressed by the arc GL on the demand curve) were to be the happy ones, a double-kinked (dashed) demand curve for the shadow economy could be derived.[20] However, as those groups will stand longest in line whose opportunity costs of time are lowest, the most likely group to obtain the goods officially supplied is MR. Fig. A2 also shows the marginal cost curve k' of the official socialist economy, where the origin 0' is relevant. If - as has been assumed here - the price p_2 is such that the average price is $(p_1+p_2)/2$, the surface A'B'C'S is equal to the loss surface C'E'X F'. This means the implicit price subsidies (losses) for preferential goods supply are compensated by the profits recorded by selling half of the goods officially produced at price p_2. The excess demand curve can be interpreted as the demand curve DD^S in the shadow economy; the intersection of the demand and the supply schedule determine the quickly established equilibrium price level in the shadow economy. The equilibrium price p^S is always above the official price, and the divergence between p^S in the shadow economy and the state-administered price provides an opportunity for "unproductive" income, namely for those who obtained goods at preferential prices - and sold those goods in the shadow economy. A rightward shift of the demand schedule (say, because of a monetary financed wage increase) in the official economy was bound to raise prices in the shadow economy, to widen the gap between administered prices and market prices and induce a devaluation in black markets. Increasing rationing problems implied rising prices of used consumer durables, e.g. used cars.

By contrast, in market economies, prices in the shadow economy are typically lower than in the official market system. The reason for this is straightforward. In the official market economy, the demand side is served "from above". Profit-maximizing firms which are free to choose their offer price (then naturally accepting the associated market demand) have an incentive to serve those clients whose marginal willingness to pay is relatively high; this holds even more if price discrimination is possible. In a market economy with an identical cost curve (k'_m) as in our socialist market economy, there would be a higher official supply at the market price p^P, where consumers A to P are satisfied.[21] In a market economy only the unsatisfied demand QZ would reflect the demand potential for the shadow economy. That this demand finds a corresponding supply in the shadow economy at a price below the official price is assured by the incentive and ability of people to avoid taxes and regulations imposed in the official sector.

---

[20] See for the case of a simple kinked demand curve as the derived demand curve for the shadow economy: WELFENS, M.J. (1988), Das Phänomen der Schattenwirtschaft im Sozialismus, Osteuropa-Wirtschaft, 33, 1-15.
[21] See WELFENS (1989). Naturally, this diverging allocation pattern of capitalist versus socialist economies explains the preferences of people with high incomes for market economy solutions in the allocation of resources.

2.5.2 The Dynamics of the Socialist Shadow Economy

The socialist shadow economy, defined as economic activities that violate the rules of the official command economy system, comprises both activities within and among socialist firms as well as activities in which private domestic households, public servants and foreign individuals engage. The shadow economy consists of illegal activities, namely in contrast to the second economy which is the small range of legal activities of the private sector in the official socialist system; there is a natural overlap as many individuals who pursue legal transactions benefit from the dual-use of their premises. Shadow economic activities can be value-adding and, in this respect, are analogous to the shadow economy in Western market economies in which moonlighting and illegal (undeclared/untaxed) production activities take place that are not recorded in the System of National Accounts. An important difference will, however, be emphasized in this contribution: in contrast to market economies, the shadow economy in socialist systems is changing the income and wealth distribution such that not only the system of official material incentives is weakened but also the goal of the official system to create a society in which major inequalities of income do not exist.

The shadow economy - the officially unrecorded amount of productive and redistributive activities in the overall economic system - has grown for many years in market economies, where the phenomenon became widely analyzed in the late 1970s. However, only in the 1980s did the considerable scope and momentum of the shadow economy in Eastern Europe and some other socialist countries, especially China, make the socialist shadow economy a more analyzed phenomenon.[22] There are, of course, some legal private business activities in socialist systems.

In Western industrialized countries the growth of informal shadow-economic activities which comprise the legal self-service economy and the illegal unofficial economy has been a consistent phenomenon of the late 1960s and the 1970s, when phases of economic stagnation

---

[22] An early assessment of the shadow economy in market economies is GUTMANN, P.M. (1977), The Subterranean Economy, Financial Analysts Journal, Vol. 33, 26-34; HEDTKAMP, G., ed. (1983), Beiträge zum Problem der Schattenwirtschaft, Berlin: Duncker & Humblot; SCHÄFER, W., ed. (1984), Schattenökonomie: Theoretische Grundlagen und wirtschaftspolitische Konsequenzen, Göttingen: Vandenhoeck; WECK, H.; POMMEREHNE, W.W. and FREY, B.S. (1984), Schattenwirtschaft, München: Vahlen. A comparative approach to the shadow economy in East and West was developed by CASSEL, D. (1986), Funktionen der Schattenwirtschaft im Koordinationsmechanismus von Markt- und Planwirtschaften, Ordo, Vol. 37, 73-104; GROSSMAN, G. (1986), ed., Studies in the Second Economy of Communist Countries, Berkeley: ICS. The phenomenon for both market economies and socialist command economies was analyzed in ALLESANDRINI, S. and DALLAGO, B., eds. (1987), The Unofficial Economy, Aldershot: Gower; GÄRTNER, W. and WENIG, A., eds. (1985); CASSEL, D. et al., eds. (1989), Inflation und Schattenwirtschaft im Sozialismus. Bestandsaufnahme, Erklärungsansätze und Reformvorschläge für die Volksrepublik Polen, Hamburg: S+W Steuer- und Wirtschaftsverlag; FEIGE, E.L., ed. (1989), The Underground Economies, Cambridge: Cambridge University Press.

of the official economy and an increasing burden of taxation and regulation of the modern welfare state characterized most OECD economies. [23]

In the shadow economy goods are produced or privately imported and durable consumer goods are exchanged as well as assets. Hence, part of shadow economic activities is value-adding and affects the allocation of factors in the overall system; other activities reflect mostly redistribution effects. KORNAI has argued that value-added in the unofficial economy amounts to roughly 20 percent of Hungary's GDP. [24] WISNIEWSKI's empirical investigation for Poland showed an acceleration of the shadow economy's share, too; from 3.8 percent in 1970 this share rose to 13.2 percent in 1982. [25] This problem is less evident for Romania, the (former) GDR and the CSSR, but there is some casual evidence that the second economy is growing in these countries, too. [26] As regards the (ex-)USSR the value of transactions made in the shadow economy is said to reach at least a third of the transaction volume in the official economy, and it seems that the majority of the population is involved in unofficial activities - including "speculation". In 1990 laws were tightened on speculation although by Western perceptions speculation is often the induced consequence of huge price divergences between state-administered prices and the higher marginal willingness to pay of many consumers. [27]

---

[23] See e.g. TANZI, V. (1980), ed., The Underground Economy in the United States and Abroad, Lexington: Lexington; FREY, B.S. and POMMEREHNE, W.W. (1983), Schattenwirtschaft und Schwarzarbeit als Folgen des Sozialstaats, in: KOSLOWSKI, P. et al. (1983), Chancen und Grenzen des Sozialstaats, Tübingen: Mohr, 135-151, FEIGE (1989), op. cit.

[24] KORNAI, J. (1986), The Hungarian Reform Process, Journal of Economic Literature, 24 (1986), 1687-1737; see also BREZINSKY, H.; ROS, C. (1985), The Development of the Second Economy in Hungary, Korean Journal of East-West European Studies, 1 (1985), 95-127.

[25] WISNIEWSKI, M. (1985), Zrodla i rozmiary drugiego obiegu gospodarczego w Polsce, Ekonomista, 1985, No. 6, 913-936. On Poland's shadow economy see also LANDAU, Z. (1987), Selected Problems of the Unofficial Economy in Poland, in: ALLESANDRINI, S.; DALLAGO, B., eds., The Unofficial Economy, Aldershot (Gower) 1987. An interesting case study in the system of Poland's parallel markets is CHAREMZA, W.; GRONICKI, M., QUANDT, R.E. (1988), Modelling Parallel Markets in Centrally Planned Economies: The Case of the Automobile Market in Poland, European Economic Review, 22 (1988), 861-884.

[26] See e.g. BREZINSKI, H.; PETRESCU, P. (1986), The Second Economy in Romania - Dynamic Sector, Discussion Paper, FB 5, Universität Paderborn, 1986. ASLUND, A. (1983), Private Enterprise in Soviet-Type Economies: A Comparison between Poland and the GDR, Osteuropa-Wirtschaft, 28 (1983), 176-193. Recently, the growing shadow economy in the PR China has become a subject of interest; see JAMANN, W.; MENKHOFF, T. (1988), Licht und Schatten - Chinas Zweite Wirtschaft, Osteuropa-Wirtschaft, 33 (1988), 16-30. For a comprehensive analysis see also my paper in Economic Systems, 1992/2.

[27] Empirical evidence of a growing economy can be gained from an analysis of money circulation which is also an approach used for the analysis of the capitalist shadow economy. The basic idea behind this approach is to take a base year in which no shadow economy exists. Denoting nominal value-added in the official and the inoffical economy as YP and ZP* (P and P* for the respective price indices of the two economies), a modified Fisher equation that represents equilibrium in the money market would be: $MV(i,..) = YP + ZP^*$. In a socialist system the state-fixed nominal interest rate on deposits is not a good measure of the opportunity cost of holding money balances - the proportional rate of the black market exchange rate could be a more meaningful variable. A seemingly occuring increase in V can than be explained by the existence and rise of the unobservable real value-added in the shadow economy (Z^*) and the increasing money demand due to high and possibly fast rising level of price in the official economy (P^*).

The question arises which forces are underlying the growing socialist shadow economy and which forces act as a boundary for its growth. In the following analysis we show that the socialist shadow economy has its roots in systemic factors and that it markedly differs from the capitalist shadow economy. So far, analysis of the second economies in both systems has shown that the shadow economy contributes to the structural flexibility of the overall system and, to the extent that it reduces the political pressure for reforms, it serves a considerable social mollifier function; the labor market is viewed as playing a central role for shadow economic growth. In market economies high unemployment and labor market regulations as well as the tax wedge encourage activities in the second economy, whereas in socialist systems lack of effective control with respect to absenteeism in the official system in combination with overmaning stimulates such activities.[28]

Growth of the Shadow Economy and Monetary Overhang
Growing consumer dissatisfaction was the consequence of a system that offered neither the amount, nor the variety, nor the quality of goods and services desired. Shortages in the official system and overall production reserves thus generated a rapidly growing shadow economy, whose supply draws on overmaning and reserves of factor inputs in the socialist system as well as on leisure. Contrary to certain groups of the population which had privileged access to goods at low state-administered prices, many people had to buy goods and services in the price-flexible shadow economy with its high market-clearing prices; the result was a new economic inequality among people with their very different assets and skills to be used in the shadow economy.[29] The shadow economy absorbed part of the excess money supply that was created as a consequence of the government budget deficits covered by printing money at a pace exceeding output growth. The illegal nature of most shadow-economic activities - necessary and useful as they were themselves - nurtured a growing system of bribery and profit-sharing schemes that undermined the material incentive system applied in the official economy.[30] Furthermore, as governments in all CMEA countries set up "foreign exchange shops", where goods in short supply could be bought by foreign and domestic residents, the population's demand for Western foreign currency gradually increased, especially after inflationary expectations spread in the 1980s. The effective money supply was raised by devaluations in the foreign exchange market since the total money supply is composed of the stock of domestic money M + eM* (e=exchange rate, M* amount of unofficial foreign

[28] CASSEL, D. (1986), Funktionen der Schattenwirtschaft im Koordinationsmechanismus von Markt- und Planwirtschaften, Ordo, 37 (1986), 73-104; CASSEL, D.; CICHY, E.U. (1986), Explaining the Growing Shadow Economy in East and West: A Comparative Systems Approach, Comparative Economic Studies/ACES Bulletin, 28 (1986), 415-428.

[29] See WELFENS, M. (1988), Das Phänomen der Schattenwirtschaft im Sozialismus, Osteuropa Wirtschaft, Vol. 33, 1-15.

[30] See WELFENS, M. (1989), Bedingungen der Entstehung und Entwicklung der inoffiziellen Erwerbswirtschaft, in: CASSEL, D.; et al., eds., Inflation und Schattenwirtschaft im Sozialismus, Hamburg: S+W Steuer- und Wirtschaftsverlag, 375-404.

exchange). The money supply in socialism was endogenous; via the soft budget constraint and, later, via currency substitution. In the 1980s, the stock of foreign currency (evaluated at black market exchange rates) in Poland was almost as high as the stock of domestic money.[31] The Deutsche mark and the U.S. dollar were the preferred currencies in the long-observed process of currency substitution in Eastern Europe which implies reduced seigniorage gains for domestic central banks and ultimately a resource transfer to Germany and the U.S., respectively. The real devaluation of CMEA currencies in the 1980s increased the incentive to work for (foreign) cash in the shadow economy, to work abroad (mostly illegally in some EC countries) and to sell assets, goods and services to businessmen and tourists from abroad. Increasing absenteeism at the official workplace and the declining working morale reduced economic growth in the official economy, aggravated shortages and distribution conflicts in the official economic system, and furthermore eroded the political legitimacy of the socialist system.[32]

Systemic Contradictions

Parallel to the reduction of economic growth of the official net material product, the socialist shadow economy has expanded. Increasing shortages in the official economic system, the gap between the structure of output as provided by the socialist system and the preferences of people, and - in some countries (CMEA: Hungary, Poland; also Yugoslavia) - double digit inflation have stimulated activities in the shadow economy. Goods are produced or privately imported, and durable consumer goods are exchanged as well as assets. Hence, part of shadow economic activities is value-adding and affects the allocation of factors in the overall system; other activities primarily reflect redistribution effects, where there is a clear tendency for considerable income inequalities to develop which are difficult to accept for a society where equality of income and wealth has been emphasized officially.

The shadow economy is by no means a quantité négligeable. Observers argued that value-added in the unofficial economy was significant in Poland, the USSR and Hungary.[33] DALLAGO estimates that - expressed in full-time job equivalents - the socialist shadow economy represents 44 % of official registered employment in Hungary, where output reaches

[31] See BOTH, M. and WELFENS, P.J.J. (1989), Internationale Determinanten des Geldangebots, in: CASSEL, D.; et al., eds., Inflation und Schattenwirtschaft im Sozialismus, Hamburg: S+W Steuer- und Wirtschaftsverlag, 151-168.

[32] See CASSEL, D. et al., eds. (1989), Inflation und Schattenwirtschaft im Sozialismus, Hamburg: S+W Verlag.

[33] See KORNAI (1986), op. cit.; see also BREZINSKY, H. and ROS, C. (1985), The Development of the Second Economy in Hungary, Korean Journal of East-West European Studies, 1 (1985), 95-127. On the USSR see SERGEEW, A. (1987), Netrudovye dochody: ekonomiceskaja priroda, struktura, puti likvidacji, Voprosy Ekonomiki, 1987/6, 85-93.

15 % of official production.[34] The various approaches to estimate the Polish shadow economy (GORKSI and KIERCZYNSKI, 1989) put the shadow economy in 1985 in the range of 9-29 percent if one refers to personal income only. However, one should not forget that with a real percentage share of, say, 25 % and a ratio of prices in the shadow economy to those in the official economy of 4:1, the nominal income in the shadow economy is as high as the official one; and its impact on the demand for money could hence be decisive. Few authors recognized the significant redistribution effects of the socialist shadow economy.[35] Durable consumer goods and foreign exchange became preferred stores of value in socialist economies with their rationing phenomena; the depreciation rate of foreign exchange was the implicit rate of return of foreign cash balances. Currency depreciation accentuated repressed inflation - created by money-financed (or credit financed) wage increases and inefficient investment projects - which in turn fueled the expansion of the shadow economy. The labor market is viewed here as playing a central role for shadow economic growth.[36] Those who had access to foreign exchange or rationed goods at preferential prices enjoyed an extra income.

Capitalism will bring new problems: Tax evasion will spread and the sharp rise of unemployment will create a new potential of unrecorded value-adding. In the transition phase to a market economy the shadow economy - this time of the capitalist type - might again become a welcomed kind of social shock absorber. The ex-USSR is likely to witness a rapid expansion of an already large shadow economy in the 1990s; income redistribution and corruption will play a role; the incentive system will be weakened and excess demand in some sectors could increase, while excess supply in other sectors could emerge at the same time.[37]

With the near-elimination of private sector production and a full-fledged socialist sector absorbing the great majority of the active population, the mismatches between the peoples' preferences and the output bundle produced according to crude state plans became increasingly obvious. Increasing per capita incomes which support the desire for more differentiated products as well as some spill-over effects from Western countries played a role in the shadow economy in Eastern Europe from the very beginning. In the CMEA countries the legal private

---

[34] See DALLAGO, B. (1989), The Non-Socialized Sector in Hungary: An Attempt at Estimation of its Importance, Jahrbuch der Wirschafts Osteuropas, Vol. 13, No. 2, 67-92.
[35] E.g. BICANIC, I. (1987), The Inequality Impact of the Unofficial Economy in Yugoslavia, in: ALESSANDRINI, S. and DALLAGO, B., eds., 323-336; WELFENS, M. (1989).
[36] It is true that already in the 1960s and the 1970s phenomena of repressed inflation were analyzed: e.g. BERNSTEIN, M. (1950), Latent Inflation, IMF Staff Papers, Vol. 1, 1-16; HOLZMAN, F.D. (1960), Soviet Inflationary Pressures 1928-57, Causes and Cures, Quarterly Journal of Economics, Vol. 74, 167-188. PORTES raised doubts about persistant inflationary pressures: PORTES, R. (1977), The Problem of Inflation: Lessons from the East European Experience, Economica, Vol. 44, 109-130.
[37] This could undermine the credibility of a market-oriented systemic transformation. The transformation to a market economy represents a public good: many could benefit from its "provision" but nobody is willing to incur private costs or accept sacrifices as long as free-riding is attractive and as long as influential groups of the socialist economy can defend their positions via side payments and "profit-sharing".

sector's activities are concentrated in agriculture (plus in the services industry) and reached in Hungary and the GDR 36% and 24 % of overall agricultural output in 1987 (BREZINSKI, 1992). The second economy (shadow economy plus the official private sector) played the role of a flexible market-determined subsystem in the overall economy.

As long as the shadow economy is a minor phenomenon in quantitative terms, neither the people nor policymakers will be much concerned about a sector with some clear traits. Goods and services are produced in the unofficial economy - partly legally during leisure time, partly illegally by unofficially resorting to factor inputs (including working time) in the firms of the socialist sector. Scarce goods are also privately imported.

2.5.3 Differentiated Product Supply in a Command Economy

An alternative way to model the link between the official economy and the socialist shadow economy could emphasize the divergence between the product assortment supplied by the official system and the desired or most preferred goods of consumers. The official economy offers a small variety of goods supplied in uncertain amounts at a fixed state-administered price, whereas the shadow economy offers a greater variety of goods - including imported ones - at higher prices. Emphasis on product varieties suggests employing a Lancaster-type approach with two industries, where an appropriate modification of models developed by SALOP and SALANT for the case of market economies is a promising research avenue.[38]

In the SALOP-SALANT model one industry supplies differentiated goods, which are noncombinable for consumers. At the same time a homogeneous "outside good" (which can be used as a numeraire) is supplied by the second industry, possibly under perfect competitive conditions. Consumers' location in the characteristic "variety space" is defined by each consumer's most preferred product variant (see appendix for an application).

3. Stagnation and Collapse

After the 1970s economic stagnation and the negative repercussion effects of the intensive-growth-strategy became increasingly apparent in Eastern Europe, where Hungary and Poland had embarked upon a modernization strategy financed by western capital inflows. With high inflation rates in OECD countries, the associated low real interest rates greatly encouraged foreign indebtedness. This tendency was reinforced by political pressure or "encouragement"

---

[38] See SALOP, S.C. (1979), Monopolistic Competition with Outside Goods, Bell Journal of Economics, 10: 141-156; SALANT, D.J. (1980), Quality, Location Choice and Imperfect Competition, Doctoral Dissertation, University of Rochester.

to extend loans to Eastern Europe. In 1980 investment output ratios were high in the CMEA: investment ratios reached 30.6 % in the USSR, 38.1 in Hungary, 32.1 in Poland, 36.2 in the CSSR, 33.9 in the GDR, 33.9 in Bulgaria and 43.8 in Romania. Ten years later these ratios had declined by 5-15 percentage points - except for the USSR and Bulgaria.

With human and material production factor reserves increasingly exhausted, the switch to a more science-based expansion strategy became necessary - a challenge that was not met in Eastern Europe at all with the exception of a few technically successful ventures with insignificant economic pay-off, e.g. in the military industry. In addition there was no significant growth of the services industry, which had traditionally been discriminated against in socialist countries; however, without a growing service industry that supplies customer-taylored services both to business and the household sector, there is no modern manufacturing sector and thus no prospering economy.

In industrialized market economies economic growth is roughly attributed equally to labor, capital and technological progress. With increasing factor inputs an industrial country might have a sustainable economic growth of 3 percent p.a. which implies a ninefold increase of real output in one generation (75 years), whereas a country with no growth of labor and know-how might grow at only 1 percent (doubling output in 75 years) or even stagnate. The traditional command economy which relies upon a monopolistic network of state-owned firms and priority allocation of government funds for high investment might generate economic growth as long as economies of scale from standard technologies or dynamic learning effects can be mobilized and as long as political legitimacy and hence working morale in the state-owned socialist production system is preserved. However, in the late 1970s and in the 1980s the changing direction of international technological progress confronted the socialist economies with four major challenges that were basically not met for systemic reasons:[39]
- Resource-saving miniaturization (dubbed here "bonsai products", paying due attention to Japanese achievements) required sophisticated quality control and the full mobilization of individual know-how and skills at the shopfloor level; neither the intra-firm communication structures in the socialist sector and its incentive system nor the detail-neglecting command approach in R&D as well as in investment were up to this challenge. The two oil price shocks of the 1970s increased the demand for energy-saving and resource-saving products and production technologies worldwide - except for Eastern Europe where prices of oil and gas were artificially fixed below world market prices. Facing the need to integrate into the world market economy in the 1990s Eastern Europe will have to switch to world market

---

[39] See WELFENS, P.J.J.(1987), Growth, Innovation Dynamics and Welfare: A Comparative Economic Systems Approach, paper presented at the second European Economic Association meeting, Copenhagen, August 22-24; WELFENS, P.J.J. (1988), Innovationstheorie, -politik und -dynamik im Systemvergleich, in: Welfens, P.J.J.; Balcerowicz, L., eds., Innovationsdynamik im Systemvergleich, Heidelberg: Physica, 1-24.

oil/energy prices which implies that the shocks of systemic transformation will be aggravated by supply-side shocks.

- Flexible production techniques were not available which would have allowed the East European countries to meet the increasing demand for product variety which is typical for the stage after basic needs have been satisfied and which is a cornerstone for success in world markets; moreover the demand for services was not met by the slowly reacting planning system, where vested interests of heavy industry favored high investment in traditional industries. About 30 percent of national output was typically devoted to investment, but the CMEA countries never reached economic growth similar to Japan, where investment-output ratios also hovered around the 30 percent level in the 1960s and 1970s. Low interest rates and the "soft budget constraint" (KORNAI[40]) - meaning easy access to subsidies - encouraged permanent overinvestment, oftentimes in inefficient projects.

- Ambitious to meet Western technological and economic advances, the political claim of the communist party monopoly implied tremendous opportunity costs, as modern flexible communication, information and production technologies could not be applied on a wide basis. With multi-use copy machines, modems, fax-machines and printers being considered as a threat to political control, millions of people were denied valuable experience with advanced technologies and know-how, where COCOM-restrictions added problems on the hardware-side. Software as well as hardware that could have been used to build more decentralized flexible production structures was hardly used, and - apart from the shadow economy - political control over the population with modern technologies was the only growth field left.

- Non-physical investment played an increasing role in modern industry; it is increasingly the software as well as R&D which determine together with the hardware (investment goods) the growth of output in industry. Software development and R&D activities are both located within firms, but are also undertaken in specialized service industries - some of which form national and international joint ventures which require extensive exchange of information and know-how. Investment was inefficient and fully hardware-oriented in socialist Eastern Europe where investment-output ratios reached Japanese levels, but since the marginal product of capital was very low the growth of output was low, especially in terms of the growth of consumption goods (the latter partly due to a high share of investment directed toward the military-industrial complex). Tab. A8 gives an indication how high investment-GNP ratios were in 1975, and it also becomes evident that only in the 1980s did investment output ratios decline. To enter the modern computer and telecom revolution which is so closely related to the growing software-orientation of modern market economies, it would have been necessary to give up the government monopoly on photocopiers, fax-machines and

---

[40] KORNAI, J. (1980), Economics of Shortage, 2 Vols., Amsterdam (North-Holland) 1980. For a comprehensive discussion of financial and real problems in Eastern Europe see BOLZ, K., ed. (1990), Die Wirtschaft der osteuropäischen Länder an der Wende zu den 90er Jahren, Hamburg: HWWA.

the media. While the hammer and sickle were the symbols of socialist economies the chip
and the parabolic antenna symbolized modern Western ways of organizing production and
exchange worldwide. Giving up the party monopoly on the media was impossible for
systemic reasons since it implied giving room to spontaneous individualism (possibly counter-
revolutionary) and letting the population learn about the increasing East-West gap in the
standard of living in Europe. Moreover, the catching-up process of the Asian NICs, which
overtook the CMEA countries in the 1980s in per capita incomes, would have become
apparent. The party bureaucracy had no explanation for this development nor could it offer a
remedy that would not have at the same time eroded its politico-economic power basis. The
state owned the industry, and the state was "owned" by the party bureaucracy. Privatizing
part of the economy, for instance, would have weakened not only the scope of central
planning but have reduced the party's economic power which was based on the monopolistic
position in allocating management positions, jobs, consumer durables, etc.

Tab. A8: Investment GNP Ratios in Eastern Europe and West Germany

	1975	1980	1985	1987
(West Germany)	20.6	24.8	19.5	19.8*
GDR	29.8	29.6	20.4	21.8
USSR	26.0	28.0	30.0	31.0
Bulgaria	38.9	27.6	22.3	19.6
Romania	41.0	41.4	37.0	36.4
Poland	37.3	30.0	30.1	27.9
CSSR	33.8	33.3	28.0	30.5
Hungary	37.6	34.0	28.5	30.0

*Source: HEITGER (1990), based on PlanEcon Reports and ALTON, T., "Comparison of
Overall Economic Performance in the East European Countries, in: WEICHHARDT (1988),
Ed., The Economics of Eastern Europe under Gorbatchev's Influence. NATO Colloquium,
March 23-25, Brussels, 26-50. Figures for Japan and Germany are own calculations based on
IMF, International Financial Statistics. * Ratio for West Germany is based on figures in prices
of 1985: Deutsche Bundesbank, Monatsberichte der Deutschen Bundesbank; IMF,
International Financial Statistics, own calculations.*

4. Dramatic Changes in Eastern Europe

Radical politico-economic reforms had to be undertaken in several CMEA countries, most
notably in Hungary, Poland, the CSSR and the USSR. With glasnost and perestroika Mikhail
Gorbachev marked a new era of public discussion about constitutional and economic reforms.
In August 1989 under Prime Minister Mazowiecki and Minister of Finance Leszek
Balcerowicz Poland embarked upon a market-oriented drastic reform program. In late 1989,
Hungary's decision to open the border to Austria for citizens from the German Democratic

Republic made the huge potential for "voting with one's feet" in the divided Germany visible; with the Berlin wall coming down, the peaceful revolution in East Germany (and later in the CSSR), and the "two-plus four arrangement" for talks on German unification, the situation in Europe changed dramatically.

Socialist systems are based on seven fatal principles: (i) state planning for state-owned industries, demand structuring by the state budget, and state-determined monetary policy with a one-tier banking system; (ii) production in a state-run system of mostly monopolistic firms which, producing a narrow range of goods at state-administered prices, face a system of monopolistic suppliers; (iii) risk-averse managers/administrators who are reluctant to introduce innovations and qualitative improvements or novelties and instead aim at hoarding material factor inputs as the basis to easily fulfill quantitatively specified state plans; (iv) a full-employment guarantee of the state and as a consequence of the systemic impossibility of firms to go bankrupt a soft state credit policy ("soft budget constraint"[41]); (v) a state monopoly in foreign trade, administered prices and exchange rates which reflect the inconvertibility of the domestic currency and fuels the spread of black currency markets; (vi) fiscal revenues generated mainly by turnover taxes and transfers of profits (and so-called surpluses from socialist firms) to the state and "domestic exports" which means the sale of domestic goods in special state-owned foreign currency shops; part of the surplus is devoted to covering losses of inefficient firms and to subsidizing prices for mass staple goods which often represented a "cheap price strategy" in accordance with the socialist ideal of providing basic goods to everyone;[42] (vii) apart from groups having important government functions or representing important and therefore influential industries, consumers are generally not well-organized and face a narrow range of goods and services on the one hand, and, on the other hand, a limited asset menu which is comprised of domestic and foreign money as well as consumer durables (and sometimes real estate), but - in contrast to market economies - no stocks or bonds.[43]

Key Role of the Labor Market
The latter implies that sustaining state budget deficits have to be covered by printing money which creates a direct link between rising price subsidies, increasing industry inefficiencies and wage-salary spirals that stem from the pressure of public servants to keep up with powerfully organized labor groups in strategically important industries.

---

[41] See KORNAI, J. (1980), The Economics of Shortage, 2 Vols., Amsterdam: North-Holland.

[42] In Hungary the complex system of taxes and subsidies implied that 60 percent of the revenues in the socialist industry were reallocated in the late 1980s and it is also noteworthy that price subsidies for housing construction and consumer goods were equivalent to 12.5 percent of the average household income. See WASS VON CZEGE, A. (1990), Die Ungarische Wirtschaft an der Wende zu den 90er Jahren, in: BOLZ, K., Die Wirtschaft der osteuropäischen Länder an der Wende zu den 90er Jahren, Hamburg: HWWA, 1990, 319-370, here 324 and 337.

[43] In most CMEA countries cars are not only a means of transportation but are equally important as a preferred store of value which enjoy high liquidity because in secondary markets used car prices were often above those of new cars.

Socialist countries in Eastern Europe have been suffering from a long phase of economic stagnation - at least since the mid-1970s, but only in the late 1980s when Poland and later the USSR discussed radical internal and external reforms in a period of economic stagnation of output and productivity, increasing budget deficits, increasing black market exchange rates and a rising shadow economy did the systemic crisis of the socialist economies become fully apparent.[44] Despite positive growth rates of net material product, the standard of living has not increased in most CPEs; not providing for reinvestment in many cases simply implied that the capital stock was effectively consumed. Clearly all possibilities for intensive growth which was based on high investment, the full exploitation of natural resources and the full utilization of the male and female labor force had been exhausted in the 1970s.[45]

From then on the sustaining excess demand for labor translated into rising nominal wages, while at the same time the increasing official shortages in goods markets seriously reduced the motivation to work (hence repressed inflation cum stagnation). In terms of the efficiency wage hypothesis a lower probability to obtain desired goods in the official economy and a higher price level offered in the unofficial economy implies reduced efforts to work in the official sphere. At the same time planners who were eager to achieve planning goals naturally became more inclined to offer rising nominal wages; however, the most productive sectors were certainly not those who were best organized in political terms. The socialist firms' monopolistic competition for labor created a sustaining upward wage pressure which in turn reduced enterprise profits at the aggregate level, contributed to higher budget deficits and thereby induced a quasi-inflationary growth of the money supply.[46]

In the monopolistically structured inward-oriented CPEs technological progress - a growth factor of prime importance in OECD countries and the NICs - was low for systemic reasons and hence secular economic stagnation coincided with internal planning failures and external shocks in a way that led to a serious politico-economic crisis in Eastern Europe and the USSR.[47] The 1980s were particularly crisis-prone for most socialist countries.

---

[44] In 1989 per capita GNP in US dollars amounted to $ 1780 in the USSR and to $ 2465 in Eastern Europe, compared with an OECD average of $ 17606. See IMF et al. (1990), p.51.

[45] As regards the internal and external reform aspects in the Soviet Union see WAGENER H.-J. (1990), The Market and the State under Perestroika, Kyklos, Vol. 43, 359-384. WELFENS, M.J. (1990), Internationalisierung der UdSSR? Bedeutung der sowjetischen Reformpolitik für die Stellung der UdSSR im RGW und im Ost-West-Handel, in: CASSEL, D., ed., Wirtschaftssysteme im Umbruch, München: Vahlen, 196-221. For the Polish case see LIPTON, D. and SACHS, D. (1990), Creating a Market Economy in Eastern Europe: The Case of Poland, Brookings Papers on Economic Activity, 1990; WORLD BANK (1990), Poland. Economic Management in a New Era, Washington D.C., CASSEL, D. et al. (1989), op. cit.

[46] On the switch to excess demand in the official labor market see: Gontarski, Z. (1985), Bariery efektywnego zatrudienia, Zycie Gospodarcze, 5/1985, p. 10. For the Hungarian case see Sziraczki, G. (1990), Employment Policy and Labor Market in Transition: From Labour Shortage to Unemployment, Soviet Studies, Vol. 42, 701-722.

[47] The weak technological progress in CMEA countries is emphasized in WELFENS, P.J.J. and BALCEROWICZ, L., eds. (1988); POZNANSKI, K.Z. (1987), Technology, Competition & the Soviet Bloc in

Appendix A1: Quality Gaps in Socialism Modelled in a SALOP-SALANT Approach.

In the SALOP-SALANT model one industry supplies differentiated goods, which are noncombinable for consumers. At the same time a homogeneous "outside good" (which can be used as a numeraire) is supplied by the second industry, possibly under perfect competitive conditions. Consumers' location in the characteristic "variety space" is defined by each consumer's most preferred product variant. Hence, consumer j is represented by the index $j \in (0,1)$, where j is the product variant individuals would buy if all varieties were available at identical prices. Typically, consumers will buy a product variety that differs to a certain extent from the most preferred one. We denote the "distance" between product variety i and the most preferred variety j for consumer j as $a_{ij} = |\, i\text{-}j\,|$ so that a_{ij} represents the loss of utility for consumer j that results from buying i instead of j. Hence consumer utility is determined by the amount of the outside good x_i, q_{ij} and a_{ij} which means that the commodity bundle x_i, q_{ij} is given by a utility function $u_j(x_j, q_{ij}, a_{ij})$. With a given set of producers I $(1,2..i..n)$ which charges prices $p_1...p_n$ the maximization problem for the individual is:

max. via selecting q_{ij} the function $u_j(x_j, q_{ij}, a_{ij})$ for all $i \in I$

subject to the budget constraint (with the outside good taken as a numeraire and its price set to unity)

$x_j + p_i q_{ij} = R_j$.

This leads to a two-stage utility maximization where the above equations give for each product i the consumption bundle (x^i_j, q^*_{ij}) and then, in the next stage, the consumer compares all consumption bundles and decides in favor of that with the highest utility. Assume that consumption of the outside good generates surplus s_0. Consumers with the most preferred brand j will buy one unit of the differentiated product i satisfying

(1) $\quad$ max $(U(i,j)-p_i) \geq s_0$

In an analogy to utility maximization in a spatial economy one can write

(2) $\quad U(i,j) = u - b(i\text{-}j) = u - ba_{ij}$ so that the equation to be maximized is now

(2') $\quad$ max $((u-s_0) - p_i - ba_{ij}) \geq 0$

The "effective delivered price" is consequently $h_i = p_i + ba_{ij}$, where p_i is the state-administered price in the official economy; and the effective reservation price is $v = u - s_0$. Individuals with most preferred variety j will buy the differentiated brand i only if h_i is less than the reservation price v and will then actually buy i only if i maximizes $U(i,j)$. With respect to the problem of a transition to a market economy system one may note here already that such a systemic switch makes available a greater variety of goods which increases consumer surplus to the extent that a_{ij} would reduce and prices p_i would not increase; the latter could happen as a consequence of opening up the economy. Forced substitution in the sense of consumers choosing i instead of the most preferred brand j is typical for socialist systems. Even without official price inflation increasing shortages that raise a_{ij} are equivalent to "quasi- inflation" (here p^* is the price level in the shadow economy; or of imported goods):

(3) $P = (p^*)^{\alpha} (p_i + ba_{ij})^{(1-\alpha)}$; alternatively: (3') $P = (p^*)^{\alpha 1} (p_i)^{\alpha 2} (ba_{ij})^{(1-\alpha 1 - \alpha 2)}$;

An increase in the "value" of product differentiation b raises the effective price index. If one assumes that b is a positive function of wealth a given mismatch (a_{ij}) between the product desired and the brand available raises the effective price index and reduces effective real income. A crisis in the official production and distribution system raises a_{ij} above its "normal" system-specific value which is determined by planners' production preferences and consumers' desire for more differentiated products. In general one may assume that consumers will buy the good whose properties come closest to the most desired brand j. In contrast to a market economy where competition and innovation ensure that many individuals can obtain an almost customer-designed product, the socialist economies rarely provide products that closely reflect the diversified needs of millions of domestic consumers. Analogous to the previous analysis of the mismatch between the most preferred product brand desired and the brand purchased one can model the typical problem encountered by private households in a socialist economy. The most preferred product can be obtained in the shadow economy, while one has to compromise on varieties in the official system.

---

the World Market, Berkeley: Institute for International Studies; LEIPOLD, H. (1990), Technologische Modernisierung der UdSSR? Bedeutung der Reformpolitik für die Innovationsfähigkeit der sowjetischen Wirtschaft, in: CASSEL, D., op. cit., 173-195; INOTAI, A. (1988), Competition Between the European CMEA and Rapidly Industrializing Countries on the OECD Market for Manufactured Goods, Empirica, Vol. 15, 189-204; KOSTRZEWA, W. (1988), Verpaßt Osteuropa den Anschluß auf den Weltmärkten?, Institut für Weltwirtschaft, Kieler Diskussionsbeiträge Nr. 144, Institut für Weltwirtschaft, Kiel 1988; HARDT, J.P.; McMILLAN, C.H., eds. (1989), Planned Economies: Confronting the Challenges of the 1980s, Cambridge: Cambridge University Press.

References

ALLESANDRINI, S. and DALLAGO, B., eds. (1987), The Unofficial Economy, Aldershot: Gower.

ALTON, T.P. (1988), Comparison of Overall Economic Performance in the East European Countries, in: WEICHARDT, R., Ed., The Economics of Eastern Europe under Gorbatechev's Influence. NATO, Colloquium, March 23-25, Brussels, 26-50.

ASLUND, A. (1983), Private Enterprise in Soviet-Type Economies: A Comparison between Poland and the GDR, Osteuropa-Wirtschaft, 28 (1983), 176-193.

BALCEROWICZ, L. (1988), Innovationsspezifika, Wirtschaftssystem und Innovationsleistung von Wirtschaftssystemen, in: BALCEROWICZ, L. and WELFENS, P.J.J., eds., 28-59.

BALCEROWICZ, L. and WELFENS, P.J.J., eds. (1988), Innovationsdynamik im Systemvergleich, Heidelberg: Physica.

BERNSTEIN, M. (1950), Latent Inflation, IMF Staff Papers, Vol. 1, 1-16.

BICANIC, I. (1987), The Inequality Impact of the Unofficial Economy in Yugoslavia, in: ALESSANDRINI, S. and DALLAGO, B., eds., 323-336.

BOLZ, K., ed. (1990), Die Wirtschaft der osteuropäischen Länder an der Wende zu den 90er Jahren, Hamburg: HWWA.

BOTH, M. and WELFENS, P.J.J. (1989), Internationale Determinanten des Geldumlaufs, in: CASSEL, D. et al., eds., 151-168.

BRADA, J. C. (1985), The Slowdown in Soviet and East-European Economic Growth, Osteuropa Wirtschaft, Vol. 30, 116-128.

BREZINSKI, H. (1992), The Autonomous Sector in a Society of Shortage, in ADJANI, G., DALLAGO, B., GRANCELLI, B. (eds.), Self-Employment and Entrepreneurship in the Socialist Countries: Economy, Law and Society, London, Macmillan (forthcoming).

BREZINSKI, H. and PETRESCU, P. (1986), The Second Economy in Romania - Dynamic Sector, Discussion Paper, FB 5, Universität Paderborn.

BREZINSKI, H. and ROS, C. (1985), The Development of the Second Economy in Hungary, Korean Journal of East-West European Studies, Vol. 1, 95-127.

BRUS, W. and LASKI, K. (1989), From Marx to the Market, Oxford: Clarendon Press.

CANTWELL, J. (1989), Technological Innovation and Multinational Corporations, Oxford: Basil Blackwell.

CASSEL, D.; et al., eds. (1989), Inflation und Schattenwirtschaft im Sozialismus, Hamburg: S+W Steuer- und Wirtschaftsverlag.

CASSEL, D. (1986), Funktionen der Schattenwirtschaft im Koordinationsmechanismus von Markt- und Plan- wirtschaften, Ordo, Vol. 37, 73-104.

CASSEL, D., ed. (1990), Wirtschaftssysteme im Umbruch, München: Vahlen.

CASSEL, D. and CICHY, E.U. (1986), Explaining the Growing Shadow Economy in East and West: A Comparative Systems Approach, Comparative Economic Studies/ACES Bulletin, Vol. 28, 415-428.

CHAREMZA, W. and J.E. QUANDT (1982), Models and Estimation of Disequlibrium for Centrally Planned Economies, Review of Economic Studies, Vol. 49, 109-116.

CHAREMZA, W.; GRONICKI, M. and QUANDT, R.E. (1988), Modelling Parallel Markets in Centrally Planned Economies: The Case of the Automobile Market in Poland, European Economic Review, Vol. 22, 861-884.

CHARMEZA, W. and QUANDT, R.E. (1990), Dual Housing Markets in a Centrally Planned Economy: An Empirical Analysis, Kyklos, Vol. 43, 411-436

CLAASSEN, E.M., ed. (1991), Exchange Rate Policies of Developing and Socialist Countries, San Francisco: ICS 1991.

DALLAGO, B. (1989), The Non-Socialized Sector in Hungary: An Attempt at Estimation of its Importance, Jahrbuch der Wirschafts Osteuropas, Vol. 13, No. 2, 67-92.

DEMBINSKI, P. (1991), The Logic of the Planned Economy, Oxford: Clarendon Press.

FEIGE, E.L., ed. (1989), The Underground Economies, Cambridge: Cambridge University Press.

FREY, B.S. and POMMEREHNE, W.W. (1983), Schattenwirtschaft und Schwarzarbeit als Folgen des Sozialstaats, in: KOSLOWSKI, P.; KREUTZER, P.; LÖW, R., eds., Chancen und Grenzen des Sozialstaats, 135-151.

GÄRTNER, W. and WENIG, A., eds. (1985), The Economics of the Shadow Economy, Heidelberg: Springer.

GEY, P.; KOSTA, J. and QUAISSER, W., eds. (1987), Crisis and Reform in Socialist Economies, Boulder: Westview Press.

GONTARSKI, Z. (1985), Bariery efektywnego zatrudnienia, Zycie Gospodarcze, 5/1985.

GORSKI, Z. and KIERCZYNSKI, T. (1989), Erscheinungsformen und Messung der inoffiziellen Erwerbswirtschaft, in: Cassel, D. et al., eds., 349-374.

GROSFELD, I (1987), Modelling Planner's Investement Behavior: Poland, 1956-81, Journal of Comparative Economics, Vol. 11, 180-191.

GROSSMAN, G. (1986), ed., Studies in the Second Economy of Communist Countries, Berkeley: ICS.

GUTMANN, P.M. (1977), The Subterranean Economy, Financial Analysts Journal, 33/1977, 26-34.

HARDT, J.P. and McMILLAN, C.H., eds. (1989), Planned Economies: Confronting the Challenges of the 1980s, Cambridge: Cambridge University Press.

HARTWIG, K.H. (1987), Monetäre Steuerungsprobleme in sozialistischen Planwirtschaften, Stuttgart: Fischer.

HARTWIG, K.H. and THIEME, J., eds. (1992), Transformationsprozesse in sozialistischen Wirtschaftssystemen, Heidelberg: Springer.

HEDTKAMP, G., ed. (1983), Beiträge zum Problem der Schattenwirtschaft, Berlin: Duncker & Humblot.

HEITGER, B. (1990), Wirtschaftliches Wachstum in Ost und West im internationalen Vergleich seit 1950, Die Weltwirtschaft, 1990, Vol. 1, 173-192.

HEWETT, E.A. (1988), Reforming the Soviet Economy, Washington, D.C.: Brookings.

HOLZMAN, F.D. (1960), Soviet Inflationary Pressures 1928-57, Causes and Cures, Quarterly Journal of Economics, Vol. 74 (1960), 167-188.

IMF et al. (1991), The Economy of the USSR, Washington D.C.

INOTAI, A. (1988), Competition Between the European CMEA and Rapidly Industrializing Countries on the OECD Market for Manufactured Goods, Empirica, Vol. 15, 189-204.

JAMANN, W. and MENKHOFF, T. (1988), Licht und Schatten - Chinas Zweite Wirtschaft, Osteuropa-Wirtschaft, Vol. 33, 16-30.

KALICKI, K. (1989), Bestimmung und Messung der Geldnachfrage, in: CASSEL, D. et al., 195-212.

KANTOROVICH, L.V. (1965), The Best Use of Economic Resources, Oxford: Clarendon.

KEMME, D.M. (1990), Losses in Polish Industry Due to Resource Misallocation, Yearbook of East-European Economics, Vol. 14, No. 2, 129-158.

KORNAI, J. (1980), Economics of Shortage, 2 Vols., Amsterdam: North-Holland.

KORNAI, J. (1986), The Hungarian Reform Process, Journal of Economic Literature, Vol. 24, 1687-1737.

KOSTRZEWA, W. (1988), Verpaßt Osteuropa den Anschluß auf den Weltmärkten?, Institut für Weltwirtschaft, Kieler Diskussionsbeiträge Nr. 144, Institut für Weltwirtschaft, Kiel.

LANDAU, Z. (1987), Selected Problems of the Unofficial Economy in Poland, in: ALLESANDRINI, S.; DALLAGO, B., eds., The Unofficial Economy, Aldershot: Gower.

LASKI, K. (1982), "Second Economy" in sozialistischen Ländern und Inflationserscheinungen, Forschungsberichte No. 83, Vienna Institute for Comparative Economic Studies, September.

LEIPOLD, H. (1990), Technologische Modernisierung der UdSSR? Bedeutung der Reformpolitik für die Innovationsfähigkeit der sowjetischen Wirtschaft, in: CASSEL, D., ed., 173-195.

LIPTON, D. and SACHS, D. (1990), Creating a Market Economy in Eastern Europe: The Case of Poland, Brookings Papers on Economic Activity.

McKINNON, R. (1990), Financial Control During the Transition from a Centrally Planned to a Market Economy, paper presented at the AER annual meeting, Washington D.C., Dec. 28, 1990.

NOVE, A. (1986), The Soviet Economic System, 3rd ed., Boston: Unwin.

OFER, B. (1987), Soviet Economic Growth: 1928-1985, Journal of Economic Literature, Vol. 25, 1767-1850.

PORTES, R. (1977), The Problem of Inflation: Lessons from the East European Experience, Economica, Vol. 44, 109-130.

POZNANSKI, K.Z. (1987), Technology, Competition & the Soviet Bloc in the World Market, Berkeley: Institute for International Studies.

ROMER, P. (1983), Dynamic Competitive Equilibria, Increasing Returns and Unbounded Growth, Chicago: University of Chicago.

ROMER, P. (1990), Are Nonconvexities Important for Understanding Growth?, American Economic Review, Vol. 80, P&P, 97-103.

SCHÄFER, W., ed. (1984), Schattenökonomie: Theoretische Grundlagen und wirtschaftspolitische Konsequenzen, Göttingen: Vandenhoeck & Ruprecht.

SERGEEW, A. (1987), Netrudovye dochody: ekonomiceskaja priroda, struktura, puti likvidacji, Voprosy Ekonomiki, 1987/6, 85-93.

SALANT, D.J. (1980), Quality, Location Choice and Imperfect Competition, Doctoral Dissertation, University of Rochester.

SALOP, S.C. (1979), Monopolistic Competition with Outside Goods, Bell Journal of Economics, 10: 141-156.

SLAMA, J. (1988), Verwendung technisch-ökonomischer Kennziffern zur Analyse des Wirtschaftswachstums und des technischen Fortschritts sozialistischer Länder, in: WELFENS, P.J.J; BALCEROWICZ, L., eds., Innovationsdynamik im Systemvergleich, Heidelberg: Physica, 300-321.

SZIRACZKI, G. (1990), Employment Policy and Labor Market in Transition: From Labour Shortage to Unemployment, Soviet Studies, Vol. 42, 701-722.

TANZI, V. (1980), ed., The Underground Economy in the United States and Abroad, Lexington: Heath.

THIEME, H.J., ed. (1985), Geldtheorie. Entwicklung, Stand und systemvergleichende Anwendung, Baden-Baden: Nomos.

UNCE (1990), Economic Reforms in the European Centrally Planned Economies, New York.

WAGENER H.-J. (1990), The Market and the State under Perestroika, Kyklos, 43 (1990), 359-384.

WASS VON CZEGE, A. (1990), Die Ungarische Wirtschaft an der Wende zu den 90er Jahren, in: BOLZ, K., Die Wirtschaft der osteuropäischen Länder an der Wende zu den 90er Jahren, Hamburg: HWWA, 319-370

WECK, H.; POMMEREHNE, W.W.; FREY, B.S. (1984), Schattenwirtschaft, München: Vahlen.

WELFENS, M.J. (1988), Das Phänomen der Schattenwirtschaft im Sozialismus, Osteuropa-Wirtschaft, Vol. 33, 1-15.

WELFENS, M.J. (1989), Bedingungen der Entstehung und Entwicklung der inoffiziellen Erwerbswirtschaft, in: CASSEL, D.; ET AL., Eds., Inflation und Schattenwirtschaft im Sozialismus, Hamburg: S+W Steuer- und Wirtschaftsverlag, 375-404.

WELFENS, M.J. (1990), Internationalisierung der UdSSR? Bedeutung der sowjetischen Reformpolitik für die Stellung der UdSSR im RGW und im Ost-West-Handel, in: CASSEL, D., ed., Wirtschaftssysteme im Umbruch, München: Vahlen, 196-221.

WELFENS, M.J. (1992a), Systemtransformation und die Umweltpolitik in Ost- und Mitteleuropa, Osteuropa Wirtschaft, 1992/2, 1-26.

WELFENS, M.J. (1992b), Systemic Transformation and Waste Management in Poland, Berlin (Tempus Project, FU Berlin), mimeo.

WELFENS, P.J.J. (1987), Growth, Innovation and International Competitiveness, Intereconomics, 22 (1987), 168-174.

WELFENS, P.J.J. (1988), Innovationstheorie, -politik und -dynamik im Systemvergleich, in: Welfens, P.J.J.; Balcerowicz, L., eds., Innovationsdynamik im Systemvergleich, Heidelberg: Physica, 1-24.

WELFENS, P.J.J. (1989), Allocation, Pricing and the Socialist Equilibrium Shadow Economy, paper presented at the 5th annual meeting of the Associazione Italiana per lo Studio dei Sistemi Economic Comparati, Pavia, September 1988.

WELFENS, P.J.J. (1990a), Economic Reforms in Eastern Europe: Problems, Options and Opportunities, testimony before the U.S. Senate, March 23.

WELFENS, P.J.J. (1991b), The Economic Challenges of Privatization and Foreign Investment in Eastern Europe, paper presented at the Society of Government Economist Annual Meeting, Washington D.C., May 23.

WELFENS, P.J.J, ed. (1992a), Economic Aspects of German Unification. National and International Perspectives, New York: Springer.

WINIECKI, J. (1988), The Distorted Type of Soviet-Type Economies: London: Macmillan.

WISNIEWSKI, M. (1985), Zrodla i rozmiary drugiego obiegu gospodarczego w Polsce, Ekonomista, 1985, No. 6, 913-936.

WORLD BANK (1990), Poland. Economic Management in a New Era, Washington D.C.

B: Inefficiency, Instability, and Restricted Options

1. Introduction

The former socialist economies of Eastern Europe have decided to switch to a market-based economy and to thereby radically change the set of economic institutions and preferred attitudes in society. The virtues of market-based factor allocation and competition are not easy to recognize for people who lack experience with a decentralized economic system in which allocation is guided by prices and price expectations and in which individual efforts are rewarded. A market-based system means facing uncertainty and risk for the individual, and only part of it can be reduced by insurance markets.

Instead of state-owned industry directed by central plans and input allocations to the mostly monopolistic firms, a decentralized system based on private property, decentralized decision-making, individual economic freedom and responsibility as well as a new role for government are to shape the politico-economic system. After four decades of an inward-oriented command economy, there will be a switch towards outward-oriented market economies, where firms are embedded into international competition often shaped by multinational companies and growing international trade in goods, services and capital. There is a strong need for theoretical, ideological and political reorientation in Eastern Europe which faces the shattered values of traditional Marxism-Leninism and the unfulfilled claim to bring prosperity and social justice to the people by means of a central planning, state-owned firms and inward oriented economic development strategies.

The countries involved in the East European transition have embarked upon various transformation approaches which differ in scope, resolve and strategy. No country so far has been successful in developing a quick way to systemic transformation and economic recovery. Except for the prospects of an East German economic miracle - of a modest scale - to be expected in the 1990s, no former CMEA country can hope to double per capita output within a decade; the case of the former GDR obviously is a special one that is shaped by West Germany's enormous resource transfer to Eastern Germany where in 1991/92 nearly 60 % of incomes are Western resource transfers which are by no means available in Eastern Europe. Given the strong fall of real incomes in the late 1980s and early 1990s in Eastern Europe, in contrast to West European economic growth, one may anticipate a transitorily rising intra-European economic divide in Europe. This is surprising in the sense that one might expect inefficient centrally planned economies (CPEs) to rapidly improve static and dynamic efficiency (thereby raising growth rates) by switching to a market-based factor allocation. What we observe in reality is a sharp reduction of economic growth rates in the initial transformation stage. Moreover, predictions by many experts suggest only moderate economic growth in the medium term (see e.g. the assessment by the Group of Thirty in Tab. B1).

Unemployment rates sharply increased in Eastern Europe in 1991 and in the former GDR where it reached 17 percent in early 1992.

Tab. B1: GNP Growth Rates in Eastern Europe
Real gross national product, figures are in percent p.a.

	GNP Growth Rates						
	1989	1990	1991	1992	1993	1994	1995
CSFR	1.0	-3.0	-5.7	-4.8	-3.9	4.3	4.1
Hungary	-1.8	-5.6	-3.1	-0.4	1.5	2.7	3.0
Poland	-0.5	-13.0	-0.2	1.5	2.6	1.8	3.2
Bulgaria	-0.3	-11.3	-14.0	-6.7	0.6	0.8	3.0
Romania	-7.5	-10.5	-6.6	-5.1	-3.9	2.6	4.2
Yugoslavia	0.8	-6.0	-4.9	-2.6	-1.0	-0.5	0.8
USSR**	1.8	-6.4	-17.7	-	-	-	-

** *PlanEcon-estimates.*
Sources: Group of Thirty (1991), Financing Eastern Europe, Washington D.C., 51; PlanEcon (1991), PlanEcon Review and Outlook, Washington D.C.

The theoretical basis for systemic transformation is scarce so far. We will develop some new arguments for systemic reforms in socialist economies. Many of these arguments are developed within the approach of the second best theory, that is we assume that certain distortions in socialist economies cannot be removed in the short run, and then we ask for appropriate neutralizing measures. Furthermore, we want to emphasize some welfare considerations as well as the role of adjustment costs.

In developing a theoretical analysis of the transformation process in Eastern Europe a number of important topics emerges. A first set of questions to discuss is (a) why the transformation is so difficult in Eastern Europe and what type of distortions characterize the initial situation; (b) what the critical minimum scope of system transformation requires and (c) which costs and benefits one has to take into account in the transition process, so that one can derive at least a rough idea about an adequate sequencing of reform steps. These questions are analyzed in section (2). A related set of topics is of a more strategic nature and concerns the actual limited options available for systemic transition in the presence of distortions. There are not only economic distortions, but also political distortions (section 3).

2. The Scope of Transformation and the Sequencing Issue

Systemic transformation requires institutional innovations, the internal liberalization of the economy, the external liberalization and the adjustment of the real economy as well as of the monetary system. Not only a different institutional framework is needed in a market economy, but one has to remove most of the inherited institutional structures and to change the typical behavioral patterns - in industry, private households and the state.

Generally, several aspects make the transformation extremely complex:
- The transformation is starting in a deep economic crisis period of socialist systems in Eastern Europe, typically characterized by a stagnating official economy, a big shadow economy, high public deficits, strong inflationary pressures, currency substitution, high foreign indebtedness and falling terms of trade. Given the backlog of postponed structural adjustment and the inherited system of big state monopolies, systemic reforms must be comprehensive, but they could lead to a transitory period of sharply falling output and slow growth as formerly excessive investment-output ratios are reduced while efficiency gains are still limited.
- Internal adjustment measures have to be coupled with external adjustments that replace the former strategies of import substitution with a neutral trade regime or some form of export promotion. Since relative world market prices provide the required signals as to the scarcity of resources and skills worldwide, trade reforms that convey these international price signals are of prime importance. This first best solution might not be optimal in a setting with distortions in other economic sectors, especially in the nontradables sector. For the former CPEs open trade can also provide disciplinary competition for systems characterized by monopolistic producers in the home market; at the same time one might argue that dismemberment of state monopolies will be more difficult if extreme external competitive pressure is exerted. The link to internal adjustments concerns mainly the supply side that has to become more responsive and more efficient, the latter especially requiring the replacement of the CPEs' selective import and export policies by a system of convertible currency trade with a uniform real equilibrium exchange rate. As is well known the elasticity of the supply side plays a crucial role for the balance of payments effects of a devaluation, especially in the case that the trade balance is negative initially.
- The problem of convertibility is directly tied to the problem of monetary policy control - linked in turn to high public deficits and soft budget constraints of socialist firms - and price stability. Internal convertibility is in principle not required to facilitate trade since it only means that domestic residents are allowed to legally possess and use foreign exchange; the more important issue for trade creation is obviously external convertibility which means that foreigners are allowed to use foreign exchange. However, given the importance of currency substitution in many former CPEs (except for the CSFR) it is important that governments manage to control the amount of foreign exchange used as a parallel currency for transaction purposes. A first step is to legalize foreign exchange holdings and offer competitive financial returns, such that foreign exchange is primarily used as a store of value and thus becomes part of normal portfolio behavior. Only then can an effective control of the domestic money supply lead to lower inflation rates in a longer adjustment process.
- A uniform exchange rate requires a devaluation of the official exchange rate such that no divergence between official and unofficial exchange rates exists anymore, and this will

translate into an export promoting exchange rate provided that high inflation rates do not cause a real appreciation of the currency. If the nominal exchange rate is to be fixed and is to provide a nominal anchor for monetary policy in the short and medium term, the required currency devaluation will be the stronger the greater the inflation inertia is. Historical experience of the 1930s in Eastern Europe suggests that with high inflationary dynamics and fixed exchange rates there is a high risk of misalignment. If the domestic inflation rate is higher than in most other industrial countries, a fixed exchange rate implies a gradual appreciation of the currency (according to the international inflation differential) such that the export industries' competitiveness is reduced; a widening trade balance deficit means an increased net demand for foreign currency and hence calls for a depreciation which government could only avoid - as soon as foreign exchange reserves have been run down - if interest rates are raised in order to generate an increased net supply of foreign exchange via rising net capital imports; restricting capital outflows or imposing non-tariff import barriers for trade are alternative remedies that are as ill-suited as artificially high interest rates which are bound to depress investment and economic growth.

- There is the problem of exchange rate/price level shifts cum inflation dynamics. A strong devaluation in the official economy fuels inflation in the short term because then higher prices for imported input goods and intermediate products will drive costs and prices up; only if the official currency devaluation entails an appreciation of the domestic currency in black markets (i.e. a new unified exchange rate would lie between the old state-fixed official rate and the formerly much higher unofficial rate) could the devaluation effect have a dampening effect on the inflation rate provided that currency substitution and shadow economic markets do not dominate. In the shadow economy many products are traded only against hard currency or their domestic currency equivalent (at black market exchange rates). The switch from low state-administered prices to higher market-clearing levels is not inflationary in the sense that it reduces the purchasing power of money;[1] rather it makes it on average more likely that nominal income claims can be redeemed into goods. The population, however, is likely to perceive this "price level switch" as an inextractible part of inflation dynamics fueled by an existing former monetary overhang and money-financed budget deficits. All this feeds into inflationary expectations that can accelerate actual inflation. Specific monetary control problems emerge in the context of setting up a new two-stage banking system. Periodic devaluations are almost certainly necessary if a real appreciation of the currencies and hence reduced (net) exports are to be avoided. While real exchange rate instability might impair trade expansion, exchange rate variability should hardly affect foreign direct investment flows - these, however, are influenced by the actual and expected real exchange rate levels. There is only one reason why prices of some goods might fall in the short term, and this is related to the pace of opening up the economy for trade. Facing increasingly qualitatively superior and more diversified products from the West, the NICs and other foreign suppliers to which consumers tend to switch, the often poor assortment of domestic

---

[1] Indeed, the former uncertainty about the likelihood of obtaining some goods at low prices in the official distribution system is replaced with well-informed access to goods at generally higher prices.

goods can only be sold at steep price discounts. A whole range of substitute products will be affected, but at the same time the price for complementary goods will go upwards.

- Improving the supply side response, reducing costs and promoting innovations by privatization and the formation of new firms, could only compensate for a short period for a real appreciation that results from high domestic inflation (relative to the rate in major trading partners). Supply-side policies are no substitute for monetary anti-inflation policies, but they can support such a policy to the extent that higher expected real income will reduce the social conflict over income distribution and hence weaken incentives to trigger a wage-price-wage-spiral. Adjustment trajectories that impose sharp reductions in present per capita incomes are likely to meet considerable resistance - even if high long term benefits are expected from the perspective of government, economists or international organizations. There is a critical minimum economic growth rate that must be reached to cope with external indebtedness on the one hand, and, on the other hand, the growing economic aspirations of the people - all this in a period in which the economy will face high adjustment costs and the loss of individual wealth positions and income opportunities.

- The traditional intimate link between economics and politics in the socialist system - the politicization of business and the economy - implied that the economic crisis was paralleled by a severe political crisis, i.e. in fact a collapse of the existing political system. New political governance structures have to be established in a period of great economic disruptions in CPEs. This reduces policy credibility such that economic reform must apply a higher dosis of therapeutical measures than otherwise, and it implies the risk of very inefficient political competition as a consequence of lacking established politicians/parties and experienced voters' groups. Lack of functional opposition means that failure of economic reforms could result in outright collapse of the whole political democratization process since the population will blame the new political system as such for major pitfalls, conflicts and failures arising in the systemic transformation attempt.

The sequencing problem

Many problems are encountered in the transition phase, where a major problem concerns an adequate sequencing of economic reforms. Since not all reform steps can be taken at once it makes sense to consider the problems of choosing an adequate sequence of reforms and to thereby reduce adjustment costs while improving productivity in the economic system and reducing inefficiency in the political system. Since market allocation relies on price signals it is clear that price liberalization is necessarily an early step of reform; moreover, market-clearing prices (under competition) are the basis of evaluating the value of industrial assets. Price liberalization will lead to a rapid and possibly extreme rise in the general price level which in turn will affect inflation expectations that affect wage bargaining. Not allowing full indexation and reducing the possibility of monetary financing of budget deficits are important tasks for economic policy if the switch to market-clearing prices is not to translate into a sustaining hyperinflation. Inflation in turn will entail windfall profits for those who have foreign exchange and those who own real estate whose relative price will increase during inflation. Sequencing concerns also the question whether privatization, foreign economic liberalization and the formation of a competitive banking system should be implemented early on or not. Since privatization has to be prepared and requires some lead time in any case one cannot avoid focusing on the privatization problems right away. Moreover, restructuring which may be needed as a step before privatization requires time, too. Since effective monetary control in a two-stage banking system is important for a market economy the creation of a private competitive banking system must be addressed early on. Otherwise no effective inflation control can be expected and with high inflation rates relative price signals would be distorted by "inflationary noise" (if you watch a price increase one does not know whether this is simply reflecting general inflation or an increasing relative scarcity which would make additional investment profitable) on the one hand; on the other hand, the length of the capitalization horizon becomes shorter with inflation uncertainty, a phenomenon which shows up in Western market economies in declining average maturities of bonds during periods of high inflation. Hence productivity-increasing investment projects which would be profitable in the long term only could be financed only at high real interest rates that would include a risk premium such that the overall amount of profitable investment is reducing and the marginal product of capital declining faster than otherwise.

The sequencing problem has been analyzed mainly in development economics where the proper sequence of liberalizing the capital and the trade account was discussed.[2] Although one might argue that the former CMEA countries represent the biggest socialist group of developing countries, the validity of the sequencing arguments from development economics is not assured. Indeed, it will be argued here that the system-specific distortions encountered in the socialist CMEA countries must be taken into account for the sequencing issue and that the main distortions differ widely from the typical situation in developing countries. In no major Latin American economy was output produced by state-owned firms higher than 50 % of national output; few developing economies have had centralized investment decision-making to a wide extent and only some developing countries have had a monetary sector without competition in the banking system.

In the case of the socialist economies, there is a specific link between trade account liberalization in the sense of import liberalization, the real exchange rate and the capital market/capital flows. If quantitative restrictions are not replaced by equivalent import tariffs import liberalization will entail in the medium term (before supply-side adjustments) heavy price discounts for the import-competing sector since consumers will tend to shift demand to the higher quality and greater variety of imported goods unless there is a steep price discount

---

[2] See e.g. Edwards (1989a,b).

for the existing domestic product assortment. This problem was amply borne out by the radical East German liberalization in the context of economic and, later, political unification in 1990 when East German sales and production almost collapsed. From an index value of 106.9 (1985 = 100) in the first quarter of 1990 production in industry fell to 56.7 (-46.8 percent) in the third quarter in East Germany; in light industry, in the textile industry and in the foods industry, where product quality and variety are important, the reduction was relatively highest: -54.3, -53.9 and - 59.1 percent, respectively. If the GDR had maintained its own currency but had made it fully convertible the GDR would have suffered a strong depreciation of its currency vis-à-vis most market economies, especially vis-à-vis the Federal Republic of Germany.[3]

Rapid import liberalization could entail heavy losses of domestic producers and will tend to depress asset prices, while a large part of the capital stock, representing high sunk costs, will immediately become obsolete. Since the responsiveness of the supply-side in upgrading the product assortment is difficult to assess in the given unique transition phase to a market-based system, the price of industrial assets will exhibit steep discounts compared to a situation with less (normal) uncertainty. Import liberalization which renders a large part of the capital stock obsolete and depresses asset prices has two effects. The former increases required capital imports while the fall of asset prices reduces required nominal inflows. Greater capital requirements call for higher domestic interest rates and higher returns on investment for domestic and foreign investors - in turn requiring greater tax holidays and other tax favors which in turn aggravate budgetary problems (together with higher real interest rates). It seems obvious that capital exports should not be liberalized in the medium term since this is the only means to generate high domestic investments in an environment where improved efficiency should translate into strong GNP growth and hence rapidly increasing savings.

The sequencing issue is indirectly related to the speed of economic transformation (WELFENS, 1990a). If systemic transformation contains one element which is extremely time-consuming and interrelated with other core changes one would have to consider a gradual transition to be a reasonable pattern of adjustment. Moreover, if the cost of transformation increases strongly with the speed of moving towards a market economy, it would be nonoptimal to envisage a fast transition. This does not rule out that one would begin with some radical reform steps in the beginning in order to gain credibility and to deter distorting interferences from the old nomenclatura members. PETER MURRELL (1991) has strongly emphasized that a gradual transition would be appropriate for Eastern Europe because an evolutionary perspective of capitalism leads one to emphasize that capitalism means sustaining

---

[3] Computations of changes in industrial production are based on SVR (*Sachverstaendigenrat zur Begutachtung der gesamtwirtschaftlichen Entwicklung*) (1990), Tab. IV.

changes and a continuous need of updating information in a time-consuming manner while it also takes time to develop new routines in adjusting organizations.

The destruction of large organizations in industry and in the state bureaucracy is unavoidable and certainly will entail high adjustment and learning costs. However, one may raise the question whether or not the creation of many new firms in regions with oversized state firms that have to be scale down could create an endogenous speed of optimal adjustment; namely, to the extent that new firms with a high productivity of labor and capital could attract workers from big firms and whether big firms could rejuvenate at least in some cases their know-how and their routines by acquiring newly established enterprises. A major problem concerns, of course, the question whether state subsidies in favor of big business can be avoided and whether capital markets will not be dominated by state banks and "old nomenclatura networks" that would prevent an efficient allocation of capital. Since it is true that new institutions are difficult to implement one may conclude that in the immediate transition periods simplified tax codes, business laws and rules for economic policy should contribute to reduce information costs and to render the new institutions more efficient than in the full complexity of a Western market economy. Finally, one may use the price mechanism itself to influence the range of people involved in the complex transition process. E.g. in the CSFR a small nominal fee was introduced for those who wanted to get vouchers that could be used later to buy stocks, and indeed at first only about ten percent (later more than 70 percent) of the population were under these circumstances willing to get vouchers at all.

The sequencing issue can be understood in a broader sense. Here, it will be considered to consist of a broadly defined net of problems that raise the question of (i) the link between internal reforms and external economic reforms; (ii) the problem of fiscal and monetary regime switches on the one hand, and, on the other hand, the question of liberalizing the consumer and the investment goods industry; (iii) the link between liberalizing the trade and the capital account on the one hand, and, on the other hand, the question of the exchange rate regime; (iv) the question whether to address first the privatization and dismemberment of "big industry" and then to turn to the host of smaller and medium-sized firms or vice versa.

2.1 Dimensions of the Transformation Problem

If one is to assess the problem of systemic transformation one must ask first for the objective difference (or the subjective distance) between the existing institutional setting and the minimum endowment with market compatible institutions. Compared to a "minimum market economy" defined by 2/3 of output generated in competitive private industry and more than 50 % of the jobs in private industry - as a prerequisite for a functional labor market - all former

CPEs are far from what is required. There are many conflict prone decisions to be made in Eastern Europe. Poland and Hungary have made visible progress (at differential speed) towards private industrial production and private service industry, including the important banking sector, but even these fast movers in systemic transition had in 1991 less than 25 percent of aggregate output in the private sector, less than 25 % of all credits allocated by private competing banks and less than 35 percent of all jobs in the private sector. All other former CMEA countries face even wider gaps between status quo and the minimum market economy. Countries with a relatively high proportion of young age groups - the USSR, Bulgaria, and Romania - have good prospects to adjust attitudes on the aggregate level if one assumes that younger people face less difficulties in adjusting ideas and behavioral patterns than older ones; moreover, if they adjust towards the new system they can expect to benefit from a corresponding yield over a longer time span than older age groups. Finally, if education makes people more flexible to adjust in general one should expect that countries with a solid education system have an extra advantage in the difficult transition process.

It seems obvious that bridging elements in the transition between the old institutions and the new institutional setting are required. Most important in this context is the political consensus; the greater the fundamental consensus is, the greater the institutional gap with which one will be able to cope with. Weak coalition governments could render any big leap strategy impossible because radical reforms required are unfeasible. Whether efficient political competition can be generated in an early stage of political pluralism is doubtful. If the country's own history offers models for a functional market economy, transition might be more easy than otherwise, since one will find it not too conflict-prone to return to historical codes of business law and public organization. A similar reasoning holds with respect to available and accepted foreign economic role models which might be imported "en bloc", similar to the Meiji Japan that imported institutional subsets from Germany as a strategy to modernize its economy. Imitation of evolutionary processes took this en bloc form and then saved learning costs, but left enough room to develop and adjust indigenous institutions - is there an optimal institutional import?

Second one must raise the question how large the gap in individual behavior is in the old system as compared to the new system. A functional market economy requires more emphasis on individual achievements than on collective performance, and making profits must be accepted as one element guiding efficient economic behavior and generating social prosperity in a market economy. People will have to learn to exploit profitable investment opportunities and to thereby raise their personal income and wealth, at the same time the economic policy framework and new attitudes will have to encourage imitation and competition as an effective means to check profits and avoid excessive individual economic power. Behavioral patterns which were frowned upon - although practiced in the socialist shadow economy - will have to become preferred patterns, and this switch certainly would be difficult in any society. A whole new class of entrepreneurs is needed to achieve structural adjustment, launch successful catching-up with the West and develop firm-specific and regional sets of comparative advantages.

The longer the history of the command economy, the more difficult it must seem for the majority of the population to switch to a market system. Without an intact memory of market economy times, one has to learn the grammar and language of market transactions and competitive enterprise behavior all over. Certainly, the USSR and its republics face from this perspective the hardest path. Also, if trade and investment links with Western countries played a minor role one must assume that not even a critical minority in industry is aware of the standards common in Western business. From this perspective Hungary and Poland have the best basis to build upon the existing experience with a competitive marketplace. Countries with a large expatriate community in Western eonomies enjoy the potential benefit that there is an exceptional basis upon which to build up and rebuild trade and investment links with Western market economies. Again, Hungary and Poland are well positioned in this respect (in Asia China is in a relatively good position). The subjective gap between old patterns and new behavioral patterns determines how big the subjective adjustment pressure for critical groups in society is - furthermore, how quickly one may expect aggregate behavior to be shaped by new behavioral patterns.

Third, one may ask how strong external and internal adjustment pressures are which imply a high and possibly rising adjustment burden or social costs relative to the capacity for macroeconomic adjustment. If external adjustment pressures that result from opening up the economy are so strong that dismemberment of firms and the creation of new enterprises are prevented, it might be useful to first focus on the internal foundations for competition and only then open up the respective sector. As long as the housing shortage is not remedied the social costs of regional adjustment will be very high. Regional mobility of labor in turn could be a prerequisite to attract foreign investors. As regards internal liberalization it is clear that not only anti-competitive measures are required but an active pro-competitive policy stance. If big firms cannot be dismembered in a meaningful way one may consider the option to remedy this by embedding the firm(s) in bigger markets, namely regional or global markets.

Fourth, one can ask which amount of external support a country facing the transformation problem may expect. A difficult problem concerns the visible loss of income opportunities and of wealth which will be faced by many individuals as the consequence of a new set of market-clearing relative prices and new conditions on the supply-side. The move to world market energy prices will economically invalidate much of the capital stock in Eastern Europe in the 1990s, similar to what the OECD countries experienced in the 1970s. Opening up economies to Western competition will drive prices of shoddy products down and increase the pressure to upgrade the product assortment. If quantity rationing is eliminated the prices for used consumer durables - being traditionally an alternative to newly produced goods that were in scarce or no supply - will sharply fall. Income disparities will grow in the transition to a market economy such that e.g. the income share of the lowest income quintile will be similar to those in comparable western European countries. Finally, the more or less rigid social hierarchy in socialist command economies of Eastern Europe will be replaced by a new social pyramid pattern which should be more osmotic, but which also confronts the individual with more uncertainty and greater needs of mobility in a competitive economy.

With the opening up to Western trade and investment, with free access to Western information and with growing opportunities for travelling abroad the aspiration level of individuals will become shaped by Western European standards and become influenced by competitive group pressure in the respective market economy. The aspiration level which used to be controlled by the communist party and collective influences will become an endogenous variable (and became so in the 1980s due to the satellite dish and other new forms of communication), and politicians will have to increasingly respond to the demand of their voters. The whole process of transition will also entail a switch from traditional emphasis on quantitative output goals whose legitimacy is shattered. Disillusionment over a system calls for a set of new goals.

Few elements can mitigate the transition process to a market economy. As regards external bridging elements one may hope for external debt rescheduling, new opportunities emerging from membership in fully functional international organizations and at least improved market access to regional trading blocs (in particular the EC and NAFTA). In this respect Poland, Hungary and the CSFR are certainly in a favorable position compared to other former CPEs. However, in the short run each country has an incentive to focus only on its own problems, especially because new democratic systems are subject only to the direct pressure of the national electorate. As long as there is no multinational business sector in Eastern Europe and only few profitable trade links all former CPEs face prisoner dilemma problems in systemic transition. Moreover, there is a lack of regional political institutions that would provide an incentive for integrating regional economic aspects into transformation approaches. As much as for the population in each country the introduction of a market economy represents a public good the creation of a regional trade framework is an international public good which might be desired by everybody while nobody is actually willing to contribute to its provision and establishment, respectively (free rider problem).

Exhibit B1: Dimensions of the Transformation Problem

from CENTRALLY PLANNED ECONOMY   **to MARKET ECONOMY**

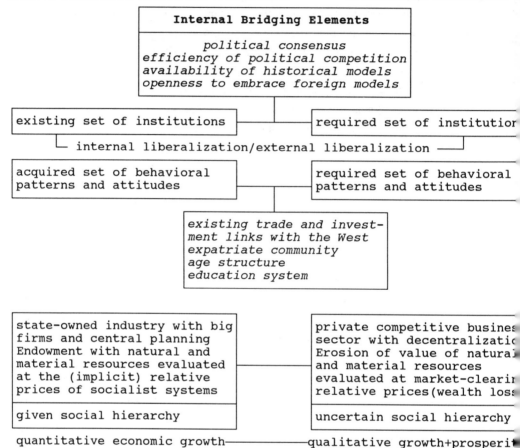

Finally, as regards international support, there is a common moral hazard problem, namely that all countries would rather overemphasize certain problems and hope that asymmetric information problems will prevent a full evaluation of the situation. E.g. in 1990/91 the EC supplied emergency food aid to Poland, although state bufferstocks were more than plenty. International bureaucracies whose employees tend to maximize their budgets are in turn not interested in systematically designing efficient aid programs. Actors involved in adjustment programs think rather of a grand design and prefer such a high profile approach than working through a myriad of gradualist reform steps that would add up to a sustaining transition. While foreign advisers or the government call for increased structural adjustment and regional reallocation of factors there is a huge housing excess demand that basically rules out high regional mobility.

2.2 Distortions and the Need for Efficiency and Stabilization

In socialist economies there is a wide range of distortions in goods markets and factor markets as well as in firms. These distortions in combination with systemic traits of the politico-economic system account for a set of complex initial problems in the transition to a market economy.

The systemic principle of guaranteed full-employment, inexistence of bankruptcies and long-followed strategies of extensive economic growth (based on increasing factor inputs) assured not only full employment in Eastern Europe, but it caused hidden unemployment and indirectly stimulated absenteeism and shadow economic activities. When record female labor participation ratios in the 1970s indicated in the CMEA countries that economic growth increasingly required reliance on technological progress and innovation, the systemic weakness of insufficient innovativeness of the dominant big firms became obvious. Moreover, there were declining world market shares in the 1980s when international competition was accentuated by new dynamic market entrants from the Newly Industrializing Countries (NICs). With the labor market supply becoming inelastic at record participation ratios the systemic hoarding tendency of the firms rapidly translated into stiff competition for labor and hence strong upward wage pressure. Since firms did not face a strict market-determined budget constraint, but could hope - even with rising losses - to continue to obtain soft loans from the state banking system (the "soft budget constraint" as KORNAI dubbed it), it seems clear that a special form of wage inflation developed in the 1970s and the 1980s. While labor productivity only modestly increased, firms accorded high wage increases that were largely credit-financed (at insignificant real interest rates) and indirectly increased money balances in the household sector. When the terms of trade vis-à-vis Western countries worsened and real interest rates on the external debt increased in the 1980s the accumulated monetary overhang faced a reduced internal supply of consumer goods; this was compounded by the fact that high investment output ratios that were 10 or more percentage points above Western figures were reduced only gradually.

In the official socialist economy there is a shortage of consumer goods and also a narrow variety of goods which is partly explained by the system's bias to favor a high investment-output ratio as a means to achieve high economic growth. The narrow product variety largely stems from lack of competition and the common phenomenon of monopolistic producers which also entails excessive plant sizes. Minimum efficient plant scales were certainly often exceeded, where the particular lack of small and medium-sized firms partly reflected attempts of the planning authorities to facilitate central planning by reducing the number of firms via state-ordered mergers. E.g., in the former GDR 2/3 of the labor force was employed in firms with more than 500 employees, a firm group which accounts in West Germany for only 1/3 of employment. In Bulgaria the share of firms with 100 to 399 employees reduced from 26.2 percent in 1965 to 4.5 percent in 1987; during the same period those with more than 5000 employees increased their share from 9.7 to 41.4 % (total number of firms in 1987: 2140).[4] In the CSFR the employment share of manufacturing firms with less than 500 employed dropped from 13.6% in 1956 to 1.4 % in 1980, and similar developments characterized Poland, Hungary, Romania and the USSR. Hence, what in Western market economies is an important ingredient for economy-wide structural and regional change as well as for innovation and flexibility is lacking in Eastern Europe - a viable set of small and medium-sized firms. To redress the balance one would have to dismember many of the big firms along efficient lines and one would have to encourage the creation of new enterprises. Even if there was a political will to dismember big state firms and privatize them, one must expect well-organized resistance from employees and managers. Moreover, there is rarely the knowledge along which lines one should split up the old giants. Only with a functional capital market and functional goods and labor markets would there be a market price vector which could guide an economically reasonable process of dismemberment; without functional internal markets only in the tradable goods sector where one can take relative world market prices as a guide on the output side, is the situation less complex. Dismemberment and privatization as steps towards allocative efficiency certainly will entail massive unemployment which in turn implies a strong resistance on the workers' side against dismemberment and privatization.

In the 1980s the CPEs in Eastern Europe recorded shares of government expenditures to GNP that were in the range of 55 to 60 percent. Hence they were more than 15 percentage points

---

[4] See AUDRETSCH, D.B. (1991), Industrial Policy and International Competitiveness: The Case of Eastern Europe, Wissenschaftszentrum Berlin für Sozialforschung, paper FS IV 91-22.

higher than in Western Europe. If one takes into account that in Western Europe government interest payment amounts to 3-5 percent of GDP, while domestic credit financing plays no major role in Eastern Europe so far, the divergence in aggregate expenditure levels of government is even bigger. Moreover, the structure of expenditures is very different, where a crucial difference concerns subsidies. In West European countries subsidies to enterprises reach between 2-5 percent of GDP, while in Eastern European CPEs figures three times as high are observed. As the capital intensive industries received the lion's share of state subsidies the basic impact has been to subsidize capital intensive production. Taking into account the low capital productivity in most East European economies there is no reasonable economic justification for this subsidization. The fact that investment-GNP ratios in Eastern Europe were in the mid-1980s about 10 percentage points above the ratios observed in Western European market economies is mainly due to well organized political influences of heavy industry and the military-industrial complex in former CPEs. High and growing subsidies to the enterprise sector were a core problem of socialist economies and have created production structures that are not in line with relative economic opportunity costs (see Tab. B2).

Tab. B2: Budgetary Subsidies* Relative to GDP in Eastern Europe

B/Y = budgetary subsidies relative to GDP;
BC/Y subsidies to consumers (relative to GDP)
BE/Y subsidies to enterprises (relative to GDP);
BF/Y subsidies for foreign trade (relative to GDP)

		1980	1985	1988	1989	1990est.	1991proj.
Bulgaria	B/Y	13.3	11.9	19.1	17.8	23.7	7.4
	BC/Y	1.2	1.4	1.6	1.6	4.2	.3
	BE/Y	12.1	10.5	17.5	16.2	19.5	7.0
	BF/Y	4.2	5.3	8.3***	3.0	2.5	1.0
CSFR		8.7	11.8	13.0	16.1	12.1	4.7
	BC/Y	2.3	5.5	5.8	7.7	4.9	1.2
	BE/Y	6.3	6.3	7.2	8.3	7.2	3.5
	BF/Y	2.2	1.9	2.5	1.8	1.0	0
Hungary		19.8**	17.1	14.0	12.6	9.8	6.5
	BC/Y	9.0****	7.1	5.7	7.2	5.7	3.9
	BE/Y	9.7****	9.9	8.2	5.4	4.1	2.6
	BF/Y	5.0****	5.4	5.6	4.0	3.3	1.4
Poland		28.7	16.5	17.0	17.1	9.8	7.2
	BC/Y	9.8	7.3	9.0	7.4	3.4	2.5
	BE/Y	18.9	9.2	7.9	9.8	6.5	4.7
	BF/Y	6.7	3.6	2.2	1.2	1.0	–
Average CPE4		19.5**	14.3	15.8	15.9	13.9	6.4
USSR	B/Y	1.4**	1.8	9.3	9.9	>10	–

* except for the USSR this includes subsidy expenditures of most, or all, extrabudgetary funds. ** refers to 1981; *** refers to 1987 (4.1 in 1988), **** refers to 1982
Source: HOLZMANN, R. (1991), Budgetary Subsidies in Central and Eastern European Economies, Economic Systems, Vol. 15, 149-176; for the USSR: PlanEcon, Washington, D.C.

In 1989 budgetary subsidies as a percentage of GDP ranged from 9.9 percent in the USSR to 17.8 percent in Bulgaria. Subsidies to the enterprises rose in the 1980s in most former CPEs as did subsidies for foreign trade. Subsidies for consumers rose sharply in the CSFR in the 1980s when political pressure induced the government to hide rising costs behind rising consumer subsidies. With open reform discussions underway in Poland and Hungary, consumer subsidization could be reduced; however, the cases of Hungary and Poland were already extreme because in 1985 consumer subsidies amounted to more than 7 percent. It is apparent that in the first transformation stage - in the early 1990s - subsidies were reduced. The transition to a market-based system did not induce short-term improvements in competitiveness, leading to reduced costs and lower subsidies; rather prices charged in the new market environment were raised to market-clearing prices (often at monopoly levels) and output was reduced.

Reducing subsidies for existing firms could be not only useful in the sense of helping to make visible the true opportunity cost of production; it would also reduce the problem of government deficits. However, there is the question whether subsidies should not only be reduced but also generally reoriented in favor of the creation of new business enterprises. Competition creates a positive sum game which means that there are positive external effects - the most important positive externality of competition being the creation of economy-wide useful knowledge; i.e. there will be a higher expected future rate of innovation and economic growth if competition is increasingly based on new market entrants. Western experience shows that a dollar invested in smaller firms yields a higher R&D rate of return than big firms (though the latter may be superior in the diffusion process). Given the difficulty of demonopolization from above - i.e. dismemberment of big firms - one might subsidize the creation of new enterprises and hence the spread of Schumpeterian forces. Another step for increasing efficiency would be a competitive private banking system that would no longer show a positive bias in favor of established state-owned firms.

The whole socialist motivation system contained strong distortionary effects. Prices did not inform buyers about the true opportunity costs nor potential market entrants about possible profit opportunities. Nominal wage claims had to be discounted by employees in accordance with the personal access opportunities to desired consumer goods. There was a widespread price discrimination in the official distribution system which supplied scarce consumer durables at reduced prices to employees in key sectors of industry and for the military plus the party bureaucracy. An ever expanding shadow economy and thriving black currency markets were only the most visible signs of distortions in the whole system of exchange and distribution. Transaction costs were often enormous and implicitly added to the officially quoted prices. As the demand side has to effectively pay the price plus (implicitly) transaction costs the demand faced by firms was lower than otherwise - the effect is similar to a commodity tax in a market economy.

Fig. B1 shows a demand curve in a perfect market economy without transaction costs such that the intersection of the demand schedule AB with the supply schedule (SS_0) would lead to the market-clearing price P^E. In a centrally planned economy there are considerable transaction costs which reduce the price a producer can obtain and indeed create a wedge between the "effective price" (including e.g. opportunity costs of standing in line) paid by the consumer and the monetary price paid. One can visualize the transaction costs by the monetary demand schedule BA' (broken lines). The new equilibrium point is E' and F, respectively; output produced is lower, the effective price paid by the consumer is higher (p^F) than before. From a consumer perspective the price has increased by the distance GF, while the producer receives a price (P^P) that was lowered by the distance GE'. If we take the ratio GF/GE' as the relative burden sharing of consumers and producers it is clear that with the introduction of a CPE (the emergence of high transaction cost) this ratio is the higher the more elastic (flat) the supply schedule is and the lower the higher the elasticity of demand is.[5] As is known from the analysis of tax incidence, the ratio of FG to GE' depends on the ratio of the supply elasticity to the elasticity of demand.

Fig. B1: Transaction Cost Problems in a Planned Economy

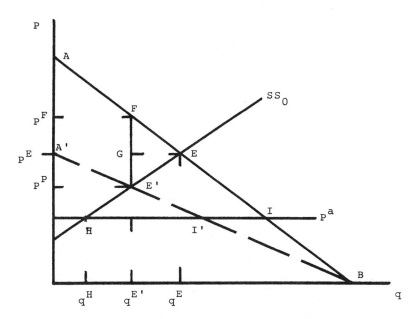

---

[5] In a socialist economy the price could be set by government at P^a such that an excess demand of HI' would be faced by the producers. However, the relevant excess demand from the perspective of a market economy is larger, namely HI.

A worsening of the official distribution system in the sense of higher transaction costs would imply a rising welfare loss from socialist central planning. It is clear that at the same time the shadow economy will expand, while the motivation of the labor force in the official system will reduce. Higher transaction costs can be interpreted as a declining probability to obtain officially produced goods at the state-administered price p^a. If the motivation of the labor force reduces and if absenteeism increases the supply curve will be negatively affected. It cannot be ruled out that while transaction costs in markets are reduced with the switch to a market economy transaction costs in (privatized) firms will transitorily increase and hence productivity reduce because established ways of organizing production are no longer useful in the new market economy. Technical and organizational skills will become obsolete in the new system, while it will take time to find out which people could be successful managers, owners, bankers, workers etc. Using an expression from PELIKAN, market competition represents tournaments for competence and many tournaments might be necessary to find out the winners in all new and old disciplines. Feed-back processes that relate market performance and organizational change will take time and require sequential learning and adjustment.

If there is an upward rotation of the supply curve SS would shift the point G upwards and hence reduce FG relative to GE'. Consequently, the switch from a socialist economy with very high transaction costs to a market economy (with no or low transaction costs) will raise the monetary price producers can obtain and lower the effective price a consumer must pay. The triangle AA'B is an approximate measure of the welfare gain from moving to an efficient distribution system with insignificant transaction costs. Reducing transaction costs by means of building up a functional retailing system should increase the price which firms can charge while effectively reducing the overall price the consumer will pay.

The accumulated inefficiencies in the final state of demise of socialism in Eastern Europe are in themselves enormous. Moreover, with the switch to a market economy and the opening up of economic systems relative output and relative factor prices rapidly are changing from their previously set ratios in the regime of state-administered prices. This implies the obsolescence of a considerable amount of real capital, of organizational structures in industry and of regional as well as structural patterns of production. Adjustment costs can be expected to be a positive function of the average size of firms and the strength of bureaucratic forces in business and public administration. Bureaucrats tend to maximize their respective budgets and politicians often are not effective in preventing bureaucratic inefficiencies. Sometimes politicians or managers of state firms might even justify state monopolies by arguing that profits from one activity are just high enough to cover the losses in some other sector (say profits from telecom services are used to cover the deficit of the postal mailing services). From an economic point of view cross-subsidization is extremely conducive to inefficiency; only private competition could determine whether profits could be even higher and services better or more diversified while unprofitable business activities might even be turned into profitable ones if provided by competing private firms. In a worst case scenario government might just cover the operating loss of a private firm that has substituted for a state provider of services. The most important - unfortunately not directly visible - cost of state bureaucracy and state monopoly is lack of innovation and a non-optimal degree of specialization which implies less sophisticated services at higher costs that in the case of private enterprise. However, private firms will be efficient only if there are clear and credible rules of the game for transactions in the market economy.

2.3 The Inefficiency Problem

If a transition to an efficient market-based system is to be achieved it is not only necessary to abolish the institutions of the command economy, but to establish market institutions, based upon a new set of well-defined property rights that are to ensure efficient allocation. Efficiency has four dimensions: (i) Efficiency in exchange or distribution, namely that the marginal rate of substitution is the inverse of relative marginal utilities and the price ratio, respectively. If relative prices are identical for all individuals - that is price discrimination is ruled out - this implies that the marginal rate of substitution is equal across individuals. (ii) Efficiency of production which requires producing at minimal costs and achieving optimum plant sizes. (iii) Production that an amount and a variety of goods and services that is actually desired by consumers. (iv) Finally, dynamic efficiency in the sense of an optimal innovation rate is required which may loosely be defined by the condition that the marginal social benefits of innovation should be equal to the marginal (social) costs of innovation. While dynamic efficiency is most important for economic growth in the long term it seems to be of limited importance in the short term transformation process in which static allocation criteria should be met first. Static efficiency criteria can contradict dynamic efficiency requirements which makes it necessary to emphasize in the short term either static efficiency or dynamic efficiency; e.g. static efficiency requires that the price of a product should be equal to marginal costs of production and by moving from a monopoly to competition one could achieve this condition in the transition stage. With dynamic efficiency product innovation plays a decisive role and hence there is a "Schumpeterian" departure from neoclassical competition scenarios in which each firm is a price taker; the innovator will be able to charge a price that exceeds marginal costs (including some R&D expenditures), and indeed innovators must be able to appropriate a risk premium for incurring the uncertainty of R&D investments. As is well known from Western literature, smaller firms are relatively more innovative than big firms. This reinforces the need to split up huge state firms and to create new enterprises in the long run.

The means to achieve efficiency in exchange is competition policy in general - hence privatization of retail sales - and an effective system of price arbitrage. Efficiency in exchange and production is one key to economic growth, the other being trade expansion and human capital formation. Here we take a look at the problem of static efficiency in production first, and only then will we briefly address the question of dynamic efficiency which is quite important in the long term because Western growth accounting shows that about 1/3 of economic growth stems from technological progress. Economic crises and reform pressure in Eastern Europe have been generated by the widening technology gap, but adopting capitalism and Schumpeterian innovation dynamics means itself a need for permanent economic changes to which Eastern European societies are not accustomed. Living in a CPE implied to forego capital income gains which raise in market economies real income above official figures. However, the transition will bring few capital gains, but high depreciation rates at first.

2.3.1 The Starting Point - Inefficiency and Adjustment Costs

Socialist systems are known for a variety of system-endemic inefficiencies which concern efficiency of production, of exchanging/distributing goods and of the structure of output. Every economic system that wants to cope with the scarcity of resources in an efficient manner must assure that for a given output input resources are minimized. This is known to require that the marginal rate of factor substitution is identical across industries, and this in turn will hold only if relative factor prices are identical across industries. This condition was clearly violated in Eastern Europe because capital was allocated at diverging (implicit) prices to industries. Firms in priority sectors and those with good connections to the political hierarchy obtained investment funds - and additional credits within the mechanism of the soft budget constraint - at favorable, subsidized rates. Efficiency of exchange or distributing goods requires that for each household the marginal rate of substitution is equal to the reciprocal of the price ratio which implies with uniform relative prices for all consumers that each consumer faces equal relative opportunity costs. If consumer A would forego one unit of good C_1 in return for 3 units of good C_2, while I would give up 1 unit for 4 units of good C_2, there is a profitable potential or an unexploited opportunity for trading. A would sell good C_1 to I (at first, say, three units in return for 3.5 units of good C_1) - obviously at falling prices with a rising amount of goods - until the relative opportunity costs were equal for both individuals who then are on the contract curve; in socialist countries there were considerable and growing black market activities which reflected individual attempts at optimizing in a second round within an illegal economic system using market-based principles of pricing and equilibrating demand and supply. However, with high transaction costs in official systems as well as in the shadow economy the feasible range of profitable private exchange was limited.

Efficiency in production requires that the economy produces on the production frontier line which is equivalent to the condition that the ratio of marginal products is equal across industries and corresponds to the factor price ratio which is uniform for all firms under perfect competition. The condition for production efficiency would be violated with cross-subsidizing and with monopoly power in factor markets. Competition again is the key to efficiency and one therefore mainly faces the problem of dismemberment of monopolistic state firms and privatization, respectively. The long term variant of the static efficiency condition is that firms realize the optimum minimum plant size and thereby minimize long term costs. We disregard here the problem of external effects and public goods. It is clear in principle that cost-minimizing firms should be induced to take into account the true production costs incurred by the economy.

What socialist economies should aim at in the medium term is to introduce relative world market prices in the tradables sector and adjust production accordingly. If firms in sectors i and j produce according to a COBB-DOUGLAS production function one can show that with uniform nominal wages across industries the ratio of labor employed in sector i relative to labor employed in j should be proportional to the ratio of the sales in sector i relative to sector j: $L^i/L^j = z \, (p^i y^i / p^j y^j)$. In market equilibrium with relative outputs produced being equal to relative output demands which in turn depends on relative prices, it is clear that relatively more jobs will be maintained and can be profitably created in sectors in which prices are relatively increasing; however, if price liberalization, occurs in an asymmetric monopoly setting, it may well be that the monopolized sector, say j, would expand, while from the long term perspective of full competition it would actually have to decline (with price differentiation at home and given world market prices there can also be distorted trade flows). If price liberalization induces in the first round under such circumstances a reallocation of labor in favor of sector j, the costly reallocation of labor would have taken place along the wrong line. It might have been better to postpone the reallocation of labor until demonopolization has been achieved and full competition been imposed. Theoretical analysis suggests that an economy consisting of monopolies will have higher prices and a lower output compared to competition - with a given capital intensity lower output also means lower employment. Labor productivity might be lower because monopolies will waste part of inputs for rent-seeking.

The third condition for a global Pareto-optimum is that the marginal rate of transformation is equal to the marginal rate of substitution in the consumption sphere which is fulfilled if prices are equal to marginal costs (relative prices equal relative marginal costs). Such an optimal production structure - at minimized costs - will be violated if the production structure is non-optimal. If there is a restricted sector j (say a monopolized sector with less production than under competition) and an unrestricted competitive sector i, a deliberate shift of resources into the unrestricted sector is not necessarily optimal. According to MISHAN's (1962) classical analysis a violation of this third efficiency condition is particularly problematic because one cannot be sure that expanding production in the unrestricted competitive sector raises welfare more than the loss accruing from the reduced output in the restricted sectors.

Role of Sunk Costs

Adjustment costs for removing distortions are high in many cases. Whenever high sunk costs of human and fixed capital formation exist, one would lose these sums by stopping production. Different industries are characterized by a different significance of sunk costs: Obviously ideosyncratic specific capital is used e.g. in the steel industry and in mining as well as in other heavy industries which played such a big role in socialist command economies. One may contrast the potential loss of capital value (sunk costs) to the costs of revitalizing the industry under the side-constraint that future investment would yield a competitive return. From an economic point of view that takes into account adjustment costs and sunk costs, respectively, one may recommend that government assume in the case of privatization the financing costs for sunk investment, so that new private owners would be responsible only for covering long-term variable costs for existing plants (assuming here for simplicity that sunk costs can be approximated by fixed costs) and total costs for all new investments.

2.3.2 Neutralizing Distortions as a Second-Best Strategy

Welfare economics has dealt with the problem of what to do when some sectors are subject to "unavoidable" distortions. The standard analysis suggests that one may remedy at least some distortions in the medium term, and try to remove the distortions themselves in the long term only. As suggested by SOHMEN[6] one can remedy problems in the restricted sector to some extent within a second-best approach which tries to offset the relative price distortion arising from distortions in the restricted sector. In the long term economic policy should aim to eliminate the sticky distortions in the restricted sectors and thereby to transform them into the set of free or effectively liberalized sectors. But it is clear that, say, eliminating a monopoly position which leads to prices above marginal costs cannot always be eliminated quickly. Then a second-best strategy is required, and this may indeed yield better results than a purist liberal Nirvana approach that wants to do all economic things right but politically gets nothing done.

If one assumes that restricted sectors are characterized by a tax (or some other distortion which creates a wedge between the market price and marginal costs) SOHMEN's formula for a neutralizing tax in the free sector N is given by:

---

[6] See SOHMEN, E. (1976), Allokationstheorie und Wirtschaftspolitik, Tübingen: Mohr.

$$t_N = \frac{\Sigma t_i p_i q_i E_{i,N}}{\Sigma p_i q_i E_{i,N}}$$

This suggests that a neutralizing tax rate is a weighted sum of all tax rates, where the cross elasticity rate $E_{i,j}$ plays an important role both because of its size and its sign (negative for complementary goods, positive for substitutes). If cars are produced in a monopolized sector and are therefore subject to an implicit tax - the divergence between monopoly price and the price under competition - gas should be subsidized; at least if no other goods that are a substitute to cars are restricted goods. Hence the consumption bundle car/gas would then be less distorted in its "price" relative to other goods. If substitutes to gas are taxed this would require as a distortion-reducing measure taxing gas, too. So, taken together the distortions stemming from complementary goods and substitutive goods, the required aggregate neutralizing tax rate could be positive. It certainly would be positive, if one could only establish competition in the car industry.

If the nontradable N-sector is the restricted sector and taxes and monopoly power entail higher prices in this sector than otherwise, one would have to tax nontradables, too, provided that tradables and nontradables are substitutes. This would include a tariff in the case of imported goods unless there is a currency devaluation which itself reflects a distortion to the disadvantage of imported goods. This finally brings us to the interdependency of asset markets. If the price of certain domestic assets is distorted this would require a neutralizing distortion in the exchange rate, too. Let us assume that real capital and investment, respectively, are subsidized while holding domestic money (a substitute for foreign exchange as we assume) is effectively taxed via a positive inflation rate. The asset bundle domestic real capital/foreign exchange - assumed to be complementary - will be less distorted than before if we increase the price of foreign exchange by a real depreciation; at the same time the inflation tax on domestic money would require neutralization of the substitution effect linking the assets domestic money and foreign exchange, again a "tax" on foreign exchange being required. One should, of course, be very careful not to use the argument for a generally interventionist strategy. However, neutralization measures might be considered with a general staggered liberalization approach.

Neutralization measures could be announced with a pre-determined phasing out plan. Hence the typical initial situation in a command economy facing transformation, namely high subsidies on capital formation and a high inflation rate calls for a deliberately strong real depreciation if one is to minimize in the short term the negative welfare effects from a second-best perspective. Exchange rate overshooting in the first stage of the transformation period would therefore be useful. In order not to let this translate into an unwarranted increase of the real burden of foreign debt one should reschedule the external debt accordingly. In the medium term when subsidies to the firms are cut, one should allow a real appreciation. This holds the more, the stronger the feasible reduction in the inflation rate is in the medium term.

Dynamic Efficiency

A fourth condition of efficiency concerns dynamic efficiency in the sense that the rate of innovation is optimal which may be interpreted as achieving an optimal variety of products (product innovations) and developing an optimal rate of process innovations. Since product innovations create a transitory monopolistic situation, the price will not be equal to marginal costs such that static efficiency is violated. Efficient competition processes are characterized by an optimal balance between static and dynamic efficiency. To achieve dynamic efficiency is probably the most difficult goal because it requires a competitive system as a whole and an adequate technology policy which takes into account positive external effects of innovations.

The new information and motivation system should be such that economic freedom as well as competition are assured and transaction costs are small. A credible and sustainable sequence of reforms would facilitate the formation of expectations and thereby widen the capitalization horizon on the one hand, and, on the other hand, reduce uncertainty and the required real rate of return on investment.

As is well known market failure can occur under certain circumstances, above all in three cases, where only one seems to be of added significance for centrally planned economies in the transition to a market economy: (a) falling marginal costs; (b) very many actors on the supply-side or the demand side such that prohibitive transaction costs are likely to prevent external effects from being fully internalized by voluntarily developed institutional arrangements; (c) public goods such that strategic behavior occurs for which game theory does not suggest Pareto-optimality of solutions to be achieved. Where the government acts via public procurement as the only or dominant actor on the demand side while only one monopolistic or a few oligopolistic suppliers exist, one might expect allocational inefficiency as a consequence of strategic behavior even after privatization of major state enterprises.

2.4 Monetary Stabilization: Need, Process and Effects

Distortions in a MUNDELL Model with BARRO-GROSSMAN Effect

One may also visualize the problem of getting relative prices right in terms of a variety of the MUNDELL model which focuses on money market equilibrium (MM line), the equilibrium in the market for nontradables (NN line) and the equilibrium in the domestic market for tradables (TT) in P^N, P^T space (Fig. B2). MUNDELL (1971, chap. 9) assumes that output and demand in both sectors depend in the standard manner on prices and that both goods are substitutes on the demand side. Hence the tradables production will increase, if the price of tradables rises or the price of nontradables falls (a similar reasoning holds for nontradables). A higher tradable price (nontradable price) will reduce demand for tradables (nontradables) and increase demand for nontradables (tradables).

An excess supply in the tradables market may be interpreted as a trade balance surplus since it implies for the case of a small country that more goods are exported. The small country assumption means both that world market prices are given and that its exports are not restricted by external demand. To the right of the MM curve there is an excess demand in the money market whose equilibrium condition is $M = Pm(Y)$, with $P = (P^N) \exp \beta (P^T) \exp(1-\beta)$. The real money demand (m) depends on real output which is given in the short term, and the nominal money demand will increase if the price of tradables P^T or that of nontradables P^N rises such that P increases. Both the TT line and the NN line have a positive slope and both products are considered as substitutes. To the right of the NN_0 curve there is an excess demand for nontradables; at a given price of tradables, say in point C at P^N_0, a price of tradables that is higher than P^T in equilibrium (point A) would imply that the demand for nontradables has grown - hence is higher than in point A - while the supply of nontradables has reduced as some firms switch from producing nontradables to producing the now more profitable tradables. A similar reasoning explains why to the right of the TT_0 line there is an excess supply of tradables. With a given external debt it is clear that the country has to reach a point to the right of the TT line in order to effect the necessary resource transfer for paying principal and interest on the foreign debt.

Government policy in this simple structural model can be monetary policy on the one hand, and, on the other hand, government expenditure policy that primarily affects the demand for nontradables; one might also consider tax policies that influence demand or supply in one or both sectors. Finally, one may take into account the BARRO-GROSSMAN effect.[7] If workers face rationing in the consumer market they will supply less labor in the official economy than otherwise. The conclusion then is that disequilibrium in the consumer market (here the market for N-goods) will lead to a reduced labor supply in both the tradables industry and the nontradables industry (implies TT_1, NN_1). In a more elaborate model one may assume that both tradables and nontradables are consumer goods. If prices are set below the market-clearing levels $P^{N'}$ and $P^{T'}$, the consequence is an excess supply in the money market which

---

[7] See BARRO, R.J. and GROSSMAN, H.I. (1973), Suppressed Inflation and the Supply Multiplier, Review of Economic Studies, Vol. 16, 87-104.

will lead to a currency devaluation in the black currency market and to rising prices in the flexible price shadow economy. The BARRO-GROSSMAN effect would mean that a point like B or C leads to an upwards shift of the NN-curve such that the excess demand increases in the N-market; a parallel rightward shift of the TT curve would raise the excess demand or reduce the excess supply in the tradables market. If firms then get extra subsidies for capital expenditures or wages - financed by soft loans and the printing press, respectively - the main consequence is that the MM-curve shifts rightward and hence the gap between state-administered prices and market-clearing prices widens. This gap will become visible as soon as price liberalization occurs. If one assumes that supply side adjustment and increasing competition first affect the tradables sector one may conclude that a first round impact of liberalization will be a steeper TT curve. This would imply that an increase in the price of tradables and a devaluation (de > 0), respectively (because $P^T = eP^{\text{world market}}$) will strongly stimulate exports in the short run. One may doubt whether systemic transition entails a reversal of the BARRO-GROSSMAN effect.

Fig. B2: Relative Price Adjustment in a MUNDELL Model with Barro-Grossman Effect

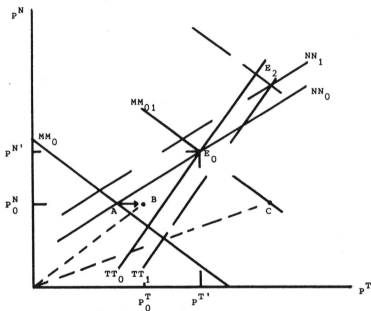

Though it is true that consumer markets are no longer characterized by shortages, but by market clearing - hence a point on the NN curve -, one must take into account the fact that commercialization and privatization will lead to rising unemployment. Employees who face redundancy will not be better motivated to work than before if they face consumer market equilibrium but at the same time the prospects of losing the job instead.

Analytically the MUNDELL model with the negative supply multiplier can be summarized as follows:[8]

p^T (p^N)= Price of (non-)tradable goods, W (W') =nominal wage rate in the official economy (in the shadow economy) e=exchange rate, M= money stock, G= government consumption

Equilibrium condition for the market for N-goods (consumption goods)
$$N^s(p^N, p^T, W, W') = N^d(p^N, p^T, \tau, M) + G \qquad (1) \quad (NN\text{-schedule})$$

Equilibrium condition for tradable T-goods
$$T^s(p^N, p^T, W, W') = T^d(p^N, p^T, \tau, M) \qquad (2) \quad (TT\text{-schedule});$$
with Barro-Grossman effect supply $T^{s'} = T^s / \acute{e}^{\sigma(Nd-Ns)}$
$\acute{e}$= Euler number; σ= labor supply elasticity

money market equilibrium (assuming that real GNP Y is given in the short run):[9]
$$M = P\, m(Y) \text{ where } P=(P^N)^\alpha (P^T)^{(1-\alpha)} \qquad (3) \quad (MM\text{-schedule}); \text{ slope } dP^N/dP^T < 0$$

slope of the NN curve:
$$\frac{dP^N}{dP^T} = \frac{(N^d_{P^T} - N^s_{P^T})}{(N^s_{P^N} - N^d_{P^N})} = (+)/[+] > 0$$

slope of the TT curve:
$$\frac{dP^N}{dP^T} = \frac{(T^d_{P^T} - T^s_{P^T})}{(T^s_{P^N} - T^d_{P^N})} = (-)/[-] > 0$$

Note: possible extreme case in the command economy is that the supply elasticity is zero.

---

[8] If relative input prices change, the economically viable capital stock will be reduced. A reduction of the sectoral capital stocks which are exogenous in this simple model basically has the same impact on the diagramm as the BARRO-GROSSMAN effect, namely that the NN curve shifts upwards and the TT curve shifts downwards such that the new equilibrium would be attained at higher prices of both goods. Analytically, a supply shock of this kind implies a once-and-for-all adjustment in relative prices and the price level P which is composed of the prices for tradables and nontradables.

[9] If one would take into account the shadow economy with value-added Z and a price level P^Z (with $P^Z > P^N$) - resulting from market-clearing and the application of the marginal product rule for factor rewards - a modified money market equlibrium schedule MMZ (not shown in the diagram) would result. The higher Z and the higher the P^Z the closer the MM curve would move to the origin. With the liberalization of the official economy, prices in the shadow economy - relative to prices in the official system - will suddenly drop and output will be reduced in the shadow economy which would imply a rightward shift of the MM(Z) curve and a corresponding excess supply in the money market that drives prices in the now flexible price official economy upwards.
$$M = P\, m'(Y+Z) \text{ mit } P=(P^N)^\alpha (P^Z)^\beta (P^T)^{(1-\alpha-\beta)} \qquad (3') \quad (MMZ\text{-schedule})$$

Inflation Problems in Systemic Transition

The transition process in Poland and other countries brought about some unexpected results in the early reform stages, e.g. the small share of unprofitable companies in Poland in 1990, the high inflation inertia in Hungary and Yugoslavia, but also the fall of the price level in East Germany immediately after unification; the latter is indeed a special case since German economic unification brought a currency conversion and the rule of an established central bank for the former GDR. In all other socialist economies inflationary pressures and even hyperinflation have been common problems of the collapse of socialism, and indeed to a wide extent hyperinflationary monetary policies reflect to a wide extent the collapse of government authority and political consensus. One should strictly distinguish between inflationary monetary policies (often directly related to government budget financing) and the apparently inflationary surge of the price level in the transition to market-clearing prices. Given the fact that the gap between market-clearing prices and state-administered prices were modest in Hungarian and Yugoslavia in the 1980s, it is clear that in this respect Hungary and Yugoslavian inflation problems of the second half of the 1980s mainly reflect monetary inflation. By contrast, the Polish hyperinflation of 1990/91 is both attributable to a monetary overhang and the switch from state-administered low prices to market-clearing price levels. Price liberalization in the sense of switching to market-clearing prices will, of course, result in windfall profits of firms.

Disinflation and Privatization

The wage indexation issue is an important problem for systemic transformation, and we will argue that it is part of the sequencing topics. The indexation problem is important for reducing the inflation inertia and for sustaining financial market reforms which necessarily will entail uncertainties in the monetary transmission process. It is clear that a short term decrease of the real wage rate that would result from an unanticipated inflationary monetary policy is not helpful in a situation in which policy credibility is at a premium. An incomes policy that acts on the expectation side can be helpful in the process of bringing down inflation rates. Social policies are also needed in cases when spiraling rents result from higher free market prices for real estate; as a preferred hedge against inflation real estate will certainly experience a relative price increase in periods of high inflation.

Governments and trade unions face considerable uncertainties about the monetary transmission process and inflationary expectation errors will be frequent. Moreover, with the gradual introduction of a two-tier banking system and new financial institutions as well as privatization the transmission uncertainties will continue, and if there is a recurrent underestimation of the inflation rate firms and their owners, respectively, will be the main beneficiaries. This then makes a case for proposing some kind of "Share Economy" arrangement, namely that workers (losing many socialist privileges anyhow) should have an equity stake in major investment funds through which windfall profits translate into higher overall incomes of workers accepting incomplete wage indexation schemes. Privatization that partly rests upon voucher schemes could indeed develop such a strategy to the extent that voucher allocation for groups not accepting de-indexation would be far less generous than for those who accept incomplete indexation schemes. Hence it is important to address the privatization problem early on, namely in the context of monetary stabilization.

What one can gain from price stabilization is obvious if one analyzes the cost of inflation. However, in contrast to the following macroeconomic argument, inflation is an invisible tax at the microeconomic level and hence political "filters" - institutions or policy rules - that prevent inflation are rarely adopted. Even without a monetary overhang, a jump in the official price level of the economy would occur in the transition from low state-administered prices to higher market clearing prices. In such a situation prices of consumer durables (e.g. used cars) and certain assets are most likely to reduce relative to the price level for newly produced goods. Ideally the emerging market economy could thus find a market-clearing relative price vector along with a new price level in a competitive environment.

There are, however, three complications concerning the price adjustment process in reality:
(1) Markets are characterized more so by monopolies than by competition. Hence prices in individual markets will be z times higher than under competition when price p equals marginal costs k'. Monopoly maximization of profits implies, with E denoting the absolute value of the price elasticity of demand, that $p(1-1/E) = k'$ and since monopoly prices will fall in the elastic range of the demand schedule $(E > 1)$, it is clear that ceteris paribus prices will be higher by a factor of $(E-1/E) > 1$. With $E=2$, the price level would be twice as high as otherwise, where we disregard the potential additional cost-push factor that emerges if process innovations in a monopoly situation are lower than under competition (k' would decline more slowly over time than otherwise).
(2) There is an existing monetary overhang in the initial period of internal liberalization, namely when quantity rationing in the official economy eases and therefore prices in the shadow economy start falling; while the socialist shadow economy might be small in terms of output volume its impact on the demand for money is considerable through the relatively high (market-clearing) prices in the shadow economy. Rising unofficial prices typically absorbed the monetary overhang created by inflationary financing of budget deficits and soft credit allocation in a "silent manner". If unofficial output was 25 % of official output while unofficial prices were four times that of the unofficial economy the shadow economy would be as important with respect to the demand for money as the official economy (assuming identical velocities). Moving from a socialist shortage economy towards a market economy system

implies that prices in the shadow economy will fall relative to the official economy, and indeed one may expect that remaining shadow economic activities would be offered at shadow economic prices below the market clearing prices in the official economy - illegal suppliers typically avoid the costly burden of taxation and regulation in the official economy. Even if there was a quasi-equilibrium in the money market in the final stage of socialism - namely with a booming shadow economy and black currency markets absorbing excess liquidity - the switch to a market economy would imply a transitory excess supply of money triggered by falling prices in the shadow economy.

(3) Inflationary expectations that are initially fueled by the unfolding of the "silent monetary overhang" can become persistent and then generate sustaining inflationary impulses if the money supply is not fully controlled by an autonomous central bank. As long as whole industries are on the government payroll and as long as civil servants strongly press for high nominal incomes as a compensation to anticipated inflation, one may presume that the nominal government budget deficit will keep growing which ceteris paribus increases the need for inflationary financing of the deficit. If the ratio of the real deficit to the real GNP (Y) is denoted by h and the official price level by P the domestic money supply M must change over time according to $dM/dt = hYP$.

Welfare Effects

From a long term perspective that assumes perfectly anticipated inflation, the nominal money supply growth will be equal to the inflation rate π in a stationary economy (to π plus the growth rate of real income in a growing economy). In a market economy an increasing monetary growth rate μ translates into a higher inflation rate and a higher nominal interest rate $i= \pi+r$ (inflation rate π plus real interest rate r, according to the FISHER-relation) such that the real money demand $m=m(i,Y,..)$ will reduce. Denoting the elasticity of the demand for money as σ, the corresponding welfare loss of inflation is according to the traditional analysis: [10]

(1) $H= \sigma(m_0/i_0)\pi(\pi/2 + r)$; [11]

The welfare loss from inflation can be considerable. With high inflation rates one may neglect r and use the inflation rate as the only relevant measure for the opportunity cost of holding money. An inflation rate of 300 % p.a. would result with $\sigma=0.02$ ($\sigma=0.01$) and $m/y= 0.8$ in an annual welfare loss of 1.2 % (0.6 %) of real output. With currency substitution the welfare loss would be much higher since the social cost of obtaining additional foreign exchange is not

---

[10] See TATOM, J.A. (1976), The Welfare Cost of Inflation, Federal Reserve Bank of St. Louis Economic Review, 58 (1976), Nov. , 9-22.

[11] Profit maximization (r=marginal product of capital) in an economy with a Cobb-Douglas production function $Y=Kexp\beta Lexp(1-\beta)$ leads to the expression $H= \sigma/(i_0V_0)\pi(\pi/2 + \beta Y/K)$.

zero; instead goods or assets have to be offered in return. To the extent that inflation reduces the efficiency of the market economy by increasing uncertainty and raising transaction costs, there are additional indirect negative welfare effects.

3. Restricted Options in Transforming Socialist Economies
3.1 Fiscal Policy and Monetary Stabilization

Socialist economies in Eastern Europe faced hyperinflationary pressures in 1990/91 - except for Hungary and Czechoslovakia. The US dollar and the Deutsche Mark were preferred currencies in the process of currency substitution in high inflation countries. If one assumes that the real government deficit G-T is money financed we have in a stationary economy, with h denoting the deficit relative to real gross national product (Y):

$$dM/dt = (hY)P$$

If, following DORNBUSCH et al. (1990) velocity - implicitly the demand for real money balances - depends on the inflation rate π such that $V = a + \beta\pi$ (β is then the semielasticity of the demand for money, relative to GNP) and such that the steady state in which money supply growth $(dM/dt)/M = \pi$, then the inflation rate will be:

$$\pi = ah/(1-\beta h)$$

Hence the inflation rate is a positive non-linear function of the budget deficit ratio h. If currency substitution plays a significant role the opportunity cost of holding money is not the domestic inflation rate but the depreciation rate α of the domestic currency. such that $V = a + \beta\alpha$ and therefore the steady state inflation rate is:

$$\pi = \frac{ah + \beta(\alpha-\pi)}{(1-\beta h)}$$

$(\alpha-\pi)$ is the real depreciation rate and it may indeed be interpreted as the expected real depreciation rate. If an increasing real depreciation rate is expected inflation will accelerate. It is obvious that the deficit GNP ratio h unambiguously increases the steady state rate of inflation. Moreover, one may ask - as done by DORNBUSCH et al. - whether in the inflation process the deficit ratio will rise, e.g. because of collection lags or because of declining real revenues from ad valorem taxes/tariffs or a rising real debt service that is entailed by a real devaluation.

As long as government tax revenues cannot be put on a predictable basis and as long as the tax base, real income, is not growing with a rate above a critical minimum rate, there will be an ongoing confidence crisis as to whether or not inflation rates will rise again. This will impede the inflow of foreign investment whose production activities partly would focus on exports - a very needed type of FDI in Eastern Europe; however, if fear of inflation is associated with fear of misalignment (a typical case under fixed exchange rates), potential exporters will be reluctant to invest. Sufficient investment inflows are, however, a key ingredient to higher economic growth and rising exports in the long run.

A grave problem is the rising financial burden of unemployment compensation and the growing number of nonprofitable firms in the medium term. That is a problem as soon as growing import competition and the creation of new firms (or dismemberment of existing ones) has destroyed the monopoly position of many suppliers. Revenues from privatization are likely to be moderate at best and can hardly compensate for the rising expenditures for social policies. Therefore it would be all the more necessary to attract foreign investors and stimulate domestic investment and innovation such that the medium term prospects for increasing revenues are improved. In any case it will be necessary to harden the enterprise budget constraint by way of establishing a competitive private banking system and to set up a relatively independent central bank. Otherwise one cannot expect to get a monetary policy framework that could effectively control the expansion of the money supply.

3.2 Side-Constraints: The Income Distribution Issue

Switching to a market economy means not only a redefinition of the role of the state, a new allocation of industrial property rights, more economic freedom and greater openness to the world market; it also means greater income differentials within the society, where in market economies the top 40 percent of income earners account for roughly 2/3 of GNP - some 5 to 10 percentage points more than in socialist economies which, however, are typically poorer than Western market economies and often even poorer than some newly industrializing countries.

The socialist centrally planned economies which always emphasized equality of incomes will not only switch to a new system of allocation of factors and goods, but they will also experience a shift to a new financial system with new financial institutions. Third, they will face more uneven or at least more transparent income distribution patterns that are conflict-prone.

With the switch to a market-based system relative income differentials will become more pronounced, and, what is more important, in a more open society they become more visible than in the socialist period such that social conflicts over income distribution are to be expected - especially since the CPEs emphasized equality of income and created a tradition of social envy that is stronger than in Western Europe (not to mention the U.S.). In the short term, greater inequality will indeed result from the few that rapidly exploit huge profit opportunities that emerge in a complex transition phase in which the value of certain skills and assets is rapidly appreciating while the human capital of many is rapidly eroding and requires a time-consuming retraining and reorientation of skills. In addition to this workers - whose status was given ideological emphasis and who often enjoyed politico-economic favors - are likely to suffer a relative loss of income and status in the switch to a market economy which will also be more a service economy than a system dominated by manufacturing industries.

Taking a look at the income distribution for socialist countries in contrast to market-oriented developing countries and some OECD countries suggests the following trend: Systemic transformation in former CPEs will mean that the lowest 20 percent in the income pyramid are likely to see a drop of their income shares while the highest 20 percent of income earners are likely to increase their share.[12] One may note that in market economies liberal professions typically play an important role in the service industry typically and are in the top 40 percent of the income group; one can indeed expect that liberal professions and the service industry, respectively, will play a greater role in the reforming CPEs. Moreover, while the 1970s and 1980s showed a continuous outsourcing of activities formerly supplied as in-house activities in manufacturing industries in OECD countries, the reforming CPEs still have to go through this process. Only then will Hungary, Poland and other CMEA countries as well as Yugoslavia raise the share of value-added in the services industry above 50 percent which nearly in all OECD countries exceed except for Germany which is Europe's leading producer of capital goods.

With greater East-West labor mobility, the falling income share of the relatively poor groups will induce in combination with considerable international income differentials a strong pressure for labor migration. The Federal Republic of Germany had more than 1 million foreign workers from Turkey in the 1980s, although geographic proximity is no supporting factor for migration in this case. If we assume an East-West income gap of 1:3 in Europe, the poorest 20 percent of households in Eastern Europe could reach the income levels of the top 40

---

[12] We disregard here the effects of the shadow economy on income distribution.

percent in their own country if (temporary) migration to the EC would on average yield the income of the lowest 20 percent in the EC host countries. The fact that Yugoslavia's income distribution did not differ much from those in market economies in the 1980s suggests that in relatively open CPEs - as regards outmigration - significant international income differences bring about a migration process that yields distribution patterns close to those in market economies.

A strong specialization in labor-intensive production could mitigate international wage differentials provided that capital were fully mobile such that international divergencies in the marginal product of labor were eliminated. However, capital import controls and other factors prevent this. Moreover, on a global scale the ownership of real capital is very uneven as the strong concentration of source countries of foreign direct investment shows (with the "I-7" U.S., U.K., Japan, Netherlands, Germany, France and Canada accounting for a share of 2/3: WELFENS, 1992a), and this suggests that economic rents coupled with capital ownership are also very unevenly distributed in the world economy.[13]

3.3 Joint Systemic Transformation and Regional Cooperation?

An important strategic question concerns the option of coordinating system transformation among at least some of the former CMEA countries. One cannot overlook that the CPEs of Eastern Europe have a long history of regional trade. The switch to a market economy invalidates the established specialization patterns and hence industrial structures whose value was determined by agreed price vectors and complementarity of production. The intra-CMEA specialization indeed prevented not only competition but also endogenous adjustments of trading patterns and economic structures. "Learning by trade" was an exception. Lack of multilateralism implied that favorable positive sum games that would have required complex multipartite (implicit) coordination and cooperation via trade were not feasible. In a period in which OECD countries and the NICs increasingly relied upon gains from international trade, the CMEA trade strategy became increasingly obsolete. The same is true with respect to the lack of international investment flows which also carry as a side-product technological know-how for which no perfect markets exist.

---

[13] Strong tax reinvestment incentives could help to solve this problem by avoiding visible and high consumption of a few in a period of general economic hardship. These reinvestment incentives should be maintained until the reform progress is beyond the point of no return and is generating high economic income growth for the broad majority of the population. One may emphasize, however, that strong reinvestment incentives will reinforce structural distortions if prices are not liberalized and competition policy (aiming at open market entry) is not enforced.

As Tab. B3 shows the percentage shares of trade were relatively high among the countries CSFR, Hungary and Poland; we disregard here the typically dominating position of the USSR since the (ex-)USSR itself is disintegrating. Since Western trade can only partially compensate for declining East European trade one may consider joint efforts in the foreign economic liberalization. A regional free trade zone or even a regional economic union could generate benefits for the countries involved; it would create bigger markets and be conducive to higher inflows of foreign investment, especially if a common framework for FDI was adopted that would reduce information costs for all investors.

Tab. B3: Bilateral CMEA Trade Flows, 1989 (percent)

(share in total exports of CMEA5 group and the USSR; growth rates of exports and [imports] of trade with the USSR/CMEA5, 1990)

	CSFR	Hungary	Poland	Bulgaria	Romania	USSR	*growth rates p.a. 1990*
							Exports[Imp.:USSR/CMEA5]
CSFR	–	8.9	17.4	4.9	3.9	64.9	18.5/-26.5[-19.4/ -2.7]
Hungary	14.8	–	8.1	2.0	4.1	71.0	-12.8/-24.6[-7.6/ -8.6]
Poland	17.7	5.5	–	4.8	3.4	86.6	31.9/ 23.5[-28.3/-27.1]
Bulgaria	5.7	1.8	4.7	–	2.6	85.2	-24.2/-32.5[-15.2/-21.5]
Romania	9.6	8.2	8.8	5.0	–	86.4	-36.8/-51.1[-22.3/ 12.8]
USSR	25.8	16.9	23.0	23.2	11.1	–	- /-19.2*[- /*-2.4]

* refers to socialist partner countries

Sources: KENEN, PETER B. (1991), Trade and Payments Among CMEA Countries, IMF Staff Papers, Vol. 38 (1991), 235-267; UN Economic Commission for Europe, Economic Survey of Europe in 1990-91, New York, 1991.

However, the prospects for growing regional trade in Eastern Europe are limited. One has to take into account that the removal of non-tariff barriers and of tariff barriers would in itself encourage trade, but not strongly improve the prospects for higher economic growth which, of course, is an important determinant of trade. Moreover, what all economies need most is a modernization of the capital stock and more sophisticated investments in order to reduce costs, produce more flexibly and offer a broader variety of goods. As Tab. B4 shows, CMEA countries produce mainly engineering goods of low technology content. The major exporters of medium and advanced technologies are the OECD economies and some newly industrializing countries. One can therefore expect that prospects for increasing trade naturally benefit East-West trade within Europe. EC countries are likely to benefit as exporters of machinery and equipment; at the same time they are bound to become increasingly important as export markets of the smaller former CPEs. With the association treaties of the EC with Hungary, the

CSFR and Poland in late 1991 a first step towards improving prospects of East-West trade has been made.

Tab. B4: Technology Intensity of Exports and Imports of Engineering-Goods, 1987 (percentage shares and percent, respectively)

	technology intensity (exports/imports:share in %)				world market share*,%
	high	advanced	medium	low	
U.S.	43.7/24.7	17.0/11.8	19.2/43.3	20.0/20.1	13.9
Japan	25.5/41.1	12.3/19.6	40.6/15.3	21.5/24.0	20.1
FRG	11.5/30.0	14.7/16.2	33.9/26.1	34.9/27.6	18.5
Spain	10.6/22.2	10.3/15.9	47.0/30.1	31.8/31.8	1.4
Korea, Rep.	31.6/32.1	4.8/22.0	35.1/ 8.7	28.5/37.1	2.2
Eastern Europe	7.6/ 8.3	18.3/23.8	19.5/ 9.5	54.3/55.6	0.4
USSR	8.4/ 6.0	11.6/23.5	49.4/ 5.3	30.5/60.6	0.2

* as a share of world exports

Source: UN COMMISSION FOR EUROPE (1990), Economic Survey for Europe in 1989-90, New York, 367-369.

3.4 Some Lessons from the Asian NICs and Latin America

Developing economies in Latin America which followed a strategy of import substitution and in which state firms played a major role were not successful in economic development. Recurrent budgetary deficits financed via the printing press have lead in almost all Latin American economies to sustaining high inflation rates or even hyperinflation, capital flight and low economic growth. State firms were often monopolies which imposed not only high prices upon consumers but which spent a considerable share of their profits on rent-seeking activities; firms would finance political campaigns or simply pay bribe payments to bureaucrates or politicians which were in a position to grant favors in the form of regulations or public procurement decisions.

In contrast to this experience of Latin America in the 1970s and the early 1980s is the outward-oriented development strategy of Asian NICs. Governments did not always open goods markets for external competition and almost always imposed restrictions on capital inflows (and sometimes capital outflows as well); however, firms were encouraged to expose themselves to world market forces via rising exports and to accept some presence of foreign investors. Moreover, human capital formation was encouraged systematically which brought not only a well-educated productive workforce but which generally improved the capabilities to adopt and emulate foreign technologies. Successful Asian NICs have all understood that low wages alone are not the decisive key to export growth and prosperity, but low wages coupled with a high rate of technological progress, be it in the form of technological imitation, diffusion or innovation. Moreover, for all countries the import of intermediate products from the huge world market is important for international competitiveness, since it allows the use of reliable and cheap components from abroad on the one hand, and, on the other hand, allows firms to specialize in certain products and offer a greater product variety which raises the average export price (improves the terms of trade). Asian NICs have relied on "positive distortions", namely those that would encourage the expansion of firms, allow them to accumulate technological know-how and international marketing experience and finally enable them to become successful foreign investors themselves.

There are some clear lessons from foreign economic liberalization in developing countries that should be kept in mind for the East European transition. A series of studies by the World Bank which looked into the experience of trade liberalization in developing countries suggests the following conclusions (PAPAGEORGIOU, CHOSKI AND MICHAELY, 1990): (i) successful programs were characterized by considerable momentum were implemented in the sense of starting boldly and implementing further measures quickly; (ii) programs that sharply reduced quantitative restrictions (QRs) - e.g. import quotas - and replaced QRs with tariff rates, sometimes with a narrower range of tariff rates, worked well; (iii) in most cases successful programs started with a real currency depreciation that assured price competitiveness - a specific trend of the real exchange rate thereafter was not observed, but successful programs avoided strong real exchange rate fluctuations; (iv) sound macroeconomic policies in the sense of small government budget deficits in relation to GNP; (v) adequate sequencing of reforms was important in the sense that early capital-market liberalization made liberalization programs derail; (vi) with unstable governments reforms were not sustainable; (vii) the transitional costs of liberalization seemed smaller than generally feared; in particular, balance-of-payments problems rarely occured as exports grew faster than imports, and, moreover, liberalization spurred economic growth and thereby promoted employment growth even in the short term.

All socialist countries have traditionally relied on import quotas or other quantitative restrictions such that a high pent-up demand will unfold - this can occur gradually only if initially a strong real devaluation is enacted. The switch from quotas to tariffs certainly would principally favor the working of the price mechanism, but without a more responsive supply side the benefits of the price mechanism cannot be reaped. The responsiveness of the supply side depends on proper incentive systems for the management and the workers, and, more generally, on a comprehensive privatization and "financial market control". A major problem with the switch from QR to uniform tariffs lies, of course, in the fact that effective protection rates will be different (and often will be much higher than nominal rates) which distorts the allocation of export-competing sectors as well as that of import-competing firms whose output is used as intermediary products for tradable goods.[14]

EDWARDS and VAN WIJNBERGEN (1986) suggest that liberalizing the capital account in an environment of trade distortion can have negative welfare effects if the capital imports are used for investments that will thereby reinforce distortions in the real economy. Focussing on the impact of tariff reduction on the real exchange rate within an intertemporal model, EDWARDS (1989a,b) maintains that capital account liberalization should be a secondary step that, causing a real appreciation of the currency, should be adopted only after the tradables sector has improved its competitiveness. LAL (1987) has argued that a liberalization of the capital account as an early reform step in LDCs can be useful, especially for the determination of some kind of equilibrium exchange rate.[15] SELL (1988, 1989, 1990) argues that gains in external competitiveness will be greater with a parallel liberalization of the capital account and the trade account.

Tradables and Nontradables

Before appropriate relative prices are achieved - above all by actual and prospective liberalization of the trade account - it is not useful to induce capital imports which otherwise could contribute to locking the economy into its inherited structural distortions. However, inflationary pressures can be limited by a progressive liberalization of foreign direct investment inflows which will allow a currency revaluation that lowers prices of imported goods and of intermediary foreign products. To absolutely fix the nominal exchange rate in the medium term is therefore not suitable provided that financial market institutions have developed some inherent stability. To fix the nominal exchange rate over a longer term can be a particular problem if the initial trade balance is in surplus and if structural aspects suggest a relative rise of nontradable N-goods (P^N relative to the price of tradables, P^T). If the latter was to be expected opening up the economy would generate an excess demand for money which would - following the monetary approach to the balance of payments - translate into an

---

[14] This point was emphasized by CORDEN (1987). For a discussion see also BRUNO (1988), BHANDARI (1989).

[15] A modified argument for a situation that starts with tariff liberalization was developed by BHANDARI (1989) who pointed out in his model the role of policymakers' preference functions, where polar cases could be represented by strict emphasis on domestic output and price goals (requiring postponed capital account liberalization) versus the goal of external competitiveness (requiring early capital account liberalization).

excess supply of tradables and this in turn possibly into an expansion of the monetary supply via foreign exchange market intervention. However, with the rise of P^N/P^T an increasing part of the production potential will be employed in the nontradables sector, and this would not only reduce the trade balance surplus in the medium term but also impair the opening up process of the economy. An ongoing opening up process is necessary for all reforming economies if potential efficiency gains from the so far underdeveloped international division of labor and hence cost reductions are to be fully exploited.

The economic catching-up process of Asian NICs is most impressive. Hong Kong, Singapore, Korea and Taiwan were the first generation of Asian NICs; Thailand, Malaysia and Indonesia belong to a second generation group. Asian NICs have used capital import controls for a long time, while practicing export promotion.[16] Despite differences in foreign investment policies and economic policy approaches, one can clearly identify four common sources of success:

- Export promotion rather than import substitution were the relevant trade policies, so that firms became exposed to world market competition and would gradually take on even leading Western firms in certain segments - not so much in the home market, but in third country markets;

- Strong emphasis was laid on human capital formation, and, in some cases, on encouraging the international inflow of capital and technologies by favorable conditions for foreign investors.

- The Asian NICs benefitted from the huge open US market which offered a highly competitive, but also strongly growing market with a host of market niches from which successful entrants could expand; Eastern European economies are so far unlikely to face a similarly favorable environment in Western Europe.

- The first generation of Asian NICs attracted considerable Japanese and U.S. foreign direct investment, while the second generation of NICs already benefits from capital inflows from the first generation NIC group. It remains doubtful whether Poland, Hungary and the CSFR could attract significant FDI inflows from Western Europe and the U.S. (Japanese investments in Eastern Europe are negligible so far), and it seems even more unlikely that these countries would become important source countries of FDI for Bulgaria, Romania and the Soviet Republics in the long run. Savings would have to be high relative to domestic investment opportunities; firms would have to have developed firm-specific advantages on a broad scale; and an outward-looking entrepreneurial class would have to be created within two decades. Moreover, potential host regions would have to show a favorable attitude

---

[16] As regards the trade liberalization strategies see eg RIEBER, W.J. and ISLAM, I. (1991), Trade Liberalization in Asian Newly Industrialized Countries, The International Trade Journal, vol. V, 471-490. On the liberalization problems of Eastern Europe see KÖVES, A. and MARER, P., eds. (1991), Foreign Economic Liberalization, Boulder, Co.: Westview.

---

towards Eastern capital inflows and improve their respective locational advantages. Under favorable circumstances, this scenario might, however, become true.[17]

Had the U.S. not been interested for political reasons in acting with its market and its political protection as a catalyst of change in East Asia the Asian NICs might have faced much greater difficulties in launching their rapid move to prosperity. The U.S. or Western Europe would never have allowed Russian or Polish students, scientists and businessmen to come, visit, learn and cooperate as it was done vis-à-vis Asian countries. Moreover, the Asian family network that still characterizes Asian societies might have facilitated the move towards international ventures and modern flexible company structures. The second half of the 20th century is certainly one in which modern communications equipment in combination with increasing (international) markets require decentralized activity and motivation, while certain "headquarter/parent" functions are centrally organized to the benefit of all subsidiaries. Eastern European societies may have to develop their own business cultures that allow them to combine efficient market transactions with efficient intra-company transactions. However, given the sharp global competition in general and the pressure from low wage economies in Asia and Latin America, where Japanese und U.S. company models dominate, it will be quite

---

[17] It is interesting to ask about the long term implications of capital mobility and asset substitutability in the portfolio approach to exchange rate determination. Money market equilibrium is given by $M/P = m(i,i^*,a,Y)A$, equilibrium in the foreign bonds markets by $eF/P = f(i,i^*,a,Y)A$ and equilibrium in the market for domestic bonds $B/P = b(i,i^*,a,Y)A$, where $A = M/P + eF/P + B/P$. In a simplified version one can assume that domestic and foreign bonds are perfect substitutes such that the nominal interest rate i must be equal to the interest rate abroad i* plus the devaluation rate a $(a=E(e)-e/e)$. One may note that capital mobility in combination with purchasing power parity (implying that the expected long term exchange rate change $E(e)-e/e = \pi-\pi^*$), the FISHER equation for the nominal interest rate $i = r+\pi$ and covered interest parity $i= i^* + (f-e/e)$ leads to the equation $r = r^* + f-E(e)/e$. One can draw this real interest rate parity (RIP) in an e/P, r diagram and draw within e/P, i space the money market equilibrium MM-line. With zero inflation, that is $\pi=0$, the intersection of the RIP line and the MM line determine the real interest rate and the real exchange rate e/P (we assume that the foreign price level is constant). With inflation the nominal interest rate is determined via the MM line and the real interest rate via the RIP line, where the difference between i and r must be equal to the inflation rate; clearly the slopes of the two lines will determine the real devaluation which will occur as a consequence of inflation (the nominal devaluation rate will, of course, be equal to the inflation rate). With profit maximization the real interest rate r must be equal to the marginal product of capital Y_K. The reduced real interest rate - and the previous switch to inflation - imply that the optimal capital stock has increased such that in Y_K, K space a higher K is realized and the area under the Y_K line - which is increasing - indicates a higher real output. This could be a meaningful way to modifiy the traditional portfolio model. One could take into account the link between a rise of the inflation rate π and the empirical observation that price uncertainty increases with the level of inflation; one could assume that beyond a certain (moderate) inflation rate the uncertainty effect would reduce the amount of profitable investment - even to the extent that reinvestment would be reduced and disinvestments be made. Asian NICs have avoided excessive inflation and maintained positive real interest rates. In Eastern Europe the forward rate f could diverge from the expected and the actual future exchange rate, and there is much doubt that domestic and foreign bonds would become close substitutes within a few years. Risk premiums will play a major role in Eastern Europe as they did in Latin America. Finally one may notice that rising unemployment rates could reduce aggregate savings which would imply for Eastern Europe that the first transformation stage - with rising unemployment (reducing savings via lower Y) and fear of rising unemployment (encouraging savings of those who have a job) - is likely to witness reduced savings; only if the desired wealth position sharply increased or if the new capitalists would strongly save would one expect a positive net effect on savings. Positive government savings would be helpful, but are unlikely.

difficult to develop its own East European variety of company organization. Instead, one might be forced - given the high degree of international capital mobility - to adjust society and its structures to the Western model of business organization.

One can certainly learn from Latin American pitfalls in catching up in the 1960s and 1970s in that the politicization of enterprises is a strong impediment to efficiency, competition cum free trade and economic growth. This is the problem of poor societies in which politicians that loose an election face few profitable opportunities of returning into normal life. Politicians tend to strongly fight for maintaining power and restricting political competition. Moreover, the permanent threat of the military to take over power in so many Latin American countries has destabilized the political process. Capital flight has been the plague of Latin America and this in turn was related to slow per capita growth and the fact that emphasis was therefore often placed on income distribution conflicts rather than income growth.

Rent-seeking problems play a major role in many Lation American countries. This is much in contrast to East Asia where economic growth has been consistently achieved by many countries with different models of market-based liberal development. The countries of the whole region were encouraged to build confidence in the ability of liberal policy approaches to yield visible long term benefits - even to the extent that in 1991 ASEAN countries discussed the option of a free trade zone that might not only stimulate regional trade but attract greater investment inflows than otherwise. In Eastern Europe there is the risk that - given the short record of historical episodes of prosperity - one might generate common pitfalls rather than common success stories. In this respect a long term option to join the EC is not only a potential Eastward extension of the EC but it would confront Eastern European countries with the success story of the manifold economic miracles in Western Europe. Moreover, it would convey the message that regional cooperation can have its benefits, and this could be a most important impulse in a period of reemerging nationalism in Eastern Europe. While we might not have a good explanation for the revolutionary dynamics in Eastern Europe we might develop stabilizing focal points which would absorb and direct the social and economic dynamism of Eastern Europe. Common institutions, two-way trade and investment links as well as common projects (say in environmental policy, health care and communication) could provide such focal points.

References

AUDRETSCH, D.B. (1991), Industrial Policy and International Competitiveness: The Case of Eastern Europe, Wissenschaftszentrum Berlin für Sozialforschung, paper FS IV 91-22.

BARRO, R.J. and GROSSMAN, H.I. (1973), Suppressed Inflation and the Supply Multiplier, Review of Economic Studies, Vol. 16, 87-104.

BHANDARI, J.S. (1989), Trade Reform under Partial Currency Convertibility, IMF Staff Papers, Vol. 36, 494-513.

BRUNO, M. (1988), Opening Up: Liberalization with Stabilization, in: Dornbusch, Rudiger and F. Leslie C.H. Helmers, eds., The Open Economy Tools for Policymakers in Developing Countries, New York: Oxford University Press/The World Bank, 223-248.

CORDEN, W.M. (1987), Protection and Liberalization: A Review of Analytical Issues, IMF Occasional Paper No. 54, Washington, DC.

DORNBUSCH, R., STURZENBERGER, F. and WOLF, H. (1990), Extreme Inflation: Dynamics and Stabilization, Brookings Papers on Economic Activity, 1990/2, 1-84.

EC COMMISSION (1990), The European Community and its Eastern Neighbours, Brussels.

EDWARDS, S. (1989a), On the Sequencing of Structural Reforms, NBER Working Paper No. 3138, Cambridge, MA.

EDWARDS, S. (1989b), Tariffs, Capital Controls, and Equilibrium Real Exchange Rates, Canadian Journal of Economics, Vol. 22, 79-92.

EDWARDS, S. AND WIJNBERGEN, S. VAN (1986), The Welfare Effects of Trade and Capital Market Liberalization, International Economic Review, Vol. 27, 141-148.

GROUP OF THIRTY (1991), Financing Eastern Europe, Washington D.C.

HOLZMANN, R. (1991), Budgetary Subsidies in Central and Eastern European Economies, Economic Systems, Vol. 15, 149-176; for the USSR: PlanEcon, Washington, D.C.

IMF (1990), World Economic Outlook, March 1990, Spring.

KENEN, P.B. (1991), Trade and Payments Among CMEA Countries, IMF Staff Papers, Vol. 38 (1991), 235-267.

KÖVES, A. and MARER, P., eds. (1991), Foreign Economic Liberalization, Boulder, Co.: Westview

MISHAN, E.J. (1962), "Second Thoughts on Second Best", Oxford Economic Papers, N.S., Vol. 14, 205-217.

MUNDELL, R.A. (1971), Monetary Theory, Pacific Palisades: Goodyear.

MURRELL, P. (1991), Evolution in Economics and in the Economic Reform of the Centrally Planned Economies, University of Maryland, mimeo, May 1991.

PAPAGEORGIOU, D., CHOSKI, A. and MICHAELY, M. (1990), Liberalizing Foreign Trade in Developing Countries, Washington, D.C.: The World Bank.

PLANECON (1991), PlanEcon Review and Outlook, Washington D.C.

RIEBER, W.J. and ISLAM, I. (1991), Trade Liberalization in Asian Newly Industrialized Countries, The International Trade Journal, vol. V, 471-490.

SELL, F.L. (1988), "True Exposure": The Analysis of Trade Liberalization in a General Equilibrium Framework, Weltwirtschaftliches Archiv, Vol. 124, 635-652.

SELL, F.L. (1989), Die Rolle ökonomischer Verhaltensweisen für "Timing" und "Sequencing" handelspolitischer Liberalisierungsprogramme, Zeitschrift für Wirtschafts- und Sozialwissenschaften, 109 (1989), 449-466.

SELL, F.L. (1990), "True Financial Opening Up": The Analysis of Capital Account Liberalization in a General Equilibrium Framework, Universität Giessen, Discussion Papers in Development Economics, No. 9, mimeo.

SOHMEN, E. (1976), Allokationstheorie und Wirtschaftspolitik, Tübingen: Mohr.

SVR (Sachverständigenrat zur Begutachtung der gesamtwirtschaftlichen Entwicklung, 1990), Jahresgutachten 1990/1991, Bonn.

TATOM, J.A. (1976), The Welfare Cost of Inflation, Federal Reserve Bank of St. Louis Economic Review, Vol. 58, Nov., 9-22.

UNCE (UN Economic Commission for Europe, 1991), Economic Survey of Europe in 1990-91, New York.

WELFENS, P.J.J. (1990), Economic Reforms in Eastern Europe: Problems, Options and Opportunities, prepared for Testimony before the United States Senate, Small Business Committee, Washington, D.C., March 23, revised draft in INTERECONOMICS, 1991/5.

Appendix B1: Tab. B5: Selected Macro Data for Eastern Europe in the late 1980s

	USSR	Bulgaria	CSFR	GDR	Hungary	Poland	Romania	OECD
population*,mill.	286.4	9.0	15.6	16.6	10.6	38.0	23.0	824.8
GNP($)/capita*#	3179.8	3774.0	5094.0	6271.9	4349.0	3654.0	2758.4	14637.0
cars/1000inhab.**	50	127	182	206	153	74	11	385
tel./1000inhab.**	124	248	246	233	152	132	111	542
investment/GNP(%)*	33.2	32.7	24.7	29.2	28.5	36.5	37.1	20.6
share of private sector in GNP*	2.5	8.9	3.1	3.5	14.6	14.7	2.5	70-80
trade/GNP **** (Imp. + Exp./GNP)	13	63	41	36	38	27	43	-
change in OECD market share,1978-89	-26.0	-18.5	-44.0	-25.2	-7.8	-32.3	-46.3	-
terms of trade change vis-à-vis USSR#	-	-38.9	-48.8	-20***	-41.0	-37.2	-46.2	-

*= 1988; **=1987; *** own estimate; ****=1980; Anmerkung: Dollareinkommen auf Basis von Kaufkraftparitäten; # in view of new statistics on the GDR we adjusted the SUMMERS/HESTON figures upon which the OECD figures are based by a factor of 1/3 downwards. Ignoring purchasing power adjustments as made by SUMMERS and HESTON we observe in 1988 a West German per capita income of $ 18480; in the Republic of Korea, Portugal and Greece per capita incomes reached $ 3600, 3650 and 4800, respectively, while Poland and Hungary reached $ 1860 and 2460, respectively (WORLD BANK, World Development Report, 1990). ## Group-of-Thirty-estimates for the transition to world market prices, where the regional and commodity structure of 1989 was used.

Source: Group of Thirty (1991), Financing Eastern Europe, Washington D.C., 17; OECD, quoted after EC COMMISSION (1990), The European Community and its Eastern Neighbours, Brussels, 20; IMF (1990), World Economic Outlook, March 1990, Spring, 65, own calculations.

C: Privatization and Foreign Investment in Eastern Europe

1. In Search of Private Owners and Entrepreneurship

Having experienced a decade of economic stagnation and increasing political and economic disruptions the East European economies - including the republics of the former USSR - have finally decided to radically change their socialist economic system and move towards a market economy. In order to achieve a market-based system a lengthy transition process must be endured in which new institutions are created, the distortions of the command economy removed and the supply-side is reorganized in a way that economic resources are efficiently produced and distributed. This transition period to a market-based system necessarily cannot be characterized by the same economic and political principles as those shaping the desired new market economy. Even the case of the former GDR is not a pure big leap strategy, although the introduction of West Germany's institutions and laws in the context of economic union on June 1, 1990 and political union on October 3, 1990 brought a radical regime switch for Eastern Germany; this switch, however, was mitigated by transitory regulations in many fields (e.g. environmental protection and labor market regulations) and a massive West-East transfer of resources in the united Germany. The privatization process as a centerpiece of systemic change was organized by the *Treuhandanstalt* ("THA", a public entity under the supervision of the Bundesministerium der Finanzen) and has made considerable progress within two years: the so-called small privatization in the retail and small service industry has been fully completed, while the "big" privatization of industry has made progress to the extent that 1/2 of the some 11,000 firms had been privatized by the May 1992 (accounting for roughly 40 % of all jobs in THA enterprises). West German firms clearly dominated as buyers of privatized firms, i.e. they accounted for 90 % of the assets that were privatized. Foreign investment has so far played a minor role even in the manufacturing industry and in the services industry where West Germany traditionally has recorded a high stock of inward foreign investment.

Compared to the former GDR the other countries of the former Council of Mutual Economic Assistance are facing a much more complex transition process to a market economy. The external transfer of resources will certainly remain modest and those countries have to develop the whole set of institutions for a market economy on their own. Moreover, the massive know-how transfer achieved in East Germany via West German firms and authorities dispatching senior management or consultants and experienced civil servants, respectively, is not a feasible avenue for the former CMEA countries. It will be more difficult to mobilize domestic and foreign investment on a sufficient scale and, even more importantly, to channel it into investment projects that would build and contribute to a prosperous private sector economy.

A modern market economy is characterized by the interplay of the invisible hand of market signals and market forces as well as the visible hand of national and multinational companies;

in such an economy government is no longer a major producer, but it is assumed to provide a credible framework of institutions, laws and regulations that define individual rights and assure that legal claims can be enforced and liability rules applied. Only then can private contracts been enforced such that the market system can work. Non-market decisions play some role in the context of the labor market in all economies, but it is obvious that wage bargaining behavior will change in the transition to a market economy. Manual labor was relatively well paid in the socialist economies, both for ideological reasons and because labor in heavy industry - favored by the command economies with their crude emphasis on manufacturing industry - was regionally quite concentrated and easy to organize within the mostly monopolistic huge firms. The bias in relative wages was effectively aggravated by the preferential supply of scarce domestic and imported goods which became available at discount prices to workers in heavy industry through firm-associated retail outlets.

Due to the lack of competition and to the coincidence of permanent shortages in the official distribution system and the impact of preferential goods supply, effective real wages could not become equal for identical jobs (say an electrician in a coal mine and an electrician in the textile industry) nor could the marginal product rule apply - at least in the official economy - not apply because firms did not maximize profits and because there were monopolies. Firms aimed at fulfilling plans and hoarding input factors, including labor via overmaning. This was to ensure that output targets could be met and premiums be obtained - even if monopolistic suppliers of intermediate products did not fulfill contracts or state-determined delivery targets. Workers in politically sensitive industries (military industrial complex, power generation, key export industries) could appropriate a politically determined rent. Entrepreneurship in the sense of risk-taking creative investment activities and innovations was never systematically encouraged, not least because individualism and individual performance were not appreciated. Moreover, it was not recognized that economic growth and technological progress as based upon millions of small improvements and some big changes in certain firms that should spill-over to or at least inspire other firms.

1.1 The Economic Challenge of Privatization

To restore a network of profitable private enterprises after more than four decades of state ownership is extremely difficult for four main reasons:
(1) There is a firm size problem, namely that most firms overextended by Western criteria of an optimum minimum production plant size. In some cases (e.g. steel) oversized production units cannot be reduced simply for technical reasons, but the more general problem lies in the fact that splitting firms and plants into smaller units automatically raises the number of

qualified managers needed to run and monitor those units - all this in a situation where management know-how already is a bottleneck factor.

(2) Expectations are running high as to the capability of market-based reforms in overcoming stagnation, but at the same time "socialist attitudes" still prevail - flexibility, performance-orientation, regional mobility and the will to improve human capital by training and job assignments in international projects certainly were not the standard qualities towards which the socialist system geared its workforce or at least a critical mass of it. Governments in eastern Europe do not have much time to implement complex reforms which, even if less ambitious, could easily fail as examples from developing countries suggest. Moreover, politics in Eastern Europe is now subject to competition in new multi-party systems which implies that any package of reform must bring about improvements of individual utility positions within a short time. Changing entrenched views and ambivalences with respect to private property and multinational company activity will be part of the systemic adjustments necessary for the evolution of a market-based system in which static and dynamic efficiency promote growth, employment and trade.

(3) The formation of new private business enterprises was an exception in the CMEA. What venture capital agencies, the banking sector and the stock markets in Western economies amount to, namely to provide a pool of risk capital for entrepreneurs was unknown in Eastern Europe. Hungary with its "liberal" enterprises law that allowed private firms with up to 5 employees was promoting at least some entrepreneurial activities which could grow further once the legal restrictions on employment are removed. However, private entrepreneurship was generally discouraged and discriminated against in the CMEA countries. Decentralized decision-making that would place considerable responsibilities with the firm were unknown in Eastern Europe - except for Hungary (since 1968) and, to some extent, Poland after 1981.

(4) Except for the Ex-USSR all East European economies face the question of how to deal with the socialization and expropriation waves that characterized Eastern Europe after World War II. The issue of restitution of industrial property is a specific problem of the transition stage. Investment on the side of new private owners will naturally remain low until clear titles of property can be established such that legal uncertainties have been removed.

East Germany has to privatize 8000, Poland about 7000 firms, the CSFR 4800, Russia 30,000, Bulgaria 1500, Romania 3500 and Hungary about 2500 to wipe out the 80-90 percent stake of the state in industry. Excluding Germany the pole position in the privatization process is taken by Hungary which plans to privatize 500-600 firms by 1993, and hopes to privatize at least 50 percent of state-owned assets by 1996 whereby foreign owners are expected to hold up to 25 percent of all industrial assets. In marked contrast to the Hungarian situation is the unstable and unclear situation in the (ex-)USSR where Lithuania was the first Republic to realize a privatization scheme in 1991.

All east European countries have recognized that improving technology transfer and accelerating capital formation require new foreign direct investment policies. However, traditional mistrust against foreign capital and fears that foreign ownership could inflict balance-of-payments problems, accentuate foreign indebtedness and create political conflicts have impaired a comprehensive and credible liberalization of investment flows. In the Polish and Czechoslovakian case there is additional fear that German investors - some of them former expellees - would dominate a privatized industry with unrestricted investment opportunities for foreigners.

Economically the basic idea of privatization of industrial assets, banks and housing is to create a more efficient, flexible and dynamic economy, namely a market system in which allocation ideally is guided by relative prices and profit expectations of producers whose dynamic competitive interaction will allow increasing per-capita consumption and sustaining economic growth. Based on a stable political framework the invisible hand of national markets and the visible hand of national and international companies have created prosperity and growth in the OECD countries and in some Newly Industrializing Countries which are all linked by a complex network of international trade and investment flows. In Eastern Europe and the USSR all five pillars of economic prosperity are non-existent, that is there is a need
- to establish a system of markets and provide an adequate institutional framework as well as a stable macroeconomic framework for this;
- to create private firms which build on domestic and investment flows to rejuvenate or expand their capital stock and improve their product lines in order to survive in a Schumpeterian competition process with its focus upon innovation and imitation.
- to organize a systemic flow and exchange of advanced knowledge, know-how and technologies which in OECD countries are strongly incorporated in multinational companies;
- to increasingly use the advantages of the international division of labor by exposing the tradables sector to global competition;
- to establish a stable monetary policy framework based on a central bank system that maintains price stability (or low inflation rates) which assure that relative price signals are not distorted or superimposed by inflation dynamics; in combination with a privatized competitive supply-side this is the basis for economic growth and structural adjustment.

Systemic transformation toward a market-based system is not only complex in the sense that a host of new institutions and reform targets have to be reached, but also extremely delicate because the starting point is marked by deep distortions of goods and factor market as well as political uncertainty. Major distortions are well-known:
(i) rationing in official consumer markets with their low state-administered prices,

(ii) high investment-output ratios in combination with low marginal products of capital and oversized investment goods industries,

(iii) an excess demand for labor and hoarding of material input in the socialist sector with its non-innovative monopolistic producers which establish and ultimately nurture a growing shadow economy;

(iv) the existence of a monetary overhang that stems from currency substitution and monetary financed past budget deficits which typically result from rising price subsidies and excessive credit allocations for unprofitable socialist firms;

(v) finally, emphasis on an autarkic economic system which - disregarding intra-CMEA trade - is reflected in the smaller East European countries by export-GNP ratios of 8-15 percent while West European countries of similar size record ratios of 30-60 percent.

Privatization as well as liberalizing FDI represent fragile liberalization attempts which not only raise economic efficiency questions but organized resistance in industry and politics as well. Some strategic issues in developing systemic reforms arise in this context. If one is to gain some insights into the problem of implementing what accentuates competition, stimulates growth and nevertheless meets entrenched resistance, it is interesting to take a look at the experiences with other comprehensive liberalization attempts, namely in the trade area.

There is little doubt that sound macroeconomic policy in general and an appropriate exchange rate policy in particular are also necessary ingredients for privatization and the inflow of foreign investment. Moreover, if it is true that capital market liberalization should follow trade liberalization only those countries which have a strong Western trade orientation or have adopted radical trade liberalization programs early on can be prime candidates for a strategy of growth by privatization-cum-FDI. Hungary and Poland are the only two countries which were open economies for world trade, while all other East European countries had relatively weak trade relations with the industrial market economies - weak as compared to West European countries of similar size. An open question, however, is to which extent enough momentum for privatization and FDI can be built up. Only if a critical minimum momentum can be achieved, may one expect that the "new train" would not derail. There will be difficulties, financial scandals and other unavoidable negative experiences, not much different from the case of the founding period of capitalism in Western Europe (on the continent) in the 1870s.

Eastern European Countries Facing Common Problems
The CMEA disintegrated in 1991 and East European economies face the risk of economic stagnation and politico-economic instability. Whatever the envisaged transformation process it is clear that there will be an extended period of rapid institutional and economic changes that create a premium on information on the one hand, and, on the other hand, sustainable and

credible policy approaches. For domestic as well as for foreign investors protracted political uncertainty must be avoided; otherwise a considerable risk premium in capital markets would depress asset prices and reduce the amount of profitable investment. However, given the enormous need of restructuring it will be almost impossible not to use new and radical approaches which themselves create uncertainty.

Privatization and the liberalization of capital flows are problems familiar to West European countries whose experiences indeed reinforce the case for comprehensive liberalization in Eastern Europe. In Western Europe privatization of state-owned firms and banks was high on the political agenda in the 1980s, when ideological reorientation towards the market economy model, endogenous disequilibria in markets and new institutional frameworks meant a changing role of government in industry. Privatization of firms and deregulation of markets were often two sides of the same coin from a new laissez-faire minting of minds (PERA, 1988). However, the demise of the state as an entrepreneur is linked less to ideological shifts than to the globalization of markets and the rise of a multinational industry. In such an environment nationally bound state-owned enterprises are at a clear disadvantage (WELFENS, 1992a).[1] In most cases state ownership implies the disadvantage of not effectively exploiting international production opportunities in a world economy with a greater mobility of technologies and capital. Even an internationally-oriented state-owned company faces the problem of political interference and capital restrictions that stem from budgetary problems of the state. This impairs its options for unbundling assets as well as for international M&As. In addition to the problem of foregoing the full set of opportunities of internationalization, state-owned companies are less exposed to the control of private capital markets.

In Eastern Europe the politico-economic transition process is taking place under difficult internal and external conditions (see Tab. C1). Inflation rates are high in all Ex-CMEA countries, except for the CSFR. The market potential is limited if one takes into account low per capita GNP figures and small absolute GNP figures for all countries, except the former USSR.

---

[1] Historically, government-owned enterprises have played in Europe a role for various reasons (AMBROSIUS, 1984). The state played an important role as an entrepreneur in Germany and Italy in the 19th century; after 1945 Italy, France, Spain and in part the U.K. emphasized the strategic role of certain public enterprises. Instead of adopting the U.S. system of controlling industries with declining costs by regulation, governments in Europe used public ownership of utility firms, the communication sector and some manufacturing activities. By public procurement decisions and in many cases by preferential allocation of credits and capital, governments had an impact on the innovativeness of upstream and downstream industries. Principal agents problems in public firms of course could not be checked by the capital market, which became a particular problem after external shocks in the 1970s required creative structural adjustment. Relying on established Olson-type redistributive coalitions with excellent access to the political system, publicly owned industries did not only accept capital yields below market rates but showed slow reactions to new technology trends and particular communication problems (PICOT and KAULMANN, 1989, FLOYD et al. 1985, BORCHERGING et al. 1982).

Net debts are high relative to exports in most countries, including Yugoslavia. Joint ventures were a dominant form of foreign investment until 1990, but were not really important economically. Industrial production sharply reduced in 1991, and unemployment rates shot up in 1991/92 (see Tab. C2). Inflation rates were very high and debt service-export ratios - except for the CSFR, Romania and the USSR - were higher than in Latin American countries. Per capita incomes relative to the OECD average were 1:2 or 1:4.

Tab. C1: Key Figures for Eastern Europe, Yugoslavia and the USSR, 1990

	GNP $ bill.	Infla-tion %	Net Hard Cur. Debt $ bill.	Net Debt/ Exports	Popula-tion (1988)	World Bank Mb.ship	Joint Ven-tures
CSFR	121.5	11.0	0.5	7.5	15.5	1990*	1300
Hungary	59.3	30.0	17.0	263	10.6	1982	1500
Poland	140.9	220.0	36.2	369	38.2	1988	2800
Bulgaria	46.0	50.0	9.9	502	9.0	1990	300
Romania	86.0	5.0	0.3	5.3	22.7	1982	2500
Yugoslavia	117.8	55.0	8.3	72	23.6	1949	2800
USSR(1989)	512.6	15-20	50-70		288.0	1992	3000

* rejoined; one may note that on average only about 50 percent
of joint ventures are operational
Sources: Planecon, Washington, IMF et al. (1990), The Economy of the USSR, Washington D.C., press releases and own estimates.

Tab. C2: Selected Macroeconomic Data for Eastern Europe (in %)

Indu.-Pro-duc-tion 1991	Unem-ploy-ment (2) 1990	Infla-tion Rate (3) '91	(4)COUNTRY	Debt Export Ser-vice 1990	GDP# per Capi-ta 1989	Growth Rates: Real GDP 1989	1990	1991*	1992*	'93*	'94
-23	1.0	6.6	58 CSFR	25	7878	1.0	-3.0	-16	-4.8	-3.9	4.3
-15	1.6	8.3	35 Hungary	65	6108	-1.8	-5.6	-8	-0.4	1.5	2.7
-12	6.1	11.4	70 Poland	71	4565	-0.5	-13.0	-9	1.5	2.6	1.8
-27	1.7	9.6	474 Bulgaria	77	5710	-0.3	-11.3	-23	-6.7	0.6	0.8
-22	1.3	3.1	219 Romania	10	3445	-7.5	-10.5	-8	-5.1-	3.9	2.6
-20	17.7	19.6	184 Yugosl.	n.a.	n.a.	0.8	-6.0	-28	-	-	-
-20	0.5	1.5	100 USSR**	29	6500	1.8	-6.4	-18	-	-	-

 # based on purchasing power parities; OECD average: $ 15565.
* Group-of-Thirty Projections; ** PlanEcon Estimates; figures for unemployment rate in the ex-USSR and the change in industrial production are my own estimates. Per capita gross domestic product figure for the USSR seems to be inflated.
Sources: Group of Thirty (1991), Financing Eastern Europe, Washington D.C., 51 (data for GNP growth rate; however, for 1991 figures of ECE are used); PlanEcon (1991), PlanEcon Review and Outlook, Washington D.C.; WIIW, Mitgliederinformationen (1992). Economic Commission for Europe, Economic Survey of Europe, Geneva 1992; OECD (1992), Reforming the Economies of Central and Eastern Europe, Paris.

Internally, there are extreme distortions of goods and factor markets as well as a capital stock and a sectoral structure which rapidly became obsolete with the opening up of the economy and the switch to world market prices. The collapse of intra-CMEA trade in 1991 which occurred with the switch to the new hard currency regime for trade is bound to accelerate trade with Western countries, but for the East European economies the switch to world market prices for imports of Soviet oil and gas will aggravate the foreign debt problem and impair regional trade. By joining the IMF and the World Bank, respectively, the Eastern European countries have gained improved access to private and official credit sources. However, one should not overlook that high debt service-export ratios will restrict the scope of Western capital good imports and narrow opportunities for liberalizing international trade and investment flows.

The fact that all East European countries, Yugoslavia and the USSR have openly embraced joint ventures in the late 1980s points to the tendency that in a period of capital scarcity and increased modernization needs foreign capital inflows are accepted in principle in all socialist economies. At the same time the emphasis on joint ventures means that there is still an ambivalence with respect to foreign investment which can only be accepted in conjunction with a domestic investor. Naturally, with the demise of the command economy there is no longer a political need to directly exercise control over foreign investors. But even so it holds that there is a need for a new strategy to control economic power and assure efficient allocation. A functional capital market and competition among foreign investors as well as between domestic and foreign investors are only gradually recognized as providing a superior organization mode to assure that no supernormal profits can be occur in the long term.

Privatization and the opening up to capital inflows is naturally difficult for economic systems which have experienced decades of socialist central planning in which individual initiative and responsibility were rarely rewarded and the virtues of a competitive market economy with private industry rarely enjoyed. Entrepreneurship, intrapreneurship (entrepreneurial initiatives of individuals within a firm) and competition in world markets are almost unknown in Eastern Europe - there is certainly a potential for this which has yet to be developed and which will require economic as well as political institutions to change accordingly. The resistance to privatization can be considerable for reasons concerning other necessary measures of a market-based transformation as well. People will be afraid that nomenclatura members and "entrepreneurs" from the shadow economy as the only two groups with considerable financial wealth will benefit from privatization, namely by gaining (again) control of industrial assets. If prices are liberalized there will be only negative effects at first in the sense that perceived real income positions erode and most groups will suffer a relative reduction of their income and wealth position. It takes time until there is a supply-side response to price liberalization.

Privatization is exactly what is urgently needed in combination with price liberalization. Only with private competition in industry can there be a positive supply side response. The USSR's price liberalization of spring 1991 was a complete failure because of lack of simultaneous privatization. Russia's program for price liberalization which was enacted on January 1, 1992, led to soaring prices - with increases of several 100 % - that expressed the switch to market-clearing price levels, but under monopoly conditions. At least the program is coupled with a privatization program.

Externally there is the problem of high real interest rates worldwide that negatively affect all the highly indebted East European countries (Romania and the CSFR are exceptions). There is continuing competitive pressure from the newly industrializing countries and global competition is widely shaped by transnational and multinational companies whose role has particularly increased in Europe as the single market evolves and Eastern Europe opens up (KLEIN and WELFENS, 1992). The existence of rivalistic multinational companies in the U.S., Japan and the post-1992 EC implies specific opportunities to attract parallel investment projects from oligopolistic competitors - e.g. in the case of the automotive industry where follow-up investments of supplier firms can be expected, too; improved access to EC and North-American markets would certainly reinforce such opportunities as would sustaining growth in the whole of Europe. This makes trade policies important for Eastern Europe.

The OECD countries have all built their prosperity on stable political institutions, stable macroeconomic policy, functional markets and entrepreneurial firms which interact in national and international trade and investment flows. Western prosperity is not only built upon domestic competition, but also on inter- and intra-industry trade as well as foreign direct investment that allows the rapid diffusion of advanced technologies despite incomplete international protection of intellectual property rights. FDI does not only allow favorably combining firm-specific advantages and locational advantages, it also provides a basis for intra-company trade which accounts for about 30 percent of total trade in the "I-7 group" (leading investor countries) of the U.S., U.K., Japan, Germany, France, the Netherlands and Canada. According to JETRO (1991) Japan was for the first time the world's biggest investor in terms of investment outflows in 1989 - reaching $ 44.1 bill. (stock value: 154.4 bill.) - while the U.S. and the U.K. both recorded 31.7 bill. (with stock values of 373 and 192 bill, respectively), followed by France with 18.1 (55.9), Germany with 13.5 (112.6), the Netherlands with 9.9 (88.2) and Canada with 4.1 (65.9); global outflows amounted to $ 198 bill. in 1989. It is important to recall that technology flows are fastest within the network of multinational companies which face imperfect markets for intellectual property rights.

Innovations which account in OECD countries for about 1/3 of economic growth were one of the weak systemic elements of the command economies in Eastern Europe.[2]

Finally, in "Schumpeterian competition" shaped by novel products and process innovations, multinational companies also take a lead, and internationally cooperative R&D ventures have reinforced this tendency; this is crucial because shortening product cycles and rising R&D costs imply rising appropriation risks for investors and innovators on the one hand, and, on the other hand, terms of trade improvements for countries whose competitiveness is largely built on successfully innovating companies (WELFENS, 1990b).[3] From this perspective multinational companies are necessary for technological progress, the diffusion of innovations and economic growth.[4] The privatization of state industries in the host countries enriches the asset menu for potential investors and contribute to a local demand for regulations that generally supports private business activities. In contrast to a two-country world with only state firms private enterprises can reorganize industry along changing lines of firm-specific and country-specific advantages and are not facing systematic political interference into business. *Murrell* (1990, 1991) has strongly emphasized the negative role which the lack of multinational companies plays for socialist economies. Lack of internal competition and oversized firms play a negative role, too, as this reduces the reaction speed, product diversity and innovativeness of industry. Hence international competitiveness is weakened.

1.2 Early Developments in Privatization and Foreign Investment in Eastern Europe

Privatization is time-consuming and complex as even the successful British approach under the Thatcher government shows when the transformation of state firms into joint stock companies was the preferred strategy of privatization. In the case of former socialist command economies everything is more complex, not least because of the changing and uncertain legal environment and because one faces extreme problems in the valuation of assets and liabilities. Under very favorable circumstances - as in the case of German unification - privatization can proceed relatively quickly.

---

[2] See on this WELFENS, P.J.J. and BALCEROWICZ, L., eds. (1988), Innovationsdynamik im Systemvergleich, Heidelberg: Physica; POZNANSKI (1987).

[3] Private ownership of capital and multinational companies have been a key ingredient of successful market-based systems, although state-owned companies have played a role in Western Europe where governments often prefer some form of ownership control in the case of natural monopolies and strategic industries rather than relying on regulations of a full-scale free enterprise model. Functional capital markets, influential banks and big institutional investors as well as the market for managers ensure that no individual firm can escape in the medium term the requirement to develop goods and services that can profitably be sold in a dynamic marketplace with Schumpeterian competition.

[4] However, small companies are quite successful as innovators, too.. See on their important role AUDRETSCH, D.B. and ACS, Z. (1990), Small Firms and Entrepreneurship in a Global Perspective: A Comparison between West and East Countries, Wissenschaftszentrum Berlin für Sozialforschung, FS IV 90-13.

In Poland the so-called small privatization whose focus is mainly on retail trade has worked well, and in 1990 almost 60 percent of the 500,000 new private enterprises are trade firms.[5] However, privatization of industry concerned in 1990/91 less than two dozen big firms of which only a few were quoted on the new Polish stock exchange. The approach envisaged after 1992 is to speed up privatization of industry by a combination of voucher schemes, public offerings and management/employee buy-outs. The Polish government's intention in early 1991 is to privatize 50 percent of state-owned firms within three years and to proceed in tranches, namely with 50-100 out of 500 large firms in a first round. In this round 20-30 percent of the shares will be offered to the public via vouchers which will be allocated to various investment funds which in turn will be allocated to individuals interested in using their vouchers. In the field of FDI there are no such bold plans of the government in Poland. So far foreign direct investment flows are insignificant so far and reached only $ 0.35 bill in 1990. The considerable number of about 3000 joint ventures (about 1/3 of which is from Germany) is not too impressive if one takes into account the fact that paid-up capital typically is below $ 1 mill. such that no decisive quantitative contribution to economic growth can be expected, while positive qualitative impacts might well be considerable.

The CSFR already attracted one mega FDI project, namely the Volkswagen-Skoda deal, but the mobilization of FDI and the privatization of industry was able to begin on a broader scale only in 1991 after the new law on restitution of property was passed in February. The CSFR's approach is to organize two privatization rounds, a first one for domestic residents - where vouchers will play a mayor role - and a second one in which domestic as well as foreign residents can participate. In Hungary privatization is also proceeding only gradually, but foreign direct investment inflows are relatively high and Hungary indeed accounts for almost 50 percent of all FDI undertaken in the CMEA in 1990. Investment inflows of almost $ 1 bill. were recorded in 1990 and another $ 1.5 bill. annually is expected for 1991/1992 and the following years. If the OECD rules for FDI were to be accepted by at least some smaller CMEA countries the amount of FDI inflows to Eastern Europe could be raised if political instability did not counteract this.

In the Hungarian case leading source countries of FDI are the U.S., Austria, Sweden, Germany, Japan and Korea (non-EC foreign investment is dominating). The government's official medium-term goal, namely to attract enough FDI that up to 25 percent of the Hungarian industry is controlled by foreign owners willing to restructure the respective companies, may well be reached in the late 1990s if $ 1.5 bill. in FDI can be attracted

---

[5] See HARE, P. and GROSFELD, I. (1991), Privatisation in Hungary, Poland and Czechoslovakia, Discussion Paper No. 544, CEPR: London. On the dynamics of industry reform in Eastern Europe see also MILANOWIC, B. (1989), Liberalization and Entrepreneurship: Dynamics of Reform in Socialism and Capitalism, Armonk, N.Y.: Sharp.

annually. It is an open question whether rising FDI inflows would accelerate the privatization program or whether privatization in turn is a prerequisite to attract higher FDI flows. Building on a liberal legislation for FDI, ethnic homogeneity and traditional outward-orientation Hungary is leading Eastern Europe's effort to attract foreign investment (INOTAI, 1992).

2. Privatization and Resistance to Systemic Change

Privatization on a massive scale not only will change ownership structures in Eastern Europe, but it will change allocation, financing and distribution of income. Allocation is supposed to become more efficient, and financing more diversified and efficient, namely in the sense that private firms would provide the basis for primary and secondary capital markets as well as help to create influential institutional investors - holding in some Western countries and Japan more than half the value of shares. Organizing a rapid, fiscally sound and equitable transfer of state-owned property is considered to be the prime task of privatization as argued by LIPTON and SACHS (1990) who emphasize that any firm-by-firm strategy in a privatization approach does not do justice to the need for quick and comprehensive privatization in Eastern Europe.[6]

It is indeed important to recognize that the privatization of a whole industry (or a whole economy) is analytically different from the privatization of single firms which occurs from time to time in Western market economies. In Eastern Europe it typically holds true that privatization of sector A (say textiles) will be influenced by the performance of branches with firms acting as suppliers of intermediate products (say, the chemicals industry). Hence the value of firm A_1 is not only affected by the output of firms A_2-A_n via falling market prices as a function of industry output, but also by the prices and quality of intermediate products supplied from firms C1, C2,...Prices of suppliers will be lower and the quality of products higher if industry C has already been privatized. If one accepts the hypothesis that private firms are more efficient and innovative than state owned firms it is clear that privatization of industry i will affect the net value of industry j (and vice versa). This is not true in the case of privatizing individual firms in Western market economies where one may assume that at the margin privatization of a firm does not change the vector of input prices and output prices in a whole industry and asset prices in the economy at large.

It is not clear whether on average the net value of firms as evaluated by discounted future profits will be higher in the short term than in the medium term. Many firms will record extra monopoly profits which should vanish in the medium term with rising import competition and greater domestic competition. This would imply higher profits in the short term than in the

---

[6] See LIPTON, D. and SACHS, J. (1990), Privatization in Eastern Europe: The Case of Poland, Brookings Papers on Economic Activity, 1990, 293-341.

long run; however, it is unclear whether intensified competition would stimulate innovativeness in individual firms and hence replace static monopoly rents by possibly higher Schumpeterian rents accruing to innovative firms. If innovations would occur mainly in the tradables sector and if capital (employed in this sector) is mobile internationally, one can conclude that labor will be able to appropriate part of static monopoly rents but not of Schumpeterian rents. At least those who are employed could therefore lobby for maintaining monopoly positions. Managers and employees could form powerful rent-seeking coalitions that put into effect distributive coalitions with their productivity impairing activities before an open system with contestable markets has been established at all.

Forms of Privatization

The basic forms and areas of privatization are summarized in exhibit C1. Privatization naturally should start where it is easiest to organize, namely at the level of retail trade and small commercial shops. An efficient distribution system - organized in a competitive way - is already one way to contribute to higher welfare since the goods produced will be distributed in such a way that the law of one price holds within the country and that marginal rates of substitution are equal across consumers (they face identical relative opportunity costs so that spontaneous resales of purchased goods become unnecessary). Local government can severely impair small privatization by holding back real estate that would be necessary to establish new outlets and shopping centers. Especially in the period of high anticipated inflation rates public authorities might be unwilling to sell real estate since waiting - while leasing meanwhile - could mean higher future prices and hence budget revenues in the case of selling later. Leasing, however, if occurring at all is often only a weak form of property rights that entails the risk that benefits expected from investments made by the user of the premise (say in the case of a hotel) cannot fully be appropriated by the present user who therefore will realize a smaller investment budget than would have been the case under full ownership.

Speculative withholding of state property is a problem in Eastern Europe. This type of privatization obstacle can be reinforced by influential members of the former nomenclatura who use their positions in the state bureaucracy to derail or at least slow down steps towards marketization. At least for the transition period - and possibly only for a pre-defined transition stage of 10 years or so - it might be useful to introduce a local sales tax on the one hand, and, on the other hand to introduce a modest capital gains tax (or just a property tax). The purpose would be to stimulate government measures that would help private business to expand and real assets to be put to their best, most valuable use quickly. Indeed incentives systems are also required that will encourage an efficient use and quasi-automatic financing of government infrastructure funds. If building a park and a new highway increases the value of real estate in area X then government should receive an implicit price for this by a capital gains tax paid by those who benefit from public investment projects or privatization schemes.

Governments that are afraid that the sale of say communal housing at preferential prices to the tenants will lead to huge windfall profits in the case that the new owners in turn sell at much higher market prices are typically inclined to impose restrictions on the use of property. E.g. as in Hungary the government has introduced binding constraints that require the present tenants to use the newly acquired housing units for at least several more years. This is certainly neither effective nor efficient compared to unrestricted use of property in combination with a capital gains tax.

Exhibit C1: Forms of Privatization

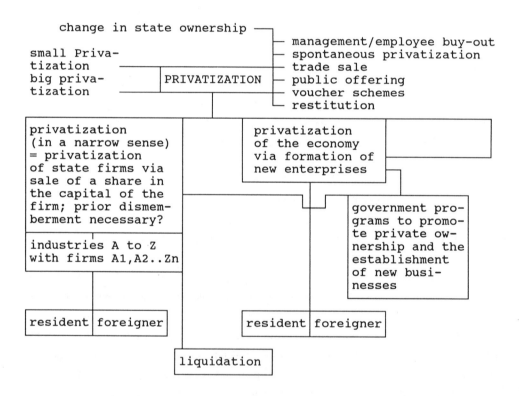

The first round in the allocation of property rights naturally is not optimal, and as economic conditions change it is only useful to allow the change of the ownership structure by means of voluntary exchange. If a housing unit could be sold at five times the original price (disregarding inflation), it is obvious that someone other than the present owner should use the property. With a 25 % capital gains tax government would receive considerable revenues that could help to finance new housing and investment projects. The basic problem with restrictions on the use of property is that the restrictions are difficult to enforce and rarely make economic sense. If present tenants are supposed to use the premises bought from the state and must use it X years in order to get it at a discount price from the state, while the market price were five times as high and therefore rents could also be high, a natural way to circumvent the restriction is that the present owner moves away (while officially still living in the housing unit) and gives a lease to somebody who offers a reasonably high rent. This still leaves the problem of windfall profits and "unjust benefits from privatization", and in contrast to a solution with a capital gains tax the situation is not transparent and society effectively gets no indirect benefit via higher tax revenues.

Big privatization raises many issues which have to treated separately. As regards the organization of big privatization, there are various possibilities: a management buy-out or an employee buy-out (possibly financed at favorable credit terms by some state bank or private venture capital agencies); a trade sale to an interested investor which would not necessarily be that firm or individual which offers the highest price but one which would make a binding promise in the contract that an amount of X currency units would be invested over Y years or that at least Z jobs would be saved or created. This type of side-constraint is typical for deals organized by the German Treuhandanstalt, which set up contracts for which failure by the new owner to keep promises brings severe penalty fees.

Public offering normally means that the assets will go to the bidder offering the highest price - the placement of bigger firms at the stock exchange is a classical way to achieve this. Voucher schemes as used in the CSFR and Poland mean that every adult or every interested citizen gets some stock for free (or at a low nominal fee). It is useful to spread individual risks by allocating vouchers only as a stake in investment funds. As the reorganization of industry proceeds and privatization is being completed the real value of the vouchers and the stocks which they represent should increase over time. A voucher scheme can be expected to affect savings and investment behavior as well as labor market supply. People who perceive themselves to have become richer will tend to save less and demand a higher real wage rate for a given amount of labor supply. While these effects may not be desirable from the perspective of East European economies there is a positive counter effect. If people with some minimum endowment in real capital can afford to engage in better human capital formation/education than had been possible otherwise one may expect that productivity will be increased in the very long run by a voucher scheme. A special form of privatization is what in some East European countries is called re-privatization, namely that the former owners - once expropriated by communist governments - receive their old property back.

Privatization "from below" in the form of setting up new business establishments is much needed in all East European economies. The number of newly created firms in the U.S. in one year was typically higher than the number of all existing firms in the USSR. Structural change and innovation dynamics in market economies owe much to new firms. They are, of course, all small in the beginning and only some 50 % survive the first five years (in West Germany they then have 5.5 employees on average). However, the conclusion to be drawn is not that new business establishments are not important, but rather that one should immediately begin the task of publicly encouraging new entrepreneurs whose positive role will yield high future benefits in the long term. Venture capital agencies and programs for seed-financing and start-up financing are needed on a massive scale in Eastern Europe.

State Interference in the Transition Period Required
It might appear that state support for new entrepreneurs is a kind of industrial policy; however, one should clearly emphasize the difference between pro-enterprise and pro-market state interference in the transition period (competition-augmenting and growth-enhancing "start-up policies") as opposed to government interference in an already fully functional market economy. A major task of government would also be to organize the dismemberment of at least some of the big firms since firms in all socialist economies are way beyond an optimum minimum plant size which at the same time often implies a monopoly position for the firm. Import competition cannot always do the job of providing competition impulses that should in many cases be firmly rooted in at least some domestic competition among several suppliers as well. Moreover, there is the risk that foreign suppliers will follow the price-leadership of domestic monopolies such that the survival of domestic monopolies implies not only a welfare loss in terms of traditional monopoly analysis but also in the transfer of extra monopoly profits to foreign suppliers. Firms that cannot be restructured in the medium term or in the long term must be liquidated. Bankruptcy procedures have to be established in Eastern European countries urgently. The greater the expected loss of jobs in a region with restructuring or liquidated companies, the more urgent is it to increase labor mobility across regions and to encourage the formation of new business establishments.

Privatization as Competition Policy
Privatization of state industry can achieve the main goal of economic efficiency and economic growth only if privatization is embedded into a pro-competitive economic policy concept. This

means that any strategy which leads to the privatization of individual firms from different industries makes limited sense - as in the case of Poland in 1991 when 16 major firms from totally different industries were privatized. Only in 1992 did Poland envisage to privatizing whole branches, allegedly because privatization so far has gone so slowly; however, the real argument for such a strategy is that the benefits from competition among private firms cannot be realized otherwise. One might start with those industries in which big oversized firms play a minor role. As long as less than 50 % of value-added or of supply (which would include imports) is coming from private competing firms one cannot hope to have really switched to a market economy - with competitive labor markets.

2.1 Basic Issues of Privatization

Eastern Europe is suffering from the shocks of systemic transformation, the collapse of regional trade and the switch to world market prices. There is a comprehensive need for structural adjustment and catching-up with Western Europe. All this must happen in a period of increased global dynamics since international markets are playing a greater role than ever, multinational competitors are expanding - while facing intensified competition - and firms from the OECD countries are building new forms of "strategic alliances" (e.g. Daimler-Benz and Mitsubishi). The internationalization of industry is reinforced by national deregulation attempts on many countries and the privatization of state industry on many OECD countries as well as in some developing countries (e.g. Argentina, Mexico, Taiwan).

In Eastern Europe privatization of industry does not only mean the switch from socialism to capitalism but it should be the basis for rapid modernization, economic growth and rising trade. Historically, Eastern Europe lagged behind in the industrial revolution, and again it is facing a necessary catching-up process towards a decentralized service industry - locked to a viable core of manufacturing industry - and towards an internationalized economy. In 1870 Swedish per capita incomes were as low as those in Russia, namely about $ 250 (1960 US dollars; BAIROCH, 1976), but in 1913 it had reached the British value of 1880, namely $680, whereas Russia's annual per capita income stood at 326 which was less than the British per capita income in 1830; however, this per capita income was higher than in Portugal, and if Russia had only followed the retarded Portuguese industrialization and internationalization process it might well have enjoyed the same per capita income as Portugal in 1989, namely $4250 which is slightly less than that of the Republic of Korea (per capita incomes for 1989 are in current dollars; WORLD BANK, 1991, Tab. 1). Using the figures from BAIROCH and the World Bank, respectively, we find that in 1913 Finland had a per capita income that was 60 % higher than Russia's, but in 1989 Finland had a per capita income of $ 22,120, whereas the leaders of the former CMEA area, the CSFR, Hungary and Poland, recorded per capita incomes of $ 3450, $ 2590 and $ 1790, respectively.

Using purchasing power parities the East European figures might be about twice as high as indicated; however, there is little doubt that without the socialist experiment the USSR even could have enjoyed in 1989 a per capita income close to that of Spain (also a late industrializing country), namely some $ 9300 - instead of some 4,000-5,000 at purchasing power parities. To put it in a different way: There is little doubt that the former socialist economies face a huge potential of catching up with their own potential within a market-based economy -   provided a market economy with efficiently organized firms and functional markets for decentralized coordination can be built up and people can change their attitudes. While the first experience with price signals might be the shock of price reform and price liberalization, the next step could be to witness the shock-absorbing power of price changes which bring demand and supply in line with each other under changing conditions and which convey signals for adjustment, entrepreneurship and diffusion to other market participants in private industry.

If we ask what the basic issues of privatization in Eastern Europe are, one could raise five points:
(i) privatization as a core element of the transformation to a market economy should help to establish a competitive system of well-managed private firms and thereby realize an efficient decentralized economic system; since competition is basically among firms in an industry privatization should therefore be mainly organized in such a way that industry by industry is privatized and in each industry competition policy should ensure that barriers to entry are removed. The tradables industries are first candidates for privatization if the supply elasticity is to be increased in the crucial export sector, but one might also consider starting in those industries where political resistance is least so that a critical minimum momentum can be built up. There is no economic rationale for starting the crucial privatization process with the aim to privatize the biggest 300 or 500 firms (as suggested by some authors) since such an approach cannot do justice to the aspects that competition is mainly a contest within a certain industry. Competition among private firms $A1, A2 \ldots A_n$ in industry A will encourage the diffusion of favorable production technologies and thereby make the supply curve - drawn as a stepwise function in Fig. C1 - more elastic in the medium term (SS_1). In Fig. C1 the competing firms A_2 to A_5 have an incentive to imitate the production technology of firm A1 whose marginal production costs are lowest in this industry (SS_0 is the short-term supply curve).

Fig. C1: Diffusion and Process Innovation in a Privatized Industry
(p=product price, k'= marginal costs)

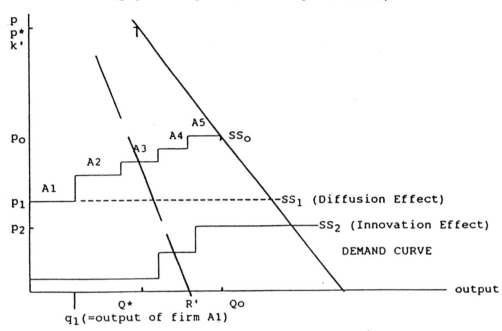

If firm A4 is still a state-owned (inflexible) firm and can use political connections - as in the socialist system before - to obtain investment credits at preferential terms, an efficient diffusion process would be impeded by a distorted capital market (A4 would expand capacity, while A1 should have done so!); clearly, a competitive capital market would allocate funds to those flexible firms that can quickly adopt the low-cost technology of firm A1.

If firms A1 to A5 were allowed to form a cartel or were actually a monopoly profit maximization would imply equating marginal revenue R' and marginal costs k' such that the higher price p* (lower output Q*) would hold, while output would be reduced; A4 and A5 would be closed, while they would actually have had a chance to survive if competition could be imposed from the start of the transformation process (starting with a state monopoly which is commercialized: managers can maximize profits, but are constrained by employees).

In the long term competition will lead to process innovations. These will shift the industry's supply curve downward (SS₂) while the slope of the supply curve might rise again until the diffusion process leads to a more flat supply curve again. Both quick diffusion and process innovations work in favor of consumers who will obtain a greater quantity at lower prices. A high supply elasticity in the medium term is required if higher market prices are to stimulate output - an important aspect both in the context of price liberalization and devaluation (the latter for the case of tradables). Competition is optimal if the diffusion process allows the initial innovator - here firm A_1 with its low-cost technology - and the fastest imitators to appropriate some extra profits that enable them to partly directly finance process innovations and thus build up a reputation as a successful innovator or fast imitator using experience, managerial resources and know-how effectively. The capital market will reflect growth options in the valuation of the firm.

The potential capital gains of privatized firms will therefore not only depend on the present amount of capital, but on perceived options to invest as well - at least if we follow MYERS, 1977 and PINDYCK, 1988. In the macroeconomic context politico-economic uncertainty and instability as factors which imply a narrowed set of options to invest will reduce the value of real assets in industrial firms.

(ii) The aim to privatize a certain number of big firms makes sense only as a secondary goal, namely as an element to establish a functional labor market. If the biggest 500 (or 1000) firms represent, say, more than 50 percent of value-added in the economy, one would have to anticipate that the marginal product rule for factor rewards would not hold such that the economy is not producing on the production possibility frontier and hence facing unexploited static efficiency gains.

(iii) Privatization requires a stable and clear legal framework that defines property rights in an unambiguous way and guarantees full ownership rights which in turn are a prerequisite to encourage high and long-term oriented investment projects. Clear liability rules should be part of a well-defined system of private property rights. The property rights system is essential for consistent incentives, while competition helps to avoid excessive market power on the one hand, and, on the other hand, will contribute to quickly melting away differential profits (firm A_1 in the above figure makes, of course, a bigger profit than all other firms which are thereby encouraged to imitate A_1's production technology - at least if profit maximization and a functional capital market, respectively, drive the other firms to quickly enter the imitation process).

(iv) Privatization as a means to achieve internal competition might be easier to implement if part of imports are subject to a tariff (and if existing quotas are replaced by equivalent tariffs). There is, of course, no sound reason to impose a tariff on imported goods in which the country is unlikely to develop a firm specific or country specific advantage; moreover, if imports that help to modernize the economy (say, computer chips) would become subject to a tariff the external competitiveness of the tradables sector would be weakened.

A certain tariff rate imposed upon a broader class of goods could be useful for the transformation process provided that a pre-announced tariff reduction scheme is introduced at the beginning of the transformation process. This would be part of a gradualist strategy, where low nominal tariffs could explicitly be stated as a constitutional economic policy goal. One should emphasize that a devaluation is not a perfect substitute for tariffs because a devaluation is equivalent to a tariff on *all* imported goods, and, as a further difference it directly will affect assets prices and interest rates. The latter is obvious from the asset market approach to exchange rate determination in the BRANSON-KOURI tradition. Finally, one may note that a given nominal tariff will, of course, raise the problem of effective protection. If the free competition/free trade price of the good were \$ 100, a 10 % tax would raise the price to \$ 110.

The effective protection rate in industry A is defined as value-added by A-firms in a regime with positive nominal tariffs ($v^{A'}$) minus value-added under free competition (v^A) divided by v^A. If imports in a free trade world were to represent \$ 60 in intermediate products used by A-firms, a 5 % tariff on imported intermediate products would raise the value of imported value-added to \$ 63, so that $(v^{A'}-v^A)/v^A$ would be - given the 10 % tariff on the final product - $(47-40)/40 = 14.9$ percent which is higher than the nominal tariff.

If we assume that instead of imported intermediate goods nontradable inputs from a monopolized industry are used there will be a somewhat different problem. If the relative difference of the monopoly price and the price under competition in the nontradables industry is 5 % privatization in the nontradables industry would raise the effective rate of protection.

The price of a unit of output in industry A would still be \$ 110, but the unit costs of intermediate inputs will have reduced to \$ 60 so that $(v^{A'}-v^A)/v^A$ is $(50-40)/40 = 25$ %. This makes clear that there is a natural link between internal competition in intermediate products and external protection of final goods. Privatization should therefore be coupled with a gradually declining nominal tariff rate.

(v) Finally, one may point to the distributive issues that play a very important role in the societies of Eastern Europe with their former emphasis on egalitarian income structures. One analytical tool to cover this issue is the ratio between the consumer surplus and the producer surplus (Fig. C3).

Fig. C2: Effective Protection under Tariffs (or with Domestic Monopoly in the Supplier Industry)

Free trade price/free competition value-added and unit costs

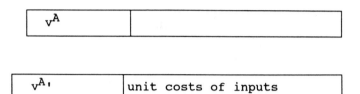

with 10 % tariff on output of industry A, 5 % tariff on inputs (or relative difference of monopoly price and competitive price equal to 5 % in the nontradables industry)

Fig. C3: Consumer Surplus and Producer Surplus

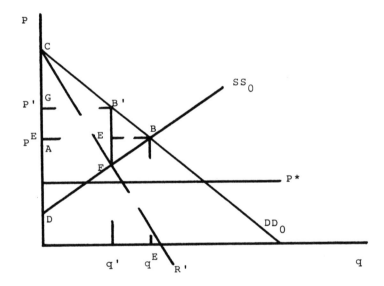

Under competition the intersection of the supply curve SS_0 and the demand curve DDo determines the market clearing-price p^E. In a competitive market economy - with no price discrimination - each consumer will obtain the good at the market-clearing price, even if an individual's willingness to pay had been higher as indicated by any point on the demand schedule above the market-clearing price. The triangle ABC reflects the "extra-gain" by the consumer group.

The supply curve reflects the industry's aggregated marginal cost curves such that the area under the curve indicates total costs (we disregard fixed costs here). Since producers will have a revenue of p^E times the market-clearing level of output q^E there will be a producer surplus equivalent to the triangle ABD. Part of income distribution conflicts can be viewed as an issue related to the ratio of the consumer surplus to the producers surplus; especially if foreigners own the capital stock of an industry and hence will benefit from an income residual like the area ABD, people (voters) could find it difficult to tolerate a low ratio of consumer surplus to producers surplus.

An effective competition policy can make the supply curve more elastic and - as will be shown below - thereby reduce the economic rents that could accrue to foreign or domestic investors. If the respective industry is a monopoly such that profit maximizing behavior leads to the Cournot point B' and the lower output q' (at price p'), there will be a reduced social surplus, namely the so-called deadweight loss equivalent to the area B'FB; but there will also be a redistribution in favor of capital owners to which part of the consumer rent (surface of the area AEB'G) will now accrue.

If the economy is opening up in a situation of internal competition a world market price of p* would imply that imports equivalent to the divergence between the amount of goods desired by consumers and that which is produced at price p* by domestic producers will emerge.

If an import tariff is imposed the price of imported goods will rise so that the import supply curve shifts upwards; there will be a deadweight loss for consumers and producers, but - taking the viewpoint of modern political economy - there will also be a tariff revenue which could be considered as a loss of social surplus; namely, if one assumes that tariff revenues will contribute to financing an expanding state bureaucracy which basically "plays social zero-sum games", it will expand loss-making activities to the extent that they can be financed from profitable activities or extra revenues.

Finally (see Fig. C4): International distribution effects can also be visualized in the MacDougall diagram which portrays the marginal product curve capital (Y_K) at home and abroad (Y_K^*; the * denotes variables abroad).

Fig. C4: International Income Distribution with Capital Flows

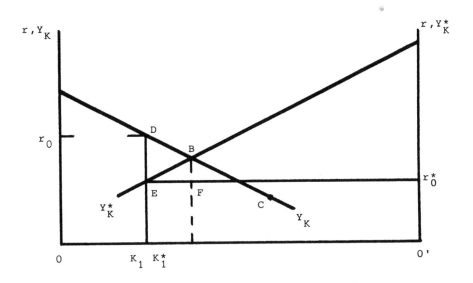

If the marginal product rule of factor rewards holds linear homogeneous production functions imply that the area under the marginal product curve will consist of capital income rK plus labor income wL (real wage rate w and labor input L) which exactly add up to real output (since the Y_K curve - a negative function of K - is the partial derivative of the production function with respect to K, the integral over this function is equal to output Y). The length of the "world capital box" OO' is determined by the amount of capital used after adopting profit maximization in Eastern Europe; it is assumed that at home K_1 is employed (origin is O), while abroad K_1* - measured from the origin O* - is employed such that diverging marginal products at first also imply internationally diverging real interest rates (profit maximization requires that in each country the marginal product of capital be equal to the real interest rate r). It may well be that in the socialist initial stage in the home country a capital stock was employed that was much higher than indicated by point D, e.g. a capital stock that would imply the very low marginal product of capital in point C. With international capital mobility marginal products will become equal in the long term such that point B will hold and the home country will have an inflow of foreign direct investment that amounts to EF (global gain: triangle EBD). The inflow of FDI would be reduced in the presence of political risk. Moreover, if the risk premium is higher than the initial difference between the marginal product at home and abroad capital outflows could occur - this indeed could be the case in some East European economies.

The traditional analysis runs as follows: Labor income in the capital importing country will rise, and there will be a uniform real interest rate. In both countries there will be changes in the functional income distribution, so that workers and capital owners in both countries have different interests in capital flows. The modernization of the capital stock is, of course, crucial for economic growth and external competitiveness. One should emphasize the need to establish competition, not just to free prices and then privatize some firms. If some temporary tariff in the tradables sector is required to set up an effective anti-monopoly agency, to privatize major branches of industry and to encourage the creation of a viable service industry, one might consider tariff protection as a strategic tool to achieve a competitive system. Moreover, the spirit of competition which is necessary for a functional market economy cannot be created over night.

Finally, a system whose people had trained for the winter olympics of the icy command economy should not be expected to immediately be winners in a totally different international summer olympics. The biggest problem might be - at least in the ex-USSR - to accept directly visible income differentials and find an attitude towards uncertainty and change in a market economy. Income differentials certainly existed in the socialist economies, however, they were much less visible than in Western societies.

2.2 Macroeconomic, Organizational and Strategic Problems

Privatization Goals

If the switch from a command economy to a market economy basically means privatizing the state a first question arising is: What should be privatized? If state-owned assets are to be sold why shouldn't liabilities be assigned, too? Who are the eligible owners - domestic residents, emigrés and former owners? The answer to many questions associated with privatization is complex because several motives are at work and because the sheer scope of privatization envisaged is without precedent. To the seven objectives which YARROW (1986, p. 327) noted in the context of privatizations in market economies we add three with which we begin our list:

(1) laying the material basis for private entrepreneurship and Schumpeterian competition;

(2) reducing the monetary overhang in the command economy;

(3) reducing the foreign debt problem by creating a profitable private industry which is more export-oriented and more easily accessible for foreign investors;

(4) improving efficiency by stronger competition and allowing companies to borrow from the capital market;

(5) reducing the public sector borrowing requirements;

(6) easing problems of public sector pay determination;

(7) reducing government involvement in enterprise decision-making;

(8) widening the ownership of assets;

(9) encouraging employee ownership of shares in their companies;

(10) redistribution of income and wealth.

The first reason clearly represents system-specific aspect of privatization. No market economy can really work without individual ownership of industrial assets. Coping with existing monetary overhang can hardly be a serious motive for privatization because in a command economy black market entrepreneurs and the nomenclatura are the two groups who enjoyed the best opportunities to accumulate monetary wealth. The reduction of the foreign debt problem - typically also a motive in developing countries - can indeed by a serious motive for privatization, namely in the case of a critical level of public foreign indebtedness. Moreover, one may envisage a first round of privatization in favor of domestic residents and then later encourage the inflow of FDI, namely if one assumes that domestic residents are more familiar with the changing local conditions and enjoy no significant disadvantage with respect to access to international market information. Economic rents accruing in the process of demonopolization as well as the benefits from the switch to free market prices and a move towards trade liberalization would then accrue to domestic residents. They would then reap higher asset prices in the course of selling a controlling stake to foreigners.

Among the seven motives mentioned by *Yarrow* one might emphasize the relevance of wage determination. A competitive labor market in which strong trade unions face creative and well-organized employers is important for a successful systemic transformation because real wage growth above productivity increases could derail the systemic transformation by causing a wage-inflation spiral. Employee ownership is probably a less relevant goal in a socialist economy, although for political reasons employee ownership might be favored. However, the enormous need for structural and regional change in a highly distorted economy implies that privatization schemes that weaken the incentive of individuals to change jobs and firms are inappropriate. Finally, the goal of a redistribution of income and wealth plays a major role in Eastern Europe. It is also clear that privileges enjoyed by the nomenclatura will vanish with the de-politicization of the economy and privatization, respectively. Selling state-owned firms is also an attempt to cope with a difficult political legacy.

2.2.1 Political Rationale versus Economic Rationale

Both political and economic motives determine the privatization process. From a purely economic point of view the fundamental idea of privatization is to allocate ownership rights in a first round to well-motivated and capable entrepreneurs who would make the best possible long term use of the existing capital stock - basically by ensuring static and dynamic efficiency. Normally, this would require that ownership titles are clearly defined, are fully tradable and "reasonably concentrated", the latter meaning that only with a controlling influence by a relatively small group of individuals or, possibly, financial intermediaries (e.g. banks as in the West German economy) could one expect that management's discretionary power remains limited on the one hand, and, on the other hand, dominated by the profit motive.

Profits must be the natural interest of private owners as those who are exclusively entitled to all residual income and all residual rights existing. As the point of departure in East European economies typically is characterized by high public deficit-GNP ratios, almost full control of industry by government entities and nascent political competition among newly created parties, political motives could dominate. Competing for voters could create a bias in favor of populist voucher schemes that might impair the emergence of controlling ownership groups in the first and second rounds. This would be particularly true if strong restrictions were applied to the tradability of ownership rights allocated in a first round via vouchers. Government might also favor privatization schemes whose focus would be on short term government revenue from privatization instead of long term benefits in the form of avoiding rising subsidies or raising future public revenues via efficient ownership structures and the associated stimulus for sustaining economic growth.

2.2.2 Devaluation, Wealth and Welfare

Privatization and FDI will create a new group of wealth owners whose decisions will affect economic development as well as economic policy in many ways. In Western market economies industrial assets are relatively concentrated, and a high mobility of financial and real capital characterizes the OECD area. Together with real money balances and the net stock of foreign bonds the real capital stock constitutes wealth which enters the demand for money function, the labor supply function and the savings function with a positive sign in the first case, while higher wealth reduces labor supply and savings. As the capital-output ratio in OECD countries (excluding housing) is about 3, while real balances, housing property and bonds amount to about the same ratio, wealth is dominated by the value of industrial assets and real estate. Net external liabilities reduce gross national wealth, of course, and in all former CMEA countries - except for the CSFR and Romania - foreign debt is the most significant external liability.

Income and Wealth Effects Decisive in the Context of Devaluation
Wealth and income effects play a crucial role for feasible systemic transformation programs. Here only one aspect should be emphasized, namely that liberalizing foreign trade in Eastern Europe typically entails a strong nominal and real devaluation which improves the "terms of capital" for foreign investors, that is foreigners obtain a given installed capital good in the host country relatively cheaper than at home; for joint ventures this means that in terms of the foreign investor's home goods the price of investment projects reduce. One particular significance of the real devaluation of trade liberalization is that in terms of the host country's nontradable goods whose prices typically rise relative to tradables the real value of assets owned by domestic residents will fall. This has an important implication for the welfare analysis of trade liberalization that so far has been overlooked.

If wealth and consumption are arguments of the individual utility function, the negative wealth effect of trade liberalization and devaluation, respectively, can outweigh the positive effect of a greater consumption goods bundle available (a devaluation raises exports and national income under well-known conditions). In the case of indebted countries the negative real wealth effect of a devaluation is particularly strong because a given external debt increases in terms of domestic goods. If the economy is already relatively open for trade at the point when devaluation occurs an additional negative real balance effect will be noted, namely to the extent that the price level defined by tradable prices P^T and nontradable prices P^N -- $P=(P^T)^\beta(P^N)^{(1-\beta)}$ -- is rising. With wealth and income as arguments of individual or political utility functions sustainable trajectories for systemic transformation must be characterized by positive expected wealth effects in case short term negative income effects should occur. A steep fall of industrial output and national income is observed in all reforming East European countries and no country, except for Poland, recorded strong net export growth as the consequence of a real devaluation.[7] Here it is obvious that although trade liberalization per se has positive welfare effects this is not necessarily true if negative wealth effects - leading to resistance to reforms - are included in the analysis.

Since a real depreciation is required in the early transformation stage the real value of foreign debt could strongly increase (in terms of domestic consumption goods). A devaluation is also necessary to stimulate exports of the tradables sector and to stimulate its expansion. The negative wealth effect from devaluation could offset the positive real income effects that are to be expected from opening up the economy and increasing trade. If the time horizon is relatively short or discount rates very high society or influential groups of the population might perceive the transition to a market economy as being associated with a net welfare effect. One step to avoid this paradox result would be to reschedule debt and apply long grace periods for new credits such that the transitory sharp real depreciation has phased out when the normal debt service is resumed.

Monetary Stability Required
In Eastern Europe the capital-GNP ratio - evaluated at world market prices - is not higher than two and real money balances per unit of output or per capita are relatively low. However, if currency substitution could be reversed and low nominal interest rates along with positive real rates could be established one would expect that the per-capita demand for real money balances will increase which from a portfolio theoretical perspective stimulates the demand for real capital. Hence price stability - also being required for allocative efficiency - is a particularly valuable macroeconomic ingredient for privatizing industry. This in turn requires institutional reforms of the banking system and regulations which ensure stability and efficiency of a competitive two-tier banking system which is open for foreign banks.[8] As long as there is no competition in financial markets there are limited prospects for avoiding serious principal-agent problems and having efficient investment policies.

---

[7] In principle strong net export growth could contribute to rising national income and increasing per capita consumption.

[8] On the problem of monetary and banking reform in Eastern Europe see THIEME, H.J. (1991), Reformen des monetären Sektors in sozialistischen Ländern: Ursachen, Transformationbedingungen und institutionelle Voraussetzungen, Kredit und Kapital, Vol. 24, 15-35.

2.2.3 Restitution without Privatizing Foreign Debt?

Privatizing Foreign Debt?

One could argue that all existing industrial and housing capital at least indirectly benefitted from capital and technology imports which are the ultimate reason for foreign indebtedness (we disregard that consumption goods imports might have been financed on foreign credits, too). Hence, the foreign debt should be proportionally assigned to all existing non-human wealth such that privatization would always include the privatization of the existing external public debt. The existing state industry often prospered from foreign indebtedness which was incurred to finance imports of Western capital goods and technology. This aspect has been disregarded so far, but it is important in the privatization issue.

The privatization of foreign debt can hardly be achieved without the consent of foreign lenders. However, one may also consider the government setting up a separate Foreign Debt Fund, while the Treasury as the present owner of industrial firms printing bonds equivalent to the domestic currency value of foreign debt, and these bonds then being assigned as a liability to all companies, namely in proportion to the value of their capital stock.

A direct assignment of foreign bonds to major companies - with cross-share holdings or common backward or forward linkages that create interdependency - in the tradable goods sector could be a preferred option. This holds to the extent that incentives that promote the export of goods and services would ultimately also favor a real appreciation of the currency and thereby a reduction of company debt in terms of domestic goods. The caveat is that this type of debt allocation and export incentive would not work with foreign owners who will calculate dividends ultimately in terms of foreign goods.

Determining the value of assets and all non-human wealth is a major problem in all formerly socialist countries. Not only does one not find a record of Western-type accounting, but there is also no experienced and well-informed banking and investment community; nor is there much expertise in how systemic changes will affect the valuation of industrial assets. Furthermore, liabilities are often uncertain, e.g. in the case of soil contamination in a chemical plant for which a future owner could be held liable. Open and hidden internal and external liabilities exist in all East European countries, and these liabilities pose particular problems for the envisaged privatization of industrial and agricultural property. Finally, determining the net worth of a firm is difficult because future factor prices and output prices are uncertain (see appendix). A similar caveat holds for tax rate and exchange rate developments.

Privatization of foreign debt would actually allow the possibility that debt reduction by means of bankruptcy could occur. A debt reduction under normal circumstances could happen only by government engaging in negotiations with the Paris Club (case of official creditors) and the London Club (private creditors). It is often overlooked that in Western market economies part of external claims and liabilities are with private firms abroad. Firms facing financial difficulties typically come under pressure from stock owners and domestic as well as foreign creditors; since they have an interest in saving at least part of their initial capital/credit stakes a financial rescue package can often be found which explicitly implies debt reduction and some rescheduling. Firms that fare well will enjoy better credit ratings over time and prices of their debt instruments in secondary markets will increase. If one would at least partly privatize foreign debt in Eastern Europe - say by allocating part of the debt to firms in the tradables sector - one would generate an endogenous interest of foreign creditors in supporting transformation and Western market opening measures allowing Eastern Europe to expand its tradables sector and to increase its net exports.

2.2.4 Compensation vs. Restitution

In Eastern Europe most industrial assets were nationalized by Communist regimes - mostly between 1945 and 1949. Other private firms were also nationalized also in the 1950s and 1960s. All the smaller CMEA countries therefore face the problem of how to deal with former private owners of land and property. Should former owners be restituted or should some form of compensation for domestic residents and emigrés be considered? In the case of the former GDR German unification largely implied a conflict-prone restitution for the former owners and their heirs, respectively - a very time-consuming and costly approach in a period where rapid adjustment of industry as well as comprehensive investment and modernization decisions in all firms are nececessary such that delays impede the chance for economic survival and decisively raise the risk of lay-offs. In Germany the initially stated principle of restitution before compensation was weakened by a special law that emphasizes that former owners filing for restitution can expect such a procedure to be adopted only if they promise as high an amount of investment as interested bidders are willing to promise.[9] Finally recognizing the problem of restitution the Bonn government issued new ordinances that now favor compensation rules.

---

[9] One may mention a strange and certainly inconsistent point of German economic policy in the restitution question - most individuals who came to West Germany immediately after World War II and in the 1950s and 1960s as refugees, expellees or migrants from the GDR and other former German territories in central and Eastern Europe benefitted from government compensation schemes ("Lastenausgleich-Zahlung", "Burden-Equalization-Payments"). E.g. if person A had owned a piece of real estate in Eastern Germany before World War II he/she might have received in 1950 successive payments of say DM 5000; if individual A is filing for restitution in 1990 he/she would have to return the money received once restitution occurs. It is a nice gift to many former real estate owners to thereby obtain their original property whose market value is rapidly increasing while repaying DM

Undisputed property rights are decisive for any new owner and investor, respectively, because uncertainty not only leads to higher required rates of return which reduce the profitable amount of investment economy-wide but also implies financing restrictions that result from a lack of acceptable collateral for bank credits. By the end of 1991 there were about 1.3 million claims for restitution filed in East Germany.

All East European countries emphasize a mix of restitution and compensation. Czechoslovakia offers former owners a restitution option, including those emigrés who returned before January 1, 1990. Poland clearly emphasizes compensation and offers former owners bonds that can be converted into equities of newly-privatized firms. Hungary offers former owners that can prove their title - including individuals living abroad - a restitution option, but prefers compensation via compensation bonds whenever possible. Bulgaria and Romania are preparing regulations and laws in this area. It is clear that legal uncertainties and unclear property rights could become a major impediment to restructuring, privatization and foreign investment. Moreover, 45 years after most expropriations it is extremely difficult to identify claims and fix appropriate compensations.[10] Hungary so far has applied in a relatively clear manner the principle that compensation goes before restitution. Fewer claims for restitution were filed than expected initially and the time period for raising such claims was therefore extended twice. Former owners receive government bonds that can be converted in the future into stock of firms. This is, of course, a weak form of compensation since the lack of competition in Hungary's banking sector and restrictions on capital exports imply that interest rates are below internationally competitive ones.

2.2.5 Ownership Structure Problems

If all individuals were to receive an equal share of industrial capital by a free allocation of vouchers in a first-round of privatization, one could expect problems from the wide dispersion of ownership of many companies whose management would then enjoy even less control and incentives for efficiency than in the command economy. A functional controlling interest or controlling representative is required to solve the principal agent problem. If voting rights were exercised by experienced banks or other financial institutions which could pool individuals' stocks - similar to the German case - the resulting market economy might well have broad ownership and strong controlling stakes. Poland intends to solve the ownership efficiency problem by a two stage approach which assumes that individuals will basically

---

5000 which should be some DM 35,000 if one would take into account that DM 5000 at prices of 1950 corresponds to roughly DM 35 000 in West German prices of 1990.
[10] With respect to Poland the vague form of privatization laws is critically evaluated by FRANZ et al. (1991), Privatization in Poland: A Property Rights Approach, in KREMER, M. and M. WEBER, eds., Transforming Economic Systems: The Case of Poland, Heidelberg: Physica. See also JASINSKI (1990, 1992).

invest in several investment funds with qualified managers whose decisions in turn take a controlling interest in industrial companies and shape financial market developments. This procedure is not generally accepted in all East European countries, but it is clear that any two-stage privatization approach implies great significance for banking and investment fund regulations.

Can one hope for a peoples' capitalism in the sense of a sustaining dispersed ownership that would represent an equitable distribution of industrial assets? This is probably neither necessary for equitable distribution of wealth and income nor desirable because lack of controlling capital stakes would imply a serious principal agent problem that could bring about inefficiency on the one hand, and, on the other hand, a redistribution of income in favor of managers. The British privatization experience suggests that any wider distribution of ownership will give way to a more concentrated pattern. British privatization aimed to spread stock ownership by preferential offer prices of firms to be privatized, and, indeed, the number of share owners increased sixfold between 1983 and 1989 when it reached almost 12 mill. which, however, does not represent more than 20 percent of the population. However, excess demand for stock emissions caused by preferential allocation in the first round led to very active secondary market trading where private and institutional investors pulled up share prices while many first owners of shares sold part of the shares obtained initially. One year after the first emission the share of remaining first owners was 57 percent (BISHOP and KAY, 1988; SCHNABEL, 1990). In formerly socialist economies one should not expect a first-round of widely dispersed share ownership to be stable, especially since considerable strata of the population are relatively poor, face unemployment or favor present consumption. Only special tax incentives for long term share ownership would stimulate the creation of a broader group of share owners. A strong middle class of property owners could reinforce the economic and political basis that would make foreign capital ownership easier to accept. Herein lies a specific complementarity of privatization and foreign direct investment (FDI).

2.2.6 Strategies for Privatization

Private industrial property is a relatively new institutional element in Eastern Europe. There is lack of experience, much uncertainty and some negative side-effects from privatization which raise the question of sustainable and efficient privatization strategies. Given the 3000 to 8000 firms which are to be privatized in the CSFR, Hungary and Poland (as well as in Bulgaria and Romania) four problems are evident:
(i) even a rapid privatization will take several years, especially if one takes into account that the comprehensive British privatization scheme in the 12 year government of Margaret

Thatcher represented 25 privatizations that reduced the share of state-determined output by 5 percentage points;

(ii) privatization of many firms implies a rapid rise of unemployment that results from the lay-offs in companies which no longer practice overmanning and hoard input factors;

(iii) in a period of rapid institutional change insider information is very much at a premium such that fraudulent operations are difficult to exclude;

(iv) a functional stock market can only emerge if reputation is gradually acquired and positive examples developed. This would require that only the so-called crown jewels of state industry be privatized, but at the same time a functional capital market needs a minimum market depth in the sense that at least several dozen firms should be competing on the stock exchange. Moreover, only if a critical minimum number of firms is privatized will the whole industry enjoy benefits from improved efficiency such that sustaining growth is not generally impeded by rigid bottlenecks. Finally, dismemberment of big and oversized firms is necessary in order to contain the risk that privatization would simply lead to the substitution of state monopolies by private monopolies. The Polish approach of a two-stage privatization scheme that gives employees preferential access to shares of the would-be privatized company and otherwise encourages individuals to buy shares of investment banks or investment funds is reasonable. However, the slow pace of the present Polish program poses the risk that the program will not gain enough initial momentum to be realized in a comprehensive way. To cope with this problem one might indeed envisage a predetermined time frame.[11]

The workers' councils which exist in some form in most formerly socialist countries represent a particular problem for privatization. Since they naturally fear that privatization means a high risk that workers will be laid off one must expect strong resistance from within the firm. This barrier to privatization can only be overcome if there are codified rights for outside parties to initiate the privatization process in a firm and if at the same time those losing their jobs as the consequence of privatization receive a higher unemployment compensation than in the case that the firm has gone bankrupt. For those who become unemployed as the consequence of privatization one might also consider introducing a limited tax credit for taking a new job within a pre-determined time (say one year).

As the East German, Polish and the Hungarian experiences have shown privatization from within the company often is associated with fraudulent operations and the desire to avoid taxes. Moreover, formerly communist managers often take advantage of their position and arrange deals that benefit themselves or their friends of the old nomenclatura. There were limited problems in Hungary's privatization program although there were major delays. However, the

---

[11] A predetermined time frame is also suggested by SCHMIEDING H. and M.J. KOOP (1991), Privatisierung in Mittel- und Osteuropa: Konzept für den Hindernislauf zur Marktwirtschaft, Kiel Discussion Papers, No. 165.

advantage of having some decentralization of the economy over many years makes the switch to a market economy and hence privatization less difficult than in Poland, Bulgaria or the Commonwealth of Independent States. Hungary also relies mostly on conventional privatization strategies. In Poland many privatizations are initiated by the workforces and the managers who no longer want to pay dividends to the Treasury and who want to get rid of wage restrictions valid for state firms. In this context it is interesting that 90 percent of worker-management buy-outs are arranged with the Treasury as an inflation-indexed "lease-purchase". This raises the problem that the state budget deficit is rising on the one hand, while, on the other hand, no additional capital is invested in the privatized companies which almost all need comprehensive modernization. The list of profitable firms to be privatized via free share distributions remains limited in Poland. In Poland workers have the right to obtain 20 percent of the firm's shares at a discount, and vouchers can indeed help to achieve the goal to involve a broader part of the population whose forced savings financed socialist investment.

Vouchers (as used in the CSFR) are a way to distribute ownership rights relatively equitably in the first round and to reindividualize property that once was nationalized. If individuals were to make a declaration on their net wealth position (with strong sanctions on wrong declarations), one could also allocate an overproportional share of vouchers to groups that were neither part of the nomenclatura nor active in the shadow economy.

Creation of New Firms Indispensable for Comprehensive Privatization
Competitive markets cannot be expected from rapid and comprehensive privatization alone since such a strategy - implemented as an isolated step - would create fear of mass unemployment and thereby reinforce resistance to the competition-enhancing break-up of big firms and privatization. On average one may expect every second job to go if firms are privatized, and it is clear that if economic and social stability is to be maintained additional jobs in newly established firms must be created. To open up new opportunities for business start-ups comprehensive deregulation is necessary on the one hand; on the other hand, adequate prudential supervision and therefore new regulations are required to create financial markets in which domestic and foreign banks as well as investment banks with high reputation can play an important role.

Building Confidence
Reducing information and transaction costs by reliable, but not too complex rules of the game is a necessary ingredient in a period in which macroeconomic uncertainties such as unstable inflation and real exchange rates can hardly be avoided. Deregulation of the state service industry could be a key element in building a new service sector that is internationally competitive and supports the economic viability of the whole economy. Strong reinvestment

incentives are required if the initially growing income disparities in the transition to a market-based system are not to cause politico-economic conflicts and derail the whole reform process.

Privatization requires that individuals are willing to invest in capital of uncertain value. In a society in which a broader property owning class is yet to emerge the risk of losses in financial markets are a serious problem. A series of successful privatizations and placements will be necessary to build confidence among individuals, but the task of rapid systemic transformation does not leave much time. Reducing complexity and uncertainty in the first stage of the transition process by adopting a two stage privatization scheme in which investment funds play a role as a link between individual investors and many firms whose market risks can more easily be pooled by institutional investors than by individuals is therefore an attractive privatization strategy. Such a strategy is considered in Poland and has been advocated by LIPTON and SACHS (1990).

Deregulation

In the difficult and unique transition period it would be useful to exploit growth opportunities to the fullest possible extent and to remove obstacles for the development of a competitive and flexible market system. In Western Europe state-owned services have impeded economic growth, while privatization has been almost impossible because of entrenched defensive coalitions between employees, state bureaucracy and politicians. In the field of public services one might actually suggest going beyond West European attempts where privatization and deregulation attempts have met the resistance of organized labor and powerful lobby groups - postal services, telecom and utilities are outstanding in this respect. Especially the underdeveloped postal and telecom services in Eastern Europe which are both important for efficient business transactions and international competitiveness are prospective growth fields that can easily be opened for private competition. Venture capital financing in Eastern Europe has been very much neglected so far. Creating new firms that provide additional jobs, enriching the pool of available technologies and creating positive forward and backward linkages to other industries are indeed important for successful systemic transformation.

Deregulation of so far neglected service industries can be considered as a key not only to improving competitiveness, but also as a decisive measure to accelerate the provision of infrastructure capital which is needed to improve international trade links and to raise the marginal product of capital.

Service Industry Growth Requires Successful Privatization of Manufacturing Industry

Outsourcing of industrial services has provided growth impulses for an innovative, flexible and highly productive service industry in Western Europe, and this is what is needed in Eastern Europe, too. For the service industry to flourish a profitable and competitive manufacturing industry is necessary and the fact that 2/3 of all services are industrial services in the EC suggests that a successful privatization strategy for the manufacturing sector is decisive for the service industry to expand in any significant way.

2.3 Rent-Seeking and Wage Bargaining: The Role of Privatization

Socialist command economies are characterized by a bureaucracy coalition in the political administration and management of the socialist economy whose interests are feeding into the branch ministries which provide the relevant information for the central planning authorities. Rent-seeking activities are a common phenomenon in socialist systems and preferential allocation of goods at very low state-administered prices, the discretionary allocation of input factors and access to modern capital equipment or foreign exchange reserves are elements of socialist rent-seeking activities which directly stimulated the socialist shadow economy. Regionally concentrated labor in heavy industry and other sectors deemed to be of strategic importance for the planners' goals enjoys not only high earnings but massive fringe benefits. Moreover, the labor market in a command economy is typically characterized by excess demand such that there is continuous wage pressure. Certain groups are not well-paid and are discriminated against by the Marxian bias against so-called nonproductive activities; the latter are comprised of most services, especially banking and insurance, schooling and tourism (also the health care industry), namely those services which play a key role for modern Western market economies with highly qualified and productive labor and capital. From a market economy perspective this bias also represents serious labor market distortions which are difficult to correct from within even a reformed system. The wage structure and hence the incentive structure in the economy could remain very distorted if the privileges of workers were to be unaltered and the traditionally weak position of academics wert to remain unchanged.

A functional labor market requires competition in industry on the basis of diversified ownership, while labor may be organized in trade unions under an institutional framework that ensures that workers' preferences are expressed and taken into account by trade union leaders. Moreover, there is the need for true unemployment insurance in the long term that would regionally differentiate the contributions in order to provide incentives for avoiding unemployment risks. Regions with above-average unemployment would have to anticipate above-average contributions. A functional labor market would ensure that labor is rewarded according to its marginal product. Here only privatization on a broad scale lets one expect that this efficiency condition could be realized. Any strong remaining state sector would distort wage bargaining towards various politically motivated outcomes. Finally, it is necessary that no big state monopolies in consumer industries and investment goods industries are left because otherwise there would be the risk that efficiency gains realized by private suppliers and producers of intermediate goods would contribute to excessive profits (actually static rents) of state monopolies which in turn might dominate wage bargaining. The less feasible the privatization of big state monopolies is the more important would be the liberalization of trade and investment flows in the respective areas, namely in order to create countervailing world market pressure.

FDI and foreign firms, respectively, can help to create competitive wage bargaining conditions in a situation in which for political reasons state-owned industries are likely to concede pay rises above productivity growth. Especially if state-owned industries in the non-tradables sector (N sector) dominate there is a risk that can be expressed in terms of the Scandinavian model of inflation as follows. With the N sector adopting a key bargaining position relatively rising N prices translate into high nominal wage rates that affect the whole economy. In the tradables sector (T sector) which is exposed to given world market prices the wage spill-over reduces the amount of profitable production such that frequent devaluations become necessary to restore price competitiveness and avoid balance of payments crises. If in the systemic transition period nominal exchange rate stability or a smooth crawling peg does not provide an anchor for the evolving price system and monetary policy, respectively, there is the risk of a vicious devaluation-inflation spiral and economic stagnation and reduced allocation efficiency stemming from excessive relative price instability. Only if many private firms in all sectors including foreign-owned ones face trade unions can one expect a functional labor market.

2.4 Asset Prices and Sequencing

A major problem of privatization concerns the sequencing problem, at least as long as it is unrealistic to envisage a quick full-scale privatization of the whole economy. If not all industries are privatized at the same time, one should carefully analyze the question of spill-over effects from privatization; if goods produced by two industries are substitutes the case is different from that when products are complements. Let us take a brief look at the case of substitutive goods like beer and wine. If the beer industry is privatized the rate of innovation will increase and prices will fall - relative to the development of the general price level - and the wine industry would come under adjustment pressure even if it still were state owned and in the form of a monopoly. If the wine industry were privatized first, a similar reasoning would hold for the beer industry. This is important to recognize since it may be easier, for whatever reasons, to first privatize the beer industry (or the wine industry). In the case of complementary goods, like e.g. automobiles and gas, it would not be useful to organize privatization in only one industry. If the automobile industry is privatized first, prices will come down and the increasing demand for cars will pull up gas prices and thereby raise the profits of the gas suppliers that may still represent a state owned monopoly system.

With subsidies, state-administered prices, quantity rationing and inherent monopolies there are many distortions in the socialist system and with reform requiring a host of institutional changes of uncertain scope to be implemented, privatization of industry is extremely complex and difficult to organize. With no functional banking system and capital market several thousand firms are supposed to find private owners which should ensure higher efficiency and improved competitiveness in international markets. Privatization under such circumstances almost always implies redundancies and rising unemployment as well as the need to reorganize production and upgrade product lines which would make the respective firm profitable and is the only way to ensure a positive net worth of a firm such that it can be sold at a positive price.

One important element in the price determination of assets is the length of the time horizon over which investors can capitalize future profits. In addition to this marginal productivities and output prices plus exchange rates as well as factor costs are, of course, the basis for prices of industrial assets in markets - and this leads to the core problem of price determination in any privatization scheme. If systemic transition is credible and implemented progressively investors will expect lower real wages because of anticipated unemployment but will be uncertain as to output prices and productivities which are uncertain as we will see - with growing uncertainty the price discount of industrial assets will rise and hence an adequate privatization strategy would try to avoid uncertainties. Nominal wage claims will increase as tradables reach world market prices in the long term, and real wages will rise, too, because nontradables' prices will increase relatively slowly.

The perspective of the individual investor is most important here. If one considers investing in firm F which has e.g. important backward linkages with still state-owned firms anticipated privatization of suppliers implies that certain efficiency gains on the intermediary goods level can be expected, but it is uncertain whether supplier prices will increase or not; obviously this is a problem which depends both on changes in the market form in the intermediate goods industry and, equally important, on the opening up process of the economy.

Standard economic analysis suggests that a monopolistic supplier which becomes free to also deliver to the world market will increase domestic prices such that domestic marginal revenue is equal to the given world market price evaluated at the current exchange rate.

A firm F whose suppliers already were exporting to the West (and importing from world markets) faces no relative price risk from the intermediate goods level except the favorable case that a state-monopoly turns into a firm fully exposed to competition which entails lower domestic prices.

Finally if firm F already had been exporting to the West and importing from the West as a socialist firm it is clear that systemic transformation does not alter the output price vector, except for the exchange rate which is a macroeconomic phenomenon which, of course, is affected itself by trade, international investment and expectations. Hence marginal product values are less uncertain in the tradables sector and this holds the more the stronger the respective firm already had been exposed to Western markets.

The normative conclusion is straightforward, namely that privatization should begin in the tradables sector whose scope, however, is variable. As regards the latter aspect one may conclude that opening up the economy for trade is in itself a step that helps to eliminate uncertainty about asset prices. This, however, holds only if opening up does not lead to unstable exchange rates and inflationary volatile monetary policies.

3. Economic Challenges of Foreign Direct Investment in Eastern Europe

Traditionally foreign investors played no role in the CMEA countries until the late 1980s and private ownership of capital and real estate was strictly restricted. All CMEA countries were characterized by state monopolies, relatively big firms and a state trading monopoly which together with import substitution policies and low export-GNP ratios contributed to stagnation and inefficiency in Eastern Europe and the USSR. There was no modern service sector, partly because Marxist theories suggest that most services are non-productive and because consumer preferences were disregarded in the command economies. All this is to change now in a complex transformation process in which privatization and foreign direct investment will play key roles.

Foreign direct investment can be a two-way phenomenon as it typically is within the OECD country group (however, with strong asymmetries). In the case of Eastern Europe one may expect for many years mainly a potential inflow of foreign direct investment. Subsidiaries of

EC, US or Japanese multinationals could decisively contribute to economic growth and trade in Eastern Europe. However, in many industries there is a global quest for capital inflows, and locational advantages in Eastern Europe are limited in the short term. Infrastructure is generally weak, income levels are low and national markets small - the latter holds except for Poland, the Ukraine and Russia. If the host countries' market is relatively big the countries concerned may hope to attract FDI whose profitability will be based in the first stage on producing and selling in the host country; in order to attract significant foreign investment not only economic stabilization and a credible economic policy will be required, but import tariffs as well (otherwise strong import competition would render FDI unsufficiently profitable). In such cases the countries concerned will find it difficult to obtain free access for their export products since the principle of reciprocity typically is applied in international trade negotiations.

Only in the long term may countries in Eastern Europe generally hope to attract investment projects whose envisaged production will strongly be oriented towards foreign markets and thus could help to improve Eastern Europe's trade balance.

An interesting question concerns international price discrimination. Domestic producers which want to export to OECD markets probably will be able to charge higher prices at home than abroad;[12] subsidiaries of foreign multinational companies in turn might be able to charge higher prices in the technologically not so advanced East European countries with their limited market competition.

3.1 Some Links between Privatization and FDI

At first glance there is no link between privatization and FDI except for the apparent fact that liberalizing foreign investment flows enlarges the group of potential private bidders for state-owned assets. Although local bidders enjoy better access to information in an economically, legally and politically changing setting, there is little doubt that foreign bidders - if they are present at all - will have rich financial resources that could imply that relatively poor domestic residents have no chance to obtain a stake of industrial assets.

The strong currency depreciation in the first transition stage could reinforce this problem. However, as the German hyperinflation of 1923 shows when US investors could have bought (but did not at all) the whole German industry for one year's US investment budget, cheap

---

[12] Firms in OECD countries typically charge higher prices in the home markets - where the price elasticity is lower than abroad (in other OECD countries) - than in foreign markets with their typically higher price elasticity. Empirical evidence for this is presented by PUPILLO and ZIMMERMANN (1991).

industrial assets are only one necessary condition for capital inflows (BLAICH, 1984). More important are expected future profits and the risk or uncertainty associated with the economic situation in the host country. Furthermore, a major counterargument is that foreign owners will bid only if they expect a globally competitive return on investment.

The most obvious link between privatization and the inflow of foreign capital concerns the role of a competitive group of local suppliers. Since privatization is a prerequisite to establishing innovative, cost-efficient and flexible firms that would be valuable suppliers to subsidiaries of foreign multinationals it is clear that privatization should quickly proceed especially in sectors that are of potential interest to foreign investors.

To generate sustaining FDI inflows a critical mass of initial inflows has to be mobilized in various industries; follow-up investments which typically dominate international investment in the world market could then reinforce the positive first-round and second-round impact of capital inflows. Foreign investors will increase the need to achieve at least external convertibility.

While the short-term impact on the current account balance is likely to be negative since capital goods will be imported and import substituting investment will dominate, the long term effect could be export enhancing and lead to a long term appreciation of the currency. For economic policy FDI could be a strong side-constraint. Policy credibility will be required and sustaining impulses for regulatory reform as well as for "soft" capital income taxation could be generated.

Financial market liberalization will be encouraged by FDI and it will also influence the type of monetary policy. Trade union's influence is likely to be weakened by the presence of foreign multinationals since they increase the international mobility of capital. It seems doubtful that economic rents occuring in local production of MNE's subsidiaries can be captured by employed workers. Unions could actually find it easier to extract static rents in domestic monopoly sectors.

Exhibit C2: Links between Privatization and Foreign Direct Investment in Systemic Transformation

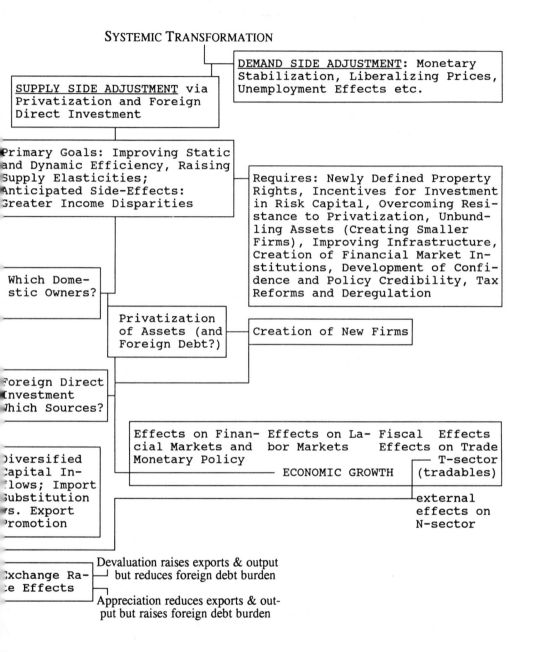

Trade unions and foreign investors could jointly lobby for tariff protection in the case of investment and firms that focus primarily on the host country market. Exhibit C2 summarizes some basic aspects of capital inflows into Eastern Europe.

Rising Economic Disparities: The Need for Economic Growth and the Case for FDI
Replacing the state industry with many private enterprises is expected to not only improve economic efficiency, help to develop efficient capital markets and contribute to economic growth; one may also emphasize three other effects, namely
(i) growing income disparities,
(ii) the role of wage restraint in an economy with internationally diversified ownership and
(iii) the trade-creating effects of FDI.

The switch to a market economy and privatization in particular will increase wealth and income disparities; they will rise because different abilities, incomes and initial wealth endowments rapidly will translate in combination with asymmetric insider information into a very skewed wealth and income distribution - this redistribution effect will be accentuated by the rise of unemployment that will result from privatization and FDI.

Wealth and income disparities in Western market economies are considerable, but Western societies are used to this phenomenon to some degree and have no history of socialist envy in income differentiation which poses political limits on privatization. Assuming that individual income and the income position relative to the median income Y' enter economic agents' utility functions, one may add that rising wealth and income disparities constitute more of a political problem, the weaker economic growth is. Such a utility function $U=U(y_i, y_i/Y')$ implies that a representative individual i remains on the same indifference curve only if a drop in his/her relative income position y_i/Y' is outweighed by a sufficient absolute rise of individual income. This means that a policy leading to greater income disparities will not meet resistance only if real per capita income growth exceeds a critical minimum level.

Here FDI could help to accelerate economic growth in a critical transition phase and thereby contribute to fewer politico-economic conflicts. Since FDI inflows typically are motivated by the attempt to appropriate in the presence of imperfect international know-how markets an economic return on firm specific advantages that are represented by advanced technologies and organization know how, FDI can indeed help to solve the inequality-growth problem. Investment inflows can, however, create balance of payments problems if the tradables sector as a whole does not become more competitive by industrial restructuring and macroeconomic adjustment. Balance of payments problems and ensuing devaluations can fuel inflationary expectations, contribute to a price-wage-price spiral and thereby destabilize the whole transformation process. From this perspective FDI is a necessary ingredient of systemic transformation but FDI inflows should be mobilized in a gradual and sustaining manner rather than in one major wave. There is a greater scope for FDI inflows if transitory local content requirements (LCRs) are applied. LCRs are economically doubtful but this problem could be eased if several East European countries would create a common free trade area and jointly apply for EC association.

Tax Aspects of Coping with Growing Income Disparities
Strong tax reinvestment incentives could help to solve the inequality problem by avoiding visible and high consumption of a few in a period of general economic hardship in the transition phase. These reinvestment incentives should be maintained until the reform progress is beyond the point of no return and is generating high economic income growth for the broad majority of the population. One may emphasize, however, that strong reinvestment incentives will reinforce structural distortions if prices are not liberalized along a preannounced and credible path. If the investment output ratio were to remain high in the initial transformation period in which most relative prices are still severely distorted and market access is limited, investments would diverge very much from an optimal long term pattern.

3.2 Role of FDI in Economic Development: Some New Aspects

The East European economies were not open for foreign capital inflows (except for minor joint venture investments) as long as they were socialist countries. Becoming open for trade and international investment certainly means opportunities not only for a faster restructuring of a widely obsolete capital stock but also a chance for an accelerated technology import. Since advanced technical knowledge and modern managerial know-how are at a premium in East European economies at large it is welcome from the host country perspective that not only industries with capital inflows will benefit but almost all sectors; there will be positive know-how spillovers and costless imitations that increase the marginal product of capital and labor.

The traditional MacDougall diagram is given in panel b) of Fig. C5, where we assume that capital is mobile internationally only in the tradables sector. Whether in each of the two countries "HOME" and "ABROAD" (variables are denoted with an asterisk *) capital is mobile across sectors - here concerning the tradables and the nontradables sector - is an open question. A pragmatic view would be to assume immobility in the short term (or some kind of putty clay effect) and full mobility in the long term. The nontradables sector is added here to the familiar MacDougall diagram which shows in panel b) that MPC^T, the marginal product of capital in the T-sector is falling with a rising capital stock K^T. The worldwide capital stock in the tradables sector is given by the length of OO', where O' is the origin from which we measure the capital stock abroad. By assumption the initial allocation of capital is such that K^T_o is employed in the home country, and $K*^T$ is the capital stock in the tradables sector ABROAD. The marginal product of capital abroad is equal to $r*_o$, while in the home country the marginal product is equal to r_o. Optimal allocation of capital and international profit maximization, respectively, would require that the marginal product of capital be equal across countries and be equal to the world real interest rate $r*^W$. $MPC^T=MPC*^T$ holds in point B where the MPC^T schedule of the home country and the foreign country ($MPC*^T$) are intersecting each other. Hence part of the capital from the home country should be exported abroad, namely the equivalent of the distance FK^T_o. The area under the marginal product schedule represents the respective output such that rewarding factors in accordance with the marginal product rule ($MPC^T=r$; $MPC^T=r*$) implies that the area under the MPC schedules minus the capital income at home (rK^T) and abroad ($r*K*^T$), respectively, is equal to labor income at home and abroad. The increase in world real income as a consequence of capital exports of country HOME is equivalent to the triangle ABC. ABC can be decomposed into BCJ which accrues to labor abroad; labor abroad also benefits from the redistribution of capital income $CJr^W_or*_o$ in favor of employed workers. If a 50 % income tax rate applies to each country's firms then the rectangle $DEFK^T$ and BCJ will accrue to the country ABROAD as a consequence of foreign direct investment inflows.

This standard view of international capital flow effects can be supplemented by some important aspects concerning (i) the nontradables N-sector abroad and (ii) the positive external effects of foreign direct investment inflows. For the country ABROAD the $MPC*^N$ schedule for the nontradables sector is given in panel c). For the home country the MPC^N schedule is indicated in panel a). Initially, at home the marginal product of capital is equal to r_o in both sectors. With international capital flows in the tradables sector the long term effect will be that the marginal product of capital in the N-sector at home has to increase to the MPC in the tradables sectors and the world real interest rate, respectively. Abroad, a similar reasoning holds.

However, one may add some interesting aspects. With positive technology spill-overs or other positive external effects from FDI inflows the MPC schedule for the N-sector abroad will shift upwards. The reduction of the real interest rate from $r*_o$ to $r*^W$ therefore means an expansion for the N-sector abroad, namely an increase in the desired capital stock $K*^N_o$ to $K*^N_1$ and hence a positive investment stimulus in the foreign country provided that mainly non-imported capital goods are employed. Moreover, the welfare gain stemming from the N-sector corresponding to the area $D*E*K*^N_1K*^N_o$ is increased by the area $A*B*F*E*$ which accrues to labor income. This holds only if the presence of FDI generates some positive spillover effects which shift the $MPC*^N$ schedule upwards $MPC**^N$. One may assume that in the medium term the MPCT schedule of the host country ABROAD is shifting upwards since imitation and costless technology flows will raise the marginal product in the whole tradables sector; that is firms owned by domestic residents will benefit as well from the presence of foreign investors, especially if they bring "diagonal" (economy-wide usable) knowledge spillovers" in the area of organizing production and distribution or finance or marketing. This would imply that a massive inflow of FDI leads to a medium term reduction in the real interest rate r and the marginal product of capital, but in the long term there should be a rise of the real interest rate (which negatively affects the tradables sector in both countries; see the new equilibrium point B_1 in panel b); if the new MPC^{*T} schedule were to run through point B_2, FDI might have no positive welfare effect for the host country provided that the MPC schedule for the N-sector is unchanged and that no taxes can effectively be imposed on foreign investors' income.[13] Such a pattern seems to be typical not only for the U.S. in the 1980s and the early 1990s when heavy Japanese and European FDI inflows occurred; this could also be the sequence of events in Eastern Europe. If FDI means buying into firms with advanced technologies there could be a transfusion of foreign-acquired know-how back home - to the parent companies. This could finally shift the MPC schedules of both sectors in the home country upwards in the very long term. This is not a likely effect in the case of Eastern Europe since multinationals' investment from the U.S., Japan or Western Europe will find very limited tacit know-how and advanced technologies in Eastern Europe which would be worthwhile to transfer back home; this would shift the MPC^T schedule upwards and imply that FDI raises real interest rates worldwide in the long term (see the dashed MPC curves)!

Fig. C5: Tradables and Nontradables Sector in a Model with International Capital Flows

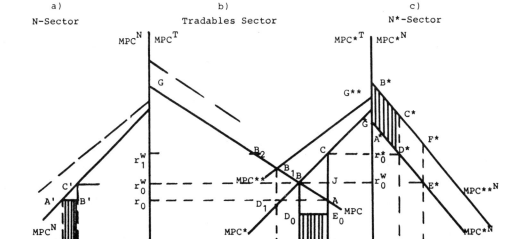

---

[13] There was such a tax problem in the U.S. in the 1980s when Japanese and European multinationals hardly paid any income taxes in the U.S.

3.3 Information Costs and Common Investment Policies

"CIR"

Only a competitive private sector can provide flexible and innovative local suppliers for subsidiaries of foreign multinationals. Only foreign multinationals are able to realize international price differentiations across national markets such that the presence of multinationals should improve the host country's terms of trade as long as FDI contributes to more diversified and innovative export products than in the case of exclusive domestic producers. Improved terms of trade are particularly important for heavily indebted countries because the required amount of domestic goods to be exported for covering the debt service is thereby reduced. In the case of small countries the size of the domestic market will be insufficient to warrant FDI of several competitors. Foreign firms in oligopolistic world markets often can be attracted in a parallel oligopolistic move if the local market volume is high. Given the small economic size of all East European countries (except for the former USSR, of course) this consideration suggests that East European countries should form a common investment region ("CIR") in order to mobilize a higher overall volume of FDI at more favorable terms, that is at lower average required rates of return on investment. This would require an explicit coordination of FDI-relevant regulations and, beyond that, a coordinated macroeconomic policy. A CIR approach would reduce the information cost for foreign investors considerably and could reinforce the credibility of investment policies by internationally coordinated policies. However, given the strong regional rivalry in attracting FDI, it seems unlikely that the smaller Ex-CMEA countries or the republics of the Ex-USSR could agree upon such an approach.

3.4 How Significant Can Foreign Direct Investment Be?

The question arises how important a role FDI could play. If one takes the CSFR government's estimate of an industrial capital stock of $ 107 bill. and $ 6903 per capita in 1990 as the point of departure to estimate an upper range of per-capita endowment in Eastern Europe, the corresponding figure for all the former socialist countries is in the range of some $ 500 bill. To put this figure into perspective one may recall that U.S. reinvested earnings and capital outflows in 1988 amounted to $ 54 bill. such that a bold assumption, namely that Eastern Europe could attract 5 percent of U.S. foreign investments would mean that in two decades less than 10 percent of Eastern Europe's capital stock would be owned by U.S. companies (provided that Eastern Europe's GNP growth at more than 4 percent p.a.). If the present foreign indebtedness would be increased in the form of foreign direct investment inflows the host countries would be much better off than in the case of simply increasing external borrowing.

Given the fact that the world's biggest source of FDI, the U.S. recorded $ 31 bill. of investment outflows in 1989 and accounted (in 1988) for a share of 30.5 percent in global FDI stocks, trailed by the U.K., Japan and Germany with 16.2, 9.8 and 9.1 percent, it is clear that even if Eastern Europe plus Yugoslavia and the USSR were to attract 5 percent of all Western and Asian FDI flows, not more than $ 5-6 bill. per year could be expected. If, however, FDI flows would concentrate on the smaller East European countries, the effects could be considerable, while positive spill-over effects in the form of stabilized or increased trade with the USSR would remain limited.

Even in Hungary which has taken the lead on foreign investment $ 1 bill. of annual FDI flows would imply that foreign capital accounts for 1.7 percent of investments relative to output. If the target investment-output ratio were 20 percent domestic investment sources would have come up with the equivalent of 12 dollars for every FDI dollar recorded. This makes clear that even under favorable circumstances privatization and domestic capital market reforms as well as measures that raise the marginal product of capital by intensified competition and technological progress are indispensable for high sustaining economic growth and successful systemic transformation.[14] In 1990 FDI inflows accounted for 15 % of overall investment in Hungary. With $ 1.5 bill. inflows in 1991 there are prospects that the share of FDI in Hungarian capital formation could even rise; however, once the most favorable FDI opportunities have been exploited it might be difficult to sustain high FDI inflows - unless very favorable conditions apply. As an extreme case in Western Europe 45 % of the assets of Belgium's manufacturing industry is controlled by foreign investors.

3.5 Regional Diversification

From a political point of view FDI will be the more acceptable the more diversified the source of FDI. Fear of German dominance poses particular problems in Eastern Europe; in Bulgaria there is a special fear of dominating Turkish investment inflows (there is a considerable Turkish minority in Bulgaria). From this perspective each U.S. dollar invested in Eastern Europe generates additional investment flows and contributes to economic growth in a double way. If FDI is viewed as a valuable contribution to a successful transformation from which not only Eastern Europe but all OECD countries could benefit the lack of Japanese FDI in Eastern Europe points to the problem of a free-rider strategy of "Nippon Inc."

---

[14] Real income growth can be approximated by dividing the investment-output ratio by the marginal capital-output ratio or by multiplying by the marginal product of capital.

As the experience of OECD countries - some of which have a foreign capital ownership of up to 25 percent (Belgium even 45 %) - suggests it is easier to accept foreign ownership if domestic companies themselves have investment stakes abroad. The conclusion to be drawn from a long term perspective is that national economic policy and international organizations should consider a new approach - namely, to support the development of firm-specific advantages of domestic firms such that they can be expected to become successful multinational companies themselves. Hungarian and Polish companies could be the first among East Europeans to follow the successful Korean example of not only accepting inward FDI but also promoting outward investment flows that yield valuable experiences in sophisticated and diversified markets.

3.6 "Club Goods" in Host Countries

Foreign investors have different interests in many respects, but they typically are also looking for local public goods to be supplied by government; infrastructure services as well as a positive image of a country provide group-specific benefits - often in favor of foreign investors. The "club goods" concerned do not only benefit foreign investors but domestic investors (and private households) as well. A modern telecom network in a market economy represents a communication network which is valuable not only for exchanging information but also as a means of intra-company coordination. The more congested communication networks are the slower the exchange and updating of information relevant to business in the market place and to organizing efficient production within firms.

It is not necessary that "club goods"/public goods are provided by the government. An efficient provision of this good simply requires that private service providers are forced to meet certain technical standards or provide some basic minimum supply in all regions. As is generally the case with public goods one cannot rule out that individual preferences are not revealed in an unbiased form; there is an incentive at least for some economic agents to take a free-rider position - that is simply to wait and see if the good is supplied - and to try to avoid paying a financial contribution for the provision of the good. If a country is too small to allow competition among private suppliers in an industry with falling marginal costs (over a certain range), the economic solution to the problem would be that neighboring countries organize a cross-border common network or several of these. Modern telecom services are an interesting example. There are competing long distance suppliers in the U.S. and Japan, with rates much lower than in Western Europe with its state-run telecom monopolies. Moreover, the range of services is narrower in Western Europe than in North-America, and the speed of innovation is much lower, too.

A specific club good is credible economic policy. Only if economic policy is designed along clear principles and if the scope for discretionary policies is limited by institutions and rules will investors develop a certain confidence in the host country's policy. Obviously, the political system itself must show some minimum stability if investors are to take the risk of long-term high investment commitments. Achieving political stability by first seeking an elaborate basic consensus as enshrined in a political constitution will be quite difficult because in the initial transformation stage there are so many conflict-prone decisions to be made that political "consensus capital" is at a premium. A 2/3 majority or any other strong voting quorum which makes the rules of the constitution indeed valuable will be difficult to obtain under such circumstances. What can be realized in the medium term is that realistic medium goals as well as long term goals are set and achieved in a gradual way.

4. Normative Conclusions for Policy Concepts

We have argued that privatization and FDI will be useful and result in higher efficiency and sustainable economic growth only if after a period used to build up credibility and reputation comprehensive projects are realized in conjunction with a program of radical macroeconomic stabilization and gradual opening up of the economy. Clear and simple procedures should be used for a transition period of about a decade and only later a more refined and complex network of regulations be applied.

The transition to a market-based system is extremely difficult for the socialist command economies of Eastern Europe. Switching to market-clearing prices and private ownership of industry creates adjustment problems in the allocation, financing and distribution spheres. In the short term privatization accelerates unemployment problems already accentuated by the cuts of government price subsidies and the steep fall of tradable prices in the phase of opening up the economy for trade with the West.

A success-promising reform program must be comprehensive and be implemented rather rigorously in the beginning in order to gain the minimum momentum necessary to overcome remaining political resistance, to be credible and not to be derailed by random shocks or unanticipated short-term problems. Internal reforms should aim at supporting the resilience of the supply-side which would not only mean privatization, but even more so the active nurturing of new enterprises that help to build a viable service sector and to create significant new employment in a period of labor market crisis. The shift from a situation with an excess demand in the labor market under the socialist system to transitorily high unemployment rates on the road to a market-based system is complicated by severe regional housing shortages which require additional wage differentials that will raise average wage levels and thereby impair price competitiveness and employment growth. Trade reforms should be rather radical to achieve both direct gains from trade and indirect gains from world market competition (the discipline argument). Given the formerly strong intra-CMEA trade links one may argue that coordinated liberalization among the smaller CMEA countries is useful. Trade diversion will result if, say, Poland switches to a market economy faster than the CSFR which will lose industrial customers in Poland. East Germany's collapse of trade with the CMEA partners in 1990 is also a warning against too rapidly opening economy. Hungary, however, is a positive model because a considerable part of its industry has been exposed to world market competition for many years. World market pressure may be a substitute for breaking-up domestic monopolies only in the case of smaller countries (such as Hungary and the CSFR), but other countries such as Poland or the USSR would have to implement a distinct competition policy that would have to include the dismemberment of state monopolies before privatization.

As regards privatization and enterprise creation it would be important to use opportunities in the modern service sector for the private provision of services. While entrenched resistance or fiscal revenue considerations have impaired progress towards privatization of telecom services in major West European countries, the former command economies could turn the disadvantage of an underdeveloped telecom system into a major asset, namely by charting a system of competing private telecom suppliers which are important for both modern industrial organization, financial services and price competitiveness of service-intensive industries. In some countries, competing private providers might require setting up joint systems with neighboring countries in order to exploit minimum firm size advantages. One may emphasize that privatization can achieve greater productive (microeconomic) and allocative (macroeconomic) efficiency only if pro-competitive policies and adequate regulations are supportive.[15] However, one may add that dynamic efficiency must be achieved in particular and hence appropriate R&D policies are equally necessary. Competition policy might indeed

---

[15] For the Polish case see on this JASINSKI, P. (1990), Two Models of Privatisation in Poland. A Critical Assessment, Communist Economies, Vol. 2, 373-401. Some aspects of foreign economic liberalization concern problems of competition policy, where some argue that flexible exchange rates are adequate in the transition period; see GRÖNER and SMEETS (1991). The theory of optimum currency areas does indeed lend little support for fixing exchange rates in the medium term transition: factor mobility is low (Mundell criterion for fixed rates as an optimum regime), the degree of openness is very low as measured by the ratio of tradable to nontradables (McKinnon criterion) and the degree of product diversity (Kenen) is also not high; finally, inflation goals are different in the former CMEA countries. On problem of EC monetary integration see WELFENS (1992b). An open question is how much regions and new countries in the former CMEA area can gain by creating their own currencies; they certainly can gain by "conservative rules" for the money supply, e.g. increasing the monetary base in accordance with the accumulation of foreign exchange - requiring export promotion. If monetary uncertainties are raised the proceeds from privatization will be lower than otherwise, moreover, it takes time to build up reputation. Political stability and functional institutions are at a premium in Eastern Europe, where international spillover effects of marketization and transformation play an important role. Creating market economies in Eastern Europe implies positive external effects from the perspective of each country involved. Again, creating a market economy has public good properties, implying that the problems of free riding and biased preferences (as publicly declared) will play a role.

encourage privatization and dynamic efficiency by allowing cooperative R&D ventures only to those companies which are owned by at least 51 percent by private owners.

The ultimate goal of privatization in Poland, Hungary, the CSFR and other East European countries should be not only private ownership, but the revival of entrepreneurship, and this at last requires replacing the spirit of Marx by that of Schumpeter. Hungary so far is relatively successful and it has indeed attractacted investment from oligopolistic industries with high innovation dynamics (*the case of the automotive industry*). One may hope that the East European countries will not only increase trade and technology flows with Western Europe, Asia and America but also exploit the opportunities of regional cooperation and coordination in order to spur economic growth and job creation.

The East-West income gap within Europe is extremely high and the still existing intra-German income gap that became fully apparent after unification in 1990 points to some dramatic problems. The intra-European income gap bears additional significance in a period in which information access has improved and barriers to mobility are falling in Eastern Europe and the (Ex-)USSR. If Western Europe does not actively support systemic transformation in Eastern Europe and encourage FDI in this region a strong westward migration pressure is to be expected. Even if immigrants from Eastern Europe were in the lowest quintile of the economically leading EC countries they would be better off than at home unless high economic growth can be achieved by privatization, FDI, stable macroeconomic policies and other measures.

References

AMBROSIUS, A. (1984), Der Staat als Unternehmer, Göttingen: Vandenhoeck.

AUDRETSCH, D.B. and ACS, Z. (1990), Small Firms and Entrepreneurship in a Global Perspective: A Comparison between West and East Countries, Wissenschaftszentrum Berlin für Sozialforschung, FS IV 90-13.

BAIROCH, P. (1976), Europe's Gross National Product, 1800-1975, Journal of European Economic History, Vol. 5, 273-329.

BISHOP, M. and KAY, J. (1988), Does Privatization Work?, London Business School.

BLAICH, F. (1984), Amerikanische Firmen in Deutschland 1890-1918, Zeitschrift für Unternehmensgeschichte, Beiheft 30, Wiesbaden: Steiner.

BORCHERDING, T.E. et al. (1982), Comparing the Efficiency of Private and Public Production: The Evidence from Five Countries, Zeitschrift für Nationaloekonomie, Supplementum 2, 127-156.

EDWARDS, S. (1990), Stabilization and Liberalization Policies in Eastern Europe: Lessons from Latin America, paper presented at the American Economic Association Annual Meetings, Washington, DC, Dec. 27-30, 1990.

FLOYD, R.H. et al. (1984), Public Enterprise in Mixed Economies, Washington, D.C.: IMF.

FRANZ, A.; SCHIPKE, A. and GROSZEK, M. (1991), Privatization in Poland: A Property Rights Approach, in M. KREMER and M. WEBER, eds., Transforming Economic Systems: The Case of Poland, Heidelberg: Physica.

GRÖNER, H. and SMEETS, H.-D. (1991), Transformation der Außenwirtschaft: Zur Öffnung und Weltmarktintegration geschlossener Volkswirtschaften, in: Hartwig, K.H. and Thieme, H.J., eds., Transformationsprozesse in sozialistischen Wirtschaftssystemen, Heidelberg: Springer, 357-406.

GROUP OF THIRTY (1991), Financing Eastern Europe, Washington D.C.

HARE, P. and GROSFELD, I (1991), Privatisation in Hungary, Poland and Czechoslovakia, London: Centre for Economic Policy Research, Discussion Paper No. 544.

INOTAI, A. (1992), Foreign Direct Investments in Reforming CMEA Countries: Facts, Lessons and Perspectives, in: Klein M.W. and Paul J.J. Welfens, eds., Multinationals in the New Europe, Heidelberg and New York, 129-138.

JASINSKI, P. (1990), Two Models of Privatisation in Poland. A Critical Assessment, Communist Economies, Vol. 2, 373-401.

JETRO (1991), JETRO White Paper on Foreign Direct Investment, Tokyo.

KLEIN, M. and WELFENS, P.J.J., eds. (1992), Multinationals in the New Europe and Global Trade, Heidelberg and New York: Springer.

LIPTON, D. and J. SACHS (1990), Privatization in Eastern Europe: The Case of Poland, Brookings Papers on Economic Activity, 1990/2, 293-341.

MILANOVIC, B. (1989), Liberalization and Entrepreneurship: Dynamics of Reform in Socialism and Capitalism, Armonk, N.Y.: Sharp.

MYERS, S.C (1977), Determinants of Corporate Borrowing, Journal of Financial Economics, 1977/5(2), 147-175.

OECD (1992), Reforming the Economies of Central and Eastern Europe, Paris.

PINDYCK, R.S. (1991), Irreversibility, Uncertainty, and Investment, Journal of Economic Literature, Vol. 29, 1110-1148.

POZNANSKI, K. (1987), Technology, Competition and the Soviet Bloc in the World Market, Berkeley: Institute of International Studies.

PERA, A. (1988), Deregulation and Privatisation in an Economy-wide Context, OECD Studies, Vol. 11, 159-197.

PICOT, A. and KAULMANN, T. (1989), Comparative Performance of Government-owned and Privately-owned Industrial Corporations - Empirical Results from Six Countries, Journal of Institutional and Theoretical Economics, Vol. 145, 298-316.

PINDYCK, R.S. (1988), Irreversible Investment, Capacity Choice, and the Value of the Firm, American Economic Review, Vol. 78, 969-985.

PUPILLO, L. and ZIMMERMANN, K.F. (1991), Relative Export Prices and Firm Size in Imperfect Markets, Open Economies Review, Vol. 2, 295-304.

SCHMIEDING H. and KOOP M.J. (1991), Privatisierung in Mittel- und Osteuropa: Konzepte für den Hindernislauf zur Marktwirtschaft, Kiel Discussion Paper No. 165: Institut für Weltwirtschaft.

SCHNABEL, C. (1990), Privatisierung und Deregulierung in Großbritannien, List Forum für Wirtschafts- und Gesellschaftspolitik, Vol. 16, 148- 166.

THIEME, H.J. (1991), Reformen des monetären Sektors in sozialistischen Ländern: Ursachen, Transformationsbedingungen und institutionelle Voraussetzungen, Kredit und Kapital, Vol. 24, 16-35.

UNCE (UN Economic Commission for Europe, 1992), Economic Survey of Europe, Geneva.

WELFENS, P.J.J. (1990b), Economic Reforms in Eastern Europe: Problems, Options and Opportunities, Testimony before the United States Senate, March 23, 1990.

WELFENS, P.J.J. (1992a), Internationalization of Production, Foreign Direct Investment and European Integration: Free Trade in Goods, Technology and Assets?, in: Klein, M. and Welfens, P.J.J., eds., Multinationals in the New Europe and Global Trade, 9-54.

WELFENS, P.J.J., ed. (1992b), European Monetary Integration. From German Dominance to an EC Central Bank, New York: Springer.

WELFENS, P.J.J. and BALCEROWICZ, L., eds. (1988), Innovationsdynamik im Systemvergleich, Heidelberg: Physica.

WORLD BANK (1991), World Development Report, New York 1991.

YARROW, G. (1986), Privatisation in Theory and Practice, Economic Policy, Vol. 2, 323-364 and 373-379.

Appendix C1: Competition and Prices in Systemic Transition

Firms in Eastern Europe may be assumed to maximize profits, although other motives could play a role, too; e.g. some firms strongly influenced by workers' councils may be assumed to maximize workers' income. With increasing foreign investment, import liberalization and privatization profit maximization may be assumed to become a more representative strategy for firms which might act in an oligopoly. A firm i that maximizes profits $H^{\#} = p(Q) q_i - K_i(q_i)$ will take the demand falling on competitors j as given and plan its output q_i in such a way that it takes into account the remaining demand; total output in industry is Q. This is a simple approach which follows COURNOT's monopoly model. The firm maximizes profits if the marginal revenue MR = k' (k' = marginal costs which depend on the quantity produced).

$$p(Q) + q_i \, \delta p/\delta Q(Q) = k'_i(q_i) \tag{1}$$

or

$$p(Q) - k'_i(q_i) = -q_i \, \delta p/\delta Q(Q) \tag{2}$$

We define the market share $s_i = q_i/Q$ and use the definition of the price elasticity of demand $E_{q,p} = 1/E_{p,Q} = [[p(Q)/Q] \, \delta Q/\delta p]^{-1}$ such that equation (2), after dividing by p, is rewritten as:

$$\frac{p(Q) - k'_i(q_i)}{p} = s_i/(-E_{q,p})$$

The relative price-cost margin of the individual firm (the mark-up factor) will be the higher the greater the market share s_i in the oligopoly is the lower the absolute value of the price elasticity of demand. The weighted mark-up factor $\Sigma s_i[p-k'_i]/p = \Sigma(s_i)^2/(-E_{q,p})$, where $\Sigma (s_i)^2$ is the HERFINDAHL index of concentration. In a monopoly the market share is 1 and the price cost margin is maximal. Hence if privatization means turning a state monopoly into a private monopoly and to later move to an oligopoly and finally "full competition", the price cost margin should reduce in the course of time. What is the consequence if aggregate monetary demand is given? The FISHER equation $M \, V = P \, Y_r$ (M= money stock; V= velocity; P = price level, Y_r = real GNP) can be modified to include transactions in the stock market that bind liquidity, too. $M \, V = P \, Y_r + P^{\#}Zz$, where $P^{\#}$ is the price of stocks and Z the amount of stocks and z the share of stocks traded. Let us assume a development towards intensified competition in the goods market. One may expect that falling prices in goods markets and hence a lower P will channel any excess supply in the money market that is not absorbed by a rising output Q or Y_r, respectively, into stock markets such that with given Z and z stock prices would increase. This is a paradox because a move from an oligopoly towards competition means lower aggregate profits at first sight; however, competition could mean increased investment options for all firms which are more free to undertake mergers and acquisitions or to pursue innovation projects. Following PINDYCK (1991) improving investment options should increase stock prices. An appreciation of the currency is likely, too. Purchasing power parity would suggest this, namely that the exchange rate e = P/P*. Since the domestic price level (P) has fallen relative to the price level abroad (P*) e should increase; moreover, foreign investors will have to pay higher prices for real capital they want to acquire, and the rising supply of foreign exchange will cause an appreciation, too. In reality it might be very difficult to disentangle monetary and nonmonetary reasons for exchange rate movements. A devaluation raises exports and national income under well-known conditions.

D: Foreign Economic Liberalization in Eastern Europe

1. The Challenge of Foreign Economic Liberalization

Traditionally, socialist economies in the CMEA were isolated from Western world markets. State foreign trade organizations handled the bilaterally fixed intra-CMEA trade and were responsible for trade with capitalist countries which was frequently conducted via barter trade agreements. Production was based on monopolistic intra-CMEA specialization which was further distorted by political considerations dominated by Soviet interests. This did not rule out that the USSR implicitly subsidized the smaller CMEA countries via natural resource exports that were underpriced relative to the world market. Divergences between export prices within the CMEA and domestic prices were characteristic for all CMEA countries. With inconvertible currencies, sustaining shortages in the official economy and a thriving shadow economy, black market exchange rates were well above official exchange rates, and currency substitution plagued most CMEA countries.

In the CMEA balances were settled in the non-convertible Transfer Rouble until January 1991 when a new trade regime was introduced which required hard currency settlements. Compared to Western European countries there was a lack of intra-industry trade. While smaller OECD countries as well as many outward-oriented Newly Industrializing Countries considered exports as a means to exploit static and dynamic economies of scale, exports in the CMEA countries were mainly considered as a means to cover necessary imports. The socialist import substitution and specialization strategy failed economically and explains the erosion of the CMEA countries' international trade position over time as well as its economic stagnation.

Foreign direct investment in the CMEA countries was an exception. Until 1990 primarily only joint ventures were allowed in Eastern Europe, but given the low average amounts of paid-up capital this was no major contribution to reducing the capital shortage in these economies. Moreover, since international technology transfer mainly occurs as intra-company flows and within cross-licensing arrangements among private firms, Eastern Europe's lack of foreign direct investment implied a totally insufficient rate of technology transfer. While the post-war decades were characterized by rising export-GNP ratios in the OECD countries, trade relative to national output remained relatively unimportant in Eastern Europe.

Table D1 shows in the first column the ratio of exports of goods and services to GNP of the ex-CMEA countries. Compared to countries of similar size and population in Western Europe the economies of the smaller CMEA countries were about half as open at first glance. A first problem with the figures presented concerns the value of intra-CMEA trade where the application of official exchange rates leads to different results than when cross rates or black market exchange rates are used (see Appendix for a calculation by the Bank of International

Settlements). Another caveat concerns the level of development that might distort comparisons with Western countries. E.g. COLLINS and RODRICK (1991, p.32) suggest that at average EC incomes East European economies would all be much more open than at actual incomes - except for Bulgaria. At EC average incomes the predicted ratios of merchandise exports to GNP for the CSFR, Hungary and Poland are 25, 26 and 22 percent compared to 19, 15 and 7 percent at current incomes (the approach used suggests a drop for the USSR at EC incomes which is a paradox, moreover, the role of trade as an engine of growth is not really taken into account).

Tab. D1: Openness and Trade Patterns of the CMEA Countries in 1988/89 (export-GNP ratio X/Y and country shares for imports/exports in percent)

X/Y	x^m	Eastern Europe**	USSR	GDR***FRG	All Indust. Market Econ.	Developing Countries	Other, incl.PRC
7	7	USSR 54.1/48.9	–	8/8 5/4	25.1/21.9	8.2/14.2	12.6/15.0
35	19	CSSR 32.3/29.9	40.3/43.1	9/6 5/5	18.6/16.3	3.5/ 4.7	5.3/ 6.0
21	13	Rom. 24.6/16.8	24.0/24.0	9/6 3/5	13.5/33.7	18.8/19.0	19.1/ 6.5
31	34	Bulg.20.1/18.1	53.7/62.8	5/4 3/3	15.5/ 6.4	7.8/ 9.1	2.9/ 3.6
19	7	Pol. 17.2/16.2	23.4/24.5	5/4 13/13	45.7/43.3	7.1/10.2	6.6/ 5.8
33	15	Hung.18.7/17.0	25.0/27.6	7/6 18/11	43.3/39.5	7.7/ 9.9	5.3/ 6.0
24*	–	(GDR)25.3/26.1	53.7/34.8	-/- 12/11	15.5/29.9	7.8/ 3.6	2.9/ 5.6

for comparison: in 1988 X/Y for Argentina and Chile was 20 and 37 percent (Brazil: 11 % in 1989), respectively; for Portugal, Spain and Turkey X/Y was 37, 19 and 28 percent, Thailand and Malaysia reached 36 and 74 percent, respectively.

x^m = 1988 ratio of merchandise trade to GNP according to COLLINS/RODRICK (1991)p. 9;

* manufacturing exports only: the GDR figure in 1989 was, according to the Deutsche Institut für Wirtschaftsforschung 24 percent if export of manufacturing industry is expressed as a percentage of value-added in manufacturing; ** CMEA-6; *** figures are for 1989; for the USSR, the CSSR and Bulgaria the GDR share in Ruble Trade was 16.1 % on the import side (15.8 % on the export side), 12.6 (10.8) and 7.7 (6.4), respectively. If overall trade is evaluated in dollar prices PLANECON estimates for the country's Ruble Trade share are 50 % (50 %), 69 % (61 %) and 65 % (64%) for the USSR, the CSSR and Bulgaria, respectively. Figures for X/Y are from OECD (1992). For some reason these figures slightly differ from a joint publication of the statistical offices of Poland, Hungary and the CSFR in 1991: Glowny Urzad Statystyczny/Federalni Statisticky Urad/Központi Statisztikai Hivatal, Bulletin 1991/1, Warszawa.

Sources: for regional trade shares (except for GDR and Germany in 1989) SCHRENK, MARTIN (1990), The CMEA System of Trade and Payments: Today and Tomorrow, SPR Discussion Paper No. 5, January 1990; figures represent UN estimates and official national statistics of the CMEA countries; IMF (1990), Directions of Trade Statistics, Yearbook 1990; COLLINS, S.M. and RODRIK, D. (1991), Eastern Europe and the Soviet Union in the World Economy, Institute for International Economics, Washington D.C.; DIW (1991), Wochenbericht, and PLANECON; own calculations. OECD (1992), Reforming the Economies of Central and Eastern Europe.

It is well known in economics that exports increase faster than GNP in the course of economic growth; moreover, only with increasing relative openness can high per capita incomes be achieved. Since per capita incomes of East European countries are smaller than those in

Western Europe part of the lack of openness could be explained by the East-West income gap. Although this might play a role it is contended here that Eastern Europe was generally relatively closed as regards openness for trade. While the shift to a market economy will raise per capita income in the long term and thus generate additional trade the structural change towards a larger service sector - always underdeveloped in socialist economies - leads one to expect a limited stimulus for exports per unit of GNP. Services are less tradable than goods, a fact that is only slightly mitigated by the increasing international mobility of service providers as well as users. Furthermore, one must not forget that international comparisons of export GNP ratios or import GNP ratios require that the existence of nontradables, the development of real exchange rates and other factors do not seriously impair the comparability of GNP figures. Exports - if going to the West - are easy to calculate since world market prices apply and dollar values can be determined. To get an export GNP ratio one has to either use the exchange rate to get the domestic value of exports and then divide by national output figures or one takes the dollar export values and divides by GNP after the exchange rate has been applied. The problem of using an exchange rate that is e.g. not distorted by political risk, capital controls etc. is difficult enough. However, a more straightforward problem concerns the price ratio and the relative size of the tradables (T) and the nontradables sector (N). Disregarding imports for simplicity we could derive the export GNP ratio, if we knew the percentage (a) of tradables exported and express the N-output in terms of T-goods. Real GNP in terms of tradables is $Y^* = (T + (P^N/P^T)N)$ such that the export GNP ratio x can be derived as the inverse of Y^*/aT:

$$(1/x) = \frac{T + (P^N/P^T)N}{aT} = \frac{1 + (P^N\,N)/(P^T\,T)}{a}$$

Hence $x = a/(1 + \beta)$, where β is the value of output in the N-sector relative to that in the T sector. Obviously β is determined by the relative price ratio of nontradables to tradables (P^N/P^T) and by the relative size of N and T - the latter certainly being a positive function of this relative price ratio. An international comparison would be distorted if we disregard that relative prices of nontradables differ, or, if the law of one price fully applies to tradables, that the price of nontrables is higher in one country than in the other. In poor countries the price of nontradables is relatively low; say a new house in Eastern Europe would cost 1/3 of what the same house would cost in Western Europe. Taking this into account and the fact that the tradables sector is certainly smaller in Eastern Europe than in comparable OECD countries β will be higher in the former CMEA area than in Western countries. Now, if outputs N and T would remain unchanged with the shift to a market economy while the relative price would rise the degree of openness as measured by x would fall. Since in Western economies the price ratio (P^N/P^T) so far is higher than in Eastern Europe we can conclude that at comparable relative prices the former socialist economies are even less open than suggested by the first or the second column in Tab. D1. KRAVIS and LIPSEY's (1988) empirical findings for market economies clearly suggest that with rising per capita incomes the relative price ratio (P^N/P^T) will increase.

A similar conclusion of limited economic openness in Eastern Europe is obtained by using appropriate purchasing power parities (PPP). HESTON and SUMMERS (1988) indicate on the basis of purchasing power parities for the German Democratic Republic a per-capita-income of $ 8740 in 1985; the figures for Hungary, Poland and the USSR are $ 5765, $ 4913 and $ 6266.

In early 1992 the Statistische Bundesamt published per capita income figures for the former GDR of DM 11,697 in 1991 which translates at an exchange rate of DM 1.70/$ into 5882 $ which is only 2/3 of the figure suggested by HESTON and SUMMERS for 1985.

If one assumes that the relative per capita income positions among CMEA countries are correctly reflected in the HESTON/SUMMERS figures but that the real income level was generally overestimated the implication is that one should reduce the East European figures of the two authors by about 1/3. This in turn means that World Bank figures, based on national income figures and official exchange rates have to be roughly doubled if one uses PPP. Then conventional export GNP measures derived as the ratio of exports to GNP would have to be reduced to about half the official figures. Hence, the true degree of openness of Eastern Europe is only about half as high as suggested by the first and the second column in Tab. D1.

There are further arguments which underline our assessment that the relative openness of the former CMEA countries was really low. The relative trade isolation is especially obvious if we disregard intra-CMEA trade which rarely was organized on the basis of comparative advantages, such that market-oriented trade was small.

If we take into account that the USSR and the other CMEA countries accounted for almost 40 percent of Hungary's and Poland's trade, their export-GNP ratios for the late 1980s would have to be revised downward (see Tab. D1): From 33 to 20 and from 19 to 11 percent, respectively.

This indicates that even those two countries that usually are considered as relatively open for trade were not strongly linked to international markets. Comparing Poland to Spain or the Republic of Korea one finds that their respective export-GNP share is much higher (in Korea more than twice as high). Comparing Hungary to the Netherlands or Belgium one finds that their export-GNP ratio is at least twice as high; similar reasoning applies for the import side. In addition to this observation it holds that the principle of the command economy to fix quantitative output targets implies that the general interdependency of markets - working via substitution or complementarity of products - was missing such that external price impulses would not affect the whole allocation process as in market economies. If we consider only the market-determined exports - that is we disregard the politically determined intra-CMEA trade - the degree of economic openness of Eastern European countries is much lower than a first glance at their export GNP ratios would suggest.

Taking into account only market-determined exports we find that Poland's per capita exports in 1988 were only about 1/3 of the Portuguese per capita value of 776 ECU and of the Spanish value of 812 ECU in 1987. The per capita export of the EC was 2563 ECU (with 58.7 % being intra-EC trade), while the Polish per capita export was 281 ECU in 1987.[1]

Pressures for Internationalization via Trade

The reforming East European economies are facing two internationalization pressures: (1) the need to a catch up with internationalization trends in Western Europe and the NICs; (2) the recognition that internationalization in the sense of trading in goods, services, technologies and capital plays a complementary supporting role for systemic transformation in its own right. One should keep in mind that the level of departure is relatively low in most East European economies. Hence the tradables sector can act as a catalyst for market-oriented change only in a few countries of Eastern Europe.

For internal reasons and because of high foreign indebtedness (except for the CSFR and Romania) all former CMEA countries must promote exports and open up their economies (see Tab. D2 and D3). Gross external debt increased from $ 117 bill. in 1987 to $ 162 bill. in 1991 - still not extreme compared to $ 1000 bill. in the developing countries. The CSFR and Hungary maintained debt service payments on convertible currency debt, other countries faced recurrent problems. The ex-USSR is a special case where repatriating export earnings of state firms posed specific problems; firms also sharply increased intercompany borrowing.

---

[1] Figures are taken from Glowny Urzad Statystyczny (1991), A Statistical Portrait of Poland against the Community, Warsaw.

Tab. D2: Foreign Indebtedness of Eastern Europe

(a) ratio* of net foreign debt/exports and gross debt

	1985 (a)	1986 (a)	1987 (a)	1988 (a)	1989 (a)	1990 (a)	1987 gross	1990 debt	1991 ($bill.)
CSFR	89	101	111	112	105	111	7	8	10
Poland	546	570	556	442	452	418	39	48	52
Hungary	275	352	358	331	302	343	20	21	20
Bulgaria	50	135	157	173	254	468	6	11	13
Romania	103	107	73	27	-21	38	7	1	2
All 5	224	268	263	227	237	292	79	89	97
(ex-)USSR	62	72	91	92	128	139	39	63	65
All 6	138	170	176	158	181	211	118	152	162

* (debt-reserves)/merchandise exports in convertible currencies.

Source: OECD (1991), Financial Market Trends, No. 48, Paris, Tab. 7; OECD, 1992.

Tab. D3: Ratio of Net Debt Service to Exports for Selected East European Economies

	1985	1986	1987	1988	1989	1990
CSFR	8	6	7	7	9	10
Poland	49	42	39	36	42	41
Hungary	18	20	22	24	26	35
Bulgaria	3	6	9	11	20	43
Romania	9	8	6	4	1	1
All 5	19	18	18	17	21	28
USSR	4	4	5	6	9	14
All 6	11	11	11	12	15	21

Source: OECD (1991), Financial Market Trends, No. 48, Paris, Tab. 8.

Hungary, Poland and Bulgaria, facing ratios of debt service to exports of 35-40 percent in 1990 are in a critical state because such high ratios imply a considerable vulnerability for adverse interest rate shocks and negative terms of trade shifts. Germany and other West European countries are the main creditors of Eastern Europe and this contributes to Western European interests in supporting structural adjustment, export growth and systemic reforms in Eastern Europe. The outlook for the ratio of net foreign debt to exports is more favorable in reality than in Tab. D2 if a country has high service exports and if its ability to switch from a dominantly East European trade orientation towards a West European orientation is high. Hungary and Poland have favorable prospects in both respects. The ex-USSR is in a difficult situation and no quick fix approach for the CIS is feasible. The considerable net creditor position of the USSR vis-à-vis the developing world is almost worthless since Mongolia, Cuba, Vietnam and several African and Arab countries which bought mainly weapons on credit terms will be unable to come up with any substantive debt service.

The net debt service ratio (Tab. D3) is worst in Poland and Bulgaria where 4 out of 10 dollars from export proceeds have to be earmarked for debt service. The rapid deterioration of the Bulgarian situation in the period between 1988 and 1990 is largely due to disparate attempts by the outgoing communists to borrow capital and time abroad and to create a short-lived illusion for the population of more easily available imports. Since the 1990s will be a period of high real interest rates Eastern European economies with high foreign indebtedness face serious external side constraints in their transformations.

1.1 Convertibility

To the extent that high foreign indebtedness is reinforced over time by modernization needs that have to be financed by commercial foreign credits, there will be specific risks and problems for achieving convertibility. GREENE and ISARD (1991) emphasize four requirements for convertibility: (a) an appropriate exchange rate; (b) an appropriate liquidity level (foreign exchange reserves); (c) sound macroeconomic policies and (d) an environment that stimulates economic agents to respond to undistorted market signals. Since foreign indebtedness in Eastern Europe is mainly part of government total debt budget deficits and thus indirectly monetary policies could be destabilized if international real interest rate shocks, speculative capital outflows or rising protectionism abroad increase the burden of the debt. Liquidity problems are in the short term and hence in the critical first stages of the transformation process more important than solvency problems; successful liquidity management should help to build up confidence and reputation, while the real adjustment process gradually can bolster prospects for higher growth and thereby reinforce solvency of East European economies.[2]

To overcome the system-specific socialist divide between internal transactions and external transactions it is necessary to remove state foreign trade monopolies, eliminate or reduce quantitative restrictions for imports and exports as well as to establish at least a partial convertibility of the currency. Currency convertibility means the freedom to convert a currency (including deposits) into foreign currencies which hence indirectly implies the option to buy foreign goods, services or assets. The economy is thereby exposed to international competitive pressure, both in the sense of import competition and in the sense of export incentives that naturally will affect the domestic price of tradables, too; indirectly prices of non-tradables that are (i) substitutes or (ii) complementary goods will be affected, too - at least if prices are freely determined in markets. If prices in the world markets are higher than at home exports, e.g. steel, will increase and the overall output of tradables could rise, too; tradable prices at home will be raised to the world market price level, and the demand for substitutes will increase at home (implying higher prices, say for lumber), while prices of complementary goods (say, concrete) will reduce as demand will fall. Clearly, if intensified import competition would reduce the demand for certain goods whose production is steel-intensive the price of steel could reduce both at home and abroad.

In the case of a small country, the price of tradables is considered as given for both exportables and importables, because firms from this country are in a price taker position. This assumption is not always valid, e.g. in the case of innovative industries. Switzerland is a small country, but export prices of pharmaceutical drugs developed by its pharmaceutical giants are not given, and indeed the ratio of export prices and import prices (hence the terms of trade) is much more determined by the relative innovativeness of domestic and foreign industries (relative technology levels T/T^*) than by quantitative supply changes abroad. Nevertheless the small country assumption may be useful for part of our analysis. However, taking into account Korean or Taiwanese exports improving the domestic innovation potential in the tradables industry - with favorable spill-over effects for the whole economy - has been a major ingredient for raising export market shares and improving the standard of living. The technology dimension of catching up with Western Europe must not be forgotten in the East

---

[2] Basic problems concerning convertiblity problems are analyzed in WILLIAMSON, J., ed. (1991), Currency Convertibility in Eastern Europe, Washington, D.C.: Institute for International Economics. An interesting proposal concerns McKINNON's idea - based on Chilean experiences with the switch from implicit to explicit tariff protection - that one should introduce a cascading tariff "...scaled down according to the distance from the final consumer and the degree of manufacturing complexity". See McKINNON (1991), Liberalizing Foreign Trade in a Socialist Economy: The Problem of Negative Value Added, in: WILLIAMSON, J., ed. (1991), 96-115. For specific strategies of NICs see RIEBER, W.J. and ISLAM, I. (1991), Trade Liberalization in Asian Newly Industrialized Countries, The International Trade Journal, Vol. V, 471-490; BALASSA (1978).

European case. We will briefly deal with this topic later, after we have analyzed the general problem of introducing convertibility and liberalizing trade and investment relations.

With rationing in the foreign exchange market prices do not fully convey signals on scarcity: some firms or consumers might obtain certain goods because they have access to foreign exchange; others do not enjoy this privilege (HAVRYLYSHYN and TARR, 1991); this discrimination would change with the move to convertibility. A country that wants to introduce currency convertibility will face the following problems: At some exchange rate e convertibility for domestic residents or for nonresidents has to be established, allowing trade in goods and services and/or capital account transactions. Partial capital account convertibility will certainly be useful, namely one which allows foreign direct investment inflows. IMF membership requires - according to Article VIII - that nonresident convertibility for current account transactions be established. The following exhibit shows the different kinds of convertibility, and Article VIII status corresponds to a combination of b)+a) coupled with A) in this exhibit, that is no restrictions on the making of transfers and payments for current international transactions may be imposed (unless the IMF has agreed to such restrictions).

Exhibit D1: Convertibility

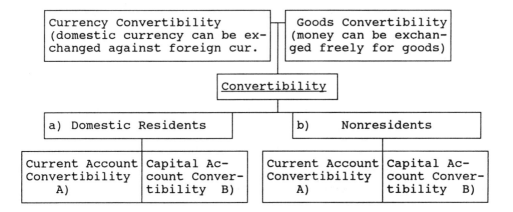

Current account convertibility is a prerequisite for trade in goods and services and ultimately for the external competitive pressure and the associated benefits, namely an efficient allocation (see GREEN and ISARD, 1991). Foreigners will provide capital only if they expect that profits and the initial capital can be repatriated which in turn implies that certain requirements be fulfilled. This means that one cannot delay capital account liberalization for nonresidents for a very long time because otherwise the initial capital could never be repatriated which could prevent Eastern European countries from receiving such capital in the first place. In the postwar reconstruction of Western Europe there was no convertibility at first since the first attempt to reestablish convertibility in the U.K. in 1947 had to be abandoned within a few months.

Instead the multilateral clearing system was established at the Bank of International Settlements in Basle, Switzerland. The West European Payments Union worked with considerable success between 1950 and 1957 in the sense that intra-European trade grew strongly in the 1950s, although 44 percent of trade in Western Europe was subject to quantitative restrictions, compared to 89 % in transatlantic trade (1959: 11 % and 28 %, respectively; see KENEN, 1991). The U.S. had helped with $ 350 mill. in Marshall Plan funds to launch the Payments Union by a generous credit for establishing a liquidity reserve. While West European-US trade grew only at about half the intra-European trade expansion rate at first, transatlantic trade picked up very strongly once nonresident convertibility had been established in most West European countries in the period 1958-1961. Establishing capital account convertibility for domestic residents and for nonresidents is certainly not easy as the West European experience or the example of Korea - achieving this status in 1988 - showed. Moreover, capital account restrictions remained in place in many West European countries until the late 1980s, and in Korea, Taiwan and other NICs they are still in place.

Important for establishing and maintaining convertibility are the following aspects:

■ (1) The initial degree of currency substitution is critical: foreign exchange used for transaction purposes should be channeled into the domestic banking system by legalizing foreign exchange holdings (domestic resident convertibility).

■ (2) The resilience of economic structures and institutions as well as the existence of a resilient market system are important because convertibility implies increased external adjustment pressure. This pressure would only destroy the economy if one had not at first created an incentive system that lets agents respond to market price signals and a network of privatized firms whose investment decisions will be influenced by the imported relative price structure for tradables in an environment of convertibility. If the domestic price structure differs strongly from that abroad, there is a risk that investments would be channeled into activities that would not and will not be profitable in the long term - once trade liberalization has been completed.

■ (3) An adequate level of official reserves (international liquidity should be high enough to create confidence in sustaining convertibility).

■ (4) Prudent macroeconomic policies in the sense of eliminating an initial monetary overhang and avoiding non-sustainable public deficits and high inflation rates (in a pragmatic view one digit inflation rates would be a success for economic policy in Eastern Europe).

■ (5) The kind of exchange rate regime chosen is important: flexible rates versus fixed rates; flexible rates invite destabilizing speculation, but as long as monetary policy is not geared towards low inflation rates fixed rates imply severe misalignment. With many adjustments in the real economy to come some exchange rate flexibility in the sense of wider parity margins will be useful and indeed flexible exchange rates might be adequate once a competitive domestic financial industry as well as a resilient real economy has been established.

■ (6) The real and nominal exchange rate in the initial situation is important for convertibility; the nominal rate should be chosen in such a way that strong future export growth is encouraged. This requires a strong devaluation which indeed should not affect the price level very much unless there is widespread currency substitution or a very high import-GNP ratio.

■ (7) An initial international interest rate differential and the development of the domestic banking system which should be competitive and offer rates of return that are not significantly lower than those abroad; otherwise massive capital outflows will occur. Typically, the point of departure in Eastern Europe is one of artificially low real interest rates and a non-competitive banking industry. As regards sequencing issues this rules out capital flows being liberalized first.

■ (8) The existence of foreign debt problems is relevant for the convertibility problem: a high debt-export proceeds ratio stimulates fear that convertibility could be suspended, especially in phases of rising international interest rates and sharply increasing imports or in the case of adverse terms of trade effects.

Eastern European countries seeking to establish current account convertibility in a medium term adjustment program have to place emphasis on both reducing monetary overhangs and increasing via privatization and the creation of new firms the adjustment capability and price responsiveness of the economy. FDI inflows could be attracted early on through a liberal FDI code; however, there is some risk that rising FDI could indeed reduce output in the remaining state industry if foreign investors attract labor and buy inputs that increase shortages in the state industry where output would then reduce; without quantitative input restrictions this effect should not occur. However, as long as there are shortages in parts of the economy, one cannot rule out that rising shortages in the state/socialist production system increase the price of goods in the shadow economy which in turn would reduce working efforts in both the state industry and the non-socialist sector (DINOPOLOUS and LANE, 1991, argue that directly unproductive profit-seeking activities - "dup" - in the shadow economy will increase; on "dup" see BHAGWATI, 1982). If FDI occurs in the nonsocialist sector under a tariff regime the reservation wage w" will increase, but what is more important, there will be an increase in the wage differential w'-w" such that the efficiency index is raised; output in the nonsocialist sector increases because there is more capital, more labor and higher work efficiency. The overall result is that the economy's national income is increased by FDI.

1.2 Expected Macroeconomic Effects of Foreign Economic Liberalization

KRUEGER (1990) has emphasized the link between outward-orientation and export growth: this may be summarized - with two additions - as follows:

(1) Replacing a protective trade regime via liberalized trade means that resources will be employed in line with comparative advantages and this creates well-known gains in efficiency and income.

(2) If comparative advantages are exploited more systematically the marginal capital-output ratio can be reduced such that even a given savings rate would allow accelerating growth.

(3) Export promotion means that economies of scale can be used even by small countries.

(4) As export-promoting trade strategies imply rising long term exports fear of balance of payments problems will be not very important for economic policy; policy could then renounce the otherwise often observed tendency for balance-of payments oriented stop and go policies (whenever there is a rising deficit, contractive monetary and fiscal policies are implemented). Reducing uncertainty would make more investment profitable.

(5) Outward orientation imposes an external discipline on economic policy which therefore will be less interventionist and volatile than otherwise; moreover, as the costs of ill-directed policies increase with the degree of openness and also become visible more quickly there is a strong external discipline on policy experiments.

(6) The benefits from free markets and free trade increase with rising per capita income and the associated more sophisticated and vast network of the division of labor; this view - a hypothesis according to KRUEGER - would imply that the degree of liberalization should increase in the course of economic development.

(7) One may add: Innovation and diffusion are accelerated by foreign investors and this contributes to economic growth, but foreign investors also increase the options for profitable domestic investors (say in the supplier industry); this will raise the market value of domestic firms (see PINDYCK, 1991) and should help to increase the price of industrial assets. Higher asset prices and more active trading in stock markets and bond markets should in turn raise the demand for money which means higher seigniorage for government or the possibility to reduce an existing monetary overhang.

(8) One may also add that smaller countries are more likely to adopt an outward-orientation because for them the world market is always bigger than the domestic market (as soon as the export sector has grown beyond a critical threshold); hence the disintegration of the USSR has not only negative aspects for Eastern Europe but could help in the long run to increase chances for liberal trade and investment regimes in the whole area.

Export promotion can be a route for catching up with leading economies; Germany in the second half of the 19th century, the Asian NICs in the 20th century and perhaps East European economies in the 21st century could be examples for such a strategy. This would mean not following Latin American or African policies of the 1960s and 1970s when import substitution was prominent. Import substitution automatically reduces export markets of others as well as one's own future export potential via the balance of payments equilibrium requirements. Export promotion means that firms are encouraged to compete in world markets. Moreover, in a two country world the firms of both countries would forego opportunities to exploit static and dynamic economies of scale on the one hand; on the other hand, they would forego the opportunity to spread R&D costs and other high fixed costs over greater output runs which would then encourage further R&D and thereby moving-up the technology ladder. Dynamic economies of scale mean that marginal costs are a negative function of cumulated output which is particularly important in the case of product cycle goods; the greater, say, the cumulated chip output is - the faster the firm has moved down its "learning curve" (reduced the failure rate in chip production) - the lower marginal costs. Before the next innovation cycle begins the firm should have reached a situation in which its marginal costs are below the world market price which will be the result of strategic pricing. No firm would set prices equal to marginal costs in an industry with dynamic economies of scale; instead the price will be set low enough to generate some demand and so deter prospective other producers and high enough to recover R&D costs and to appropriate some innovator rent if prices are falling gradually until the next product generation hits the market. Static economies of scale imply that average costs will be the lower the higher (momentary) output is. In a model of the world economy with two countries A and B both countries would gain by shifting to free trade - the consumer surplus will rise. Let us assume that only B produces the good (see the average cost curve $AC^B{}_1$), while domestic demand is given by D^B and the demand abroad - where consumers face a tariff T - by $D^A{}_T$. If one assumes for simplicity that pricing is done in accordance with average costs the intersection of the average cost curve and the world demand curve $D^B+D^A{}_T$ will determine the market-clearing price P_T. With a free trade area the price would fall because the demand in A will rise to D^A if the tariff is removed (with dynamic scale economies $AC^B{}_1 \rightarrow AC^B{}_0$).

Fig. D1: Static Economies of Scale and Liberalization

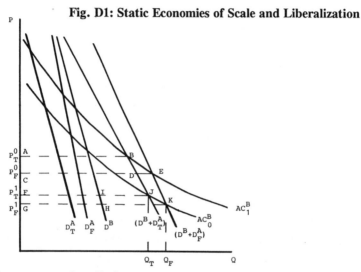

Mainly consumers benefit from such a liberalization move but one may also argue that the greater market volume will stimulate increasing R&D activities. Their costs could then be spread over a greater output volume; since R&D in a firm and more generally in the tradables sector will have positive spillover effects there will be positive output and income effects in other industries, too, and capital owners there could benefit as well. The new growth theory has emphasized both economies of scale effects for sustaining growth and the positive external effects of sector-specific R&D (e.g. ROMER, 1990; GRENBERG and HELPMAN, 1990). SENGUPTA (1991) has argued that Korea's catching-up process represents the case of a country where export expansion contributes to a kind of Harrod-neutral technological progress in the whole economy. Indeed FDI and increasing R&D expenditures - relative to GNP - have been a characteristic of the Korean development (CHAPONNIERE, 1992). However, one may also emphasize that real interest rates, in contrast with the experience of many developing countries, were positive, and this (or a functional capital market) is a prerequisite for efficient investment decisions (COLLINS, 1990). One may notice that the Keynesian macro models are not easy to reconcile with the idea that rising exports raise real output; in a standard two country-model the export multiplier is the smaller, the higher import-GNP shares are, but indeed the investment multiplier is bigger in an open economy than in a small economy.

Partial Equilibrium Analysis

The following conclusions from the partial equilibrium analysis presented are not necessarily valid in a macroeconomic context. In a strict sense one would have to corroborate all conclusions by a general equilibrium (or disequilibrium) model; one may also question some of the assumptions made, e.g. whether firms really maximize profits as opposed to the more realistic case that many firms - especially those influenced by strong workers' councils - pursue a broader concept of income maximization (not only profits are important, but labor income, too) under the constraint of some minimum job safety or explicit employment goal. We do not intend to rigorously develop a general equilibrium analysis, but rather want to raise some macroeconomic topics of foreign economic liberalization. In general we are rather confident that rational economic policies should adopt those measures that maximize social surplus (in the sense of consumer and/or producer surplus), where the presence of foreign investors naturally shifts the emphasis more on consumer surplus and the ratio of consumer surplus to producer surplus, respectively.

A major macroeconomic problem is associated with tariffs in certain industries. Tariffs will directly benefit certain industries and reduce imports. The latter reduces the demand for foreign exchange which will lead to a real appreciation in a regime of flexible exchange rates. This could reduce exports and hence the macroeconomic effect of currency appreciation would imply that the initial problem of insufficient international competitiveness in sectors D-H will have a mirror problem in the exporting sectors, say R-V. With fixed exchange rates there could be a real depreciation to the extent that higher tariffs would increase domestic demand in the import substitution industry; however, the medium term effect will be that lower exports of other countries reduce real output in the rest of the world which in turn will lead to a reduced import demand which will negatively affect the export prospects of the country which has raised tariffs.

Let us return to the problem in a flexible rate regime and assume that higher import tariffs entail an appreciation. To the extent that a currency appreciation reduces the foreign debt burden consumption demand could be stimulated by a positive wealth effect. If the consumption demand $C=C(Y, A, r)$, net real wealth of the private sector, A, will increase such that C will rise, and this tends to reduce the trade balance surplus or to aggravate an initial deficit. With a given real output Y net exports would then reduce over time. This effect could be reinforced by a reduction of labor output if the perception of a lower debt burden leads to a reduction of the labor supply; to put it differently, the same amount of labor would be only supplied at higher real wage rates and this will reduce the price competitiveness of export industries. However, to the extent that imported intermediary goods X'^* are important for production, a currency appreciation makes these imports cheaper and could raise aggregate output, but one may doubt that - given the low share of "supply-related" imports in Eastern Europe in the early 1990s - a positive supply effect would overcompensate the negative demand effects with respect to the development of the current account position. The general equilibrium condition for the economy is given by the following equation which mainly differs from standard approaches in the export and import function:

```
Y(K,L,T,X*',Z)=C(Y,A,r)+I(r,r*,q)+G+X(Y*,T/T*,q,K**/K)-X*(Y,T/T*,q,t,K**/K)(1)
  + + + +     -       + + -    - + ?         + + + +         + - - - +
```

where Y= real output (Y* output abroad; * denotes variables abroad), K= capital stock, T= technology level, X*'= imported intermediary products, Z= level of rent-seeking activities, C= consumption, A= real net wealth of the private sector, r= real interest rate (i= nominal rate), I= investment, G= government consumption, X= exports, q= terms of trade (eP*/P), K**/K is the stock of inward foreign direct investment relative to K, X*'=aX* such that a is the share of imports used for production, and t the average effective tariff rate.

Under flexible exchange rates the equilibrium condition for the foreign exchange market (we denote portfolio net capital exports as H, f= forward exchange rate) is given by:

$$dK^{**}/dt + H(i,i^*,f/e) = [X(Y^*,T/T^*,q,K^{**}/K)-X^*(Y,T/T^*,q,t,K^{**}/K)]$$

(2)

Disregarding currency substitution one can state money market equilibrium in a standard form:

$$M/P = m(i,,i^*,Y)A \tag{3}$$

Taking the labor market as the n-th market in a general equilibrium framework and treating the bond market explicitly, we obtain an interesting equilibrium condition:

$$(B/P)_{-1} + (dB/dt)/iP = b(i,i^*,Y)A \tag{4}$$

That is the stock of government debt from the period before, $(B/P)_{-1}$, plus the nonmonetary deficit must be equal to the demand for bonds. The government budget constraint in its simplest form is given by the usual equation (disregarding foreign debt):

$$G-\tau(Y+B) -(dM/dt)/P = (dB/dt)/iP \tag{5}$$

We do not want to solve the equilibrium model but rather want to emphasize some obviously useful modifications in the context of East European economies.

Immiserizing Export Growth?

All countries in Eastern Europe aim at raising their exports in order to cope with foreign debt problems and to be able to import more capital equipment for the modernization of the capital stock. However, there could be a problem of export sector expansion in combination with an insufficient consumption goods supply - a problem known from some countries in Africa and Latin America. The following figure is a modification of a well-known diagram in foreign trade theory. The production possibility frontier shows all alternative combinations of producing exportables and importables; exportables are assumed here to be consumption goods, while importables are investment goods. In the initial situation of a closed economy, a country with efficient production and a production structure in accordance with demand would produce at point Q_0'', where the community indifference curve that represents the private sector's demand structure is tangent to the production frontier line; the relative price is assumed to be such that the budget line (not shown in the figure) is also tangent at Q_0''). In reality socialist economies, of course, have not been on the production frontier line and certainly have not produced in accordance with desired demand patterns; a point like Q'_0 could have been characteristic in which there is inefficiency and in which too much is invested and consumption is much below desired levels.

Opening up the economy to international competition renders part of the capital stock and the labor force obsolete which means that the production frontier line will move towards the origin such that society can attain in the short term only a lower utility level (an indifference curve closer to the origin). Only in the case that marketization would mean a very significant jump towards the frontier line could one speculate that the efficiency gains would overcompensate the effects from factor obsolescence. We disregard these effects here, that is we start after these adjustments have already been made such that our open economy produces at Q_0 and realizes a demand pattern in accordance with point H_0 on the indifference curve II_0 which shows alternative combinations of consumption goods and investment yielding the same level of utility for the citizens. The relative price of exportables and importables - the terms of trade - is given by the the slope of the budget line B_0, that is $tg(\beta_0)$. Output in the consumption goods industry is C^S_0. However, home consumption is lower because C^S_0 minus C_0 has to be exported in order to get investment goods imports of I_0 minus I^S_0 (which is domestic output of the investment good); the domestic demand pattern is represented by point H_0. Investment goods will be employed in the exportables sector and in the importables sector. We assume that there is export-expanding factor growth such that the production frontier moves to the North-East as shown in the figure. The new demand pattern is given by point H_1 which is on an indifference curve that represents a higher utility level (II_1). The new production point is Q_1 such that C^S_1 minus the increased domestic consumption C_1 will be exported while I_1 minus I^S_1 is imported.

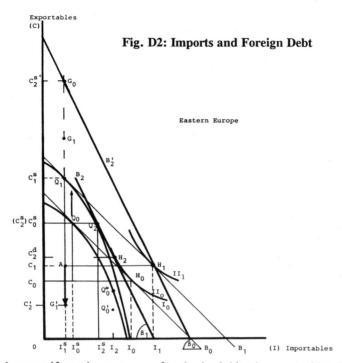

Fig. D2: Imports and Foreign Debt

What happens if an adverse terms of trade shock hits the country? Technically, the budget line will become steeper (see B_2). The traditional view is to assume that H_2 - with a lower utility level - represents the new demand pattern and Q_2 the adjusted production pattern. However, in reality structural adjustment may be very sluggish or even impossible, namely if there are "putty-clay effects" and if capital is sector specific; or, we may assume that state firms and foreign investors definitively want to maintain planned investment (I_1), while domestic investment output cannot be changed - this will be assumed in the subsequent analysis. What is the implication for consumption then? To get an answer one has to shift the new budget line B_2 in a parallel fashion to the right so that it passes through point H_1 (see line B_2'). At the new relative price unchanged consumption C_1 would require that $C^{S'}_2$ be exported to obtain initially planned investment goods imports of I_1 minus I^S_1. Moreover, consumption output is only C^S_2 such that the equivalent of the distance Q_1G_0 has to be borrowed abroad. However, if there is credit rationing in foreign capital markets there is a difficult problem. If only the equivalent of the distance Q_1G_1 can be borrowed, the domestic consumption has to be reduced by the equivalent of G_1-G_0. Hence consumption would drop down to C'_2. This could be below subsistence levels for some groups of the population.

One may assume that investment would not really reduce and therefore consumption could be so much depressed that per capita consumption could fall - for a larger group of the population - to subsistence levels. The community's utility position would be unaffected if H_1 could be realized via the increase of the previous increase of the capital stock, that is through a rightward shift of the production frontier line; H_1 would imply a reduction of investment and an increase of consumption (without a rightward shift of the production possibility line H_2 would be the domestic production point and certainly a lower utility level - with lower imports - would be realized). Now, let us assume that state firms' and foreign direct investors' investment plans for the new period are indeed not changing, so that imports are relatively price inelastic and the initial investment demand is almost sustained (I_1). The initial level of consumption could only be maintained if the new foreign indebtedness amounting to the segment GQ_2 were possible. If additional foreign credits are only Q_2G_1, the equivalent of the distance G_1G_0 would be the necessary reduction in consumption. $G_0'G_1'$ is equal to the distance G_1G_0 such that domestic consumption would fall to $C^{h'}$ if the country faces credit rationing in foreign capital markets. This would be the case of "immiserizing export growth" which is characterized by a combination of falling terms of trade and credit market rationing. Only if the capacity effect of investment were sufficiently strong would the production frontier line shift so much to the North-East that one could rule out this phenomenon.

International Equalization of Marginal Product of Capital?
How likely is it that large amounts of foreign direct investment would flow into Eastern Europe? Does historical experience suggest a strong case for high and sustaining FDI in the case of regional disparities in the marginal product of capital? Historical experience is certainly mixed in the sense that European investments financed high and sustaining current account deficits in North America in the 18th and 19th century and directly or indirectly contributed to rising investment in the U.S. and Canada. The U.K. was a major source of portfolio investment and FDI, where high long term outflows were partly financed by short term capital inflows that were attracted by the resilient and liquid British capital markets. Rates of return on capital will not equalize if capital flows are not free or if political risk plays a role - that is the mistrust in the ability of the recipient country to pay interest and principal. Political risk played no major role in the European-North American context, but it played a considerable role in the case of U.S. and European investment in Latin America in the 20th century. E.g. in the 1980s - after Mexico suspended debt service in 1982 - capital flight from Mexico to the U.S. accelerated, while U.S. FDI into Mexico reduced, even with persistent rate of return differentials. Only after a thorough restructuring program in which sound macroeconomic policies were adopted, privatization and trade liberalization pursued and international liquidity (official reserves) replenished were rising foreign capital inflows observed. An impressive $ 9.9 bill. of capital inflows were recorded in 1991. However, the current account deficit widened and raised some doubts about sustaining convertibility.

LUCAS (1990) argued that political risk cannot explain sustaining divergences in the marginal product of capital (MPC) in the North and in the South during the colonial area because a

European credit or claim on real asset income would have been equally safe in a venture in India/or of the Dutch East Indies Company as in a European investment project. However, monopsonistic market power, namely a monopoly in the colonies' labor market could then explain international MPC divergences. The monopolist would maximize profits under the constraint of a production function f(k) - with k denoting the per capita capital stock. Profit maximization means to maximize f(k)-[f(k)-kf'(k)]-rk and this implies f'=r-kf"; with a uniform (world) real interest rate r an investor would appropriate an extra rent -kf" (f" <0) in developing countries. Let per capita output be $y=Zk^{ß}$ (Z is a scale parameter). The marginal product of capital MPC must equal r: $r=Zßk^{(ß-1)}$ or, in terms of per capital output: $r= ßZ^{(1/ß)} y^{(ß-1)/ß}$, which implies with ß=0.4 for the U.S. and India and a per capita income ratio of 15:1 that MPC in India would be (15)exp.1.5 =58 times that in the U.S. which should stimulate enormous international capital flows towards India. Such flows are not observed. Indeed this contradiction is reduced if one takes into account some rough adjustments for labor quality differences which require interpreting y as GNP per effective worker; if 1 U.S. worker is equivalent to 5 unskilled Indian workers MPC differentials reduce from 58 to 3exp. 1.5=5. This still seems large. Next LUCAS considers the argument that there are positive externalities in the labor market, namely that, say an engineer working in the U.S. labor market is more productive (due to productively working together with others on a team, so that human capital h is considered separately in the production function) which leads to a modified production function $y=Zk^{ß}h^{\mu}$. This implies for the marginal product of capital under profit maximization: $r=ßZ^{(1/ß)}y^{(ß-1)/ß}h^{\mu/ß}$; the elasticity found for the positive external effect in the labor market is around 0.35 in the U.S. case which could reconcile the stylized facts with the observed low FDI flows to India. However, it seems obvious that restrictions with respect to majority foreign ownership impaired U.S. capital flows into India; moreover, weaker patent protection in India also deterred foreign investors.

What holds for the U.S. vis-à-vis India could also hold for Western Europe vis-à-vis Eastern Europe. As in Latin America there is a severe risk that debt or claims could be difficult to collect for foreigners, such that investors anticipating the uncertainties with respect to debt service or repatriation of profits will be unwilling to invest in Eastern Europe in the first place. From this perspective Eastern European countries that manage to attract a critical mass of foreign investors incur risks, namely losing the benefits in the form of jobs, exports, income and taxes associated with foreign reinvestment and net investment. While foreigners might not have access to collateral directly (or assets of the host country abroad), the benefits at stake with the presence of FDI make the host countries' commitments to service foreign debt more credible; at the same time FDI reduces the need to increase foreign debt. To prudently design a political system that assures political stability is of prime importance for East European countries that want to attract foreign investors. Political risk could otherwise deter potential inflows normally attracted by low wages; as far as political stability requires economic stability capital flight as well as speculative attacks have to be avoided in Eastern Europe. This, in turn, requires developing functional capital markets that offer competitive returns and avoiding misalignment of exchange rates. A stable political system with efficient political competition is as much an asset of a country as its endowment with natural resources can be. Therefore, the constitutional design of a country and the political rules should be carefully analyzed with respect to political stabilization and efficiency characteristics. The less useful a given political system design is in this respect, the more there is a case for full privatization and comprehensive competition policies. Rent-seeking in developing countries as in Eastern Europe has been a major problem for establishing allocation efficiency and improving international competitiveness; e.g. in India and Ghana rent-seeking costs were extremely high (up to 45 % and 25 % of GNP, respectively; see MOHAMMAD and WHALLEY, 1984; AMPOFO-TUFFUOR et al., 1991), affecting both foreign exchange markets, capital markets, goods markets and external trade controls.

2. Strategic Role of Foreign Economic Liberalization

Trade liberalization is expected to support the transformation process in three ways:
- Removing import restrictions and export barriers raises economic welfare. Only in the case of a very inelastic demand abroad could the terms of trade weaken so much with rising output that ("normal") immiserizing growth, that is a negative welfare effect, would occur.
- Import liberalization could expose the tradables sector to competitive pressure from the world market such that lack of dismemberment of giant state firms or a slow pace in privatization and the formation of new enterprises would not result in monopolistic pricing as much as otherwise. Imported intermediate goods and capital goods should also make it possible to effectively take advantage of international specialization and to thereby reduce costs and improve product quality or diversity both for domestic and foreign markets.
- Export liberalization could make it possible not only to exploit static economies of scale - much emphasized in the CMEA - but to take advantage of dynamic scale economies in R&D intensive industries in which high price cost margins are sustainable in world markets more so than in the case of standardized products. Dynamic scale economies mean that marginal costs fall as a rising cumulated output has been generated, where learning effects as in e.g. the chip or the aerospace industry play a major role. Such dynamic opportunities to improve the terms of trade require that firms move down the respective industry's learning curve relatively fast in order to position themselves successfully in the field of international competitors which all aim to realize big output volumes at home and abroad. Firms from smaller industrialized market economies, such as the Netherlands, Switzerland or Korea have

proved that even firms with a small home market can exploit dynamic economies of scale provided they have a strong focus upon world markets. An export-promotion policy might actually be adequate to encourage many firms from the smaller ex-CMEA countries to expose themselves to international market forces and to thereby improve in their entrepreneurial qualities over time; this is not only crucial for exports, but for the transfer of know-how back to the home country, too.

The liberalization of trade is not without risk for East European economies since internal convertibility is introduced at the same time and external convertibility at least envisaged. If liberalization in combination with privatization of industry and hence decentralized import decision-making would lead to imports increasing much faster than exports either a strong nominal (and real) devaluation would have to occur; this could mean "imported inflation" and, more generally, a boost to inflationary expectations for which import prices will play an increasing role as import-GNP ratios should rise in the course of economic opening up. Alternatively, the central bank could run down its foreign exchange reserves and hope that other measures rapidly restore export growth; or the central bank would raise interest rates to attract higher capital inflows. Higher interest rates would reduce profitable investment and a rising stock of short-term foreign capital would make the country more vulnerable to speculation and, in the case of flexible rates, to exchange rate overshooting that could disturb the real adjustment process. Hence, import liberalization contains in the first critical stage of transformation more risks than export liberalization. Export liberalization, however, has the consequence that domestic prices will rise to match world market prices. Indeed, in the case of a domestic monopoly, prices at home could even rise above international prices since the monopoly will equate the given world market price with the marginal revenue from sales at home. If marginal costs before opening up were below world market prices this paradox result of rising domestic prices and a short term increase in profitability will occur with export liberalization (Poland was such a case in 1990). However, in the medium term the domestic monopoly position will erode unless the firm could bloc re-importing and price arbitrage indefinitely.

Capital Account Liberalization
The liberalization of the capital account is critical in the case of short term capital flows that might be highly volatile and subject to speculative forces both at home and abroad. Some liberalization, necessary for trade financing, is, however, absolutely necessary. The natural focus of liberalizing the capital account in Eastern Europe concerns foreign direct investment flows (and, relating to the current account, profit repatriation). In Eastern Europe real interest rates were below market-clearing levels and there used to be an excess demand in the loan market, above all in the form of investment projects planned exceeding private household's

and firms' savings. The state planning bureaucracy would exploit credit market rationing to some extent and expand bureaucratic powers by discretionary intervention in favor of closely tied firms; part of the excess demand situation would be solved by the state banking system providing subsidized loans - often effectively at zero interest rates which amounts to printing more money. This latter mechanism of soft credit financing - KORNAI dubbed it the soft budget constraint - must change in the course of transformation in which a two-tier banking system with competitive private banks is to be established. As long as most credits still go through state-owned banks even the presence of many foreign banks, as in Poland, can contribute little to building a functional credit market that selects investment projects on efficiency and profitability grounds and thereby contributes to economic growth.

Trade Liberalization

There is ample theoretical evidence that trade can be an important engine of growth (e.g. RIEDEL, 1990). The developments of exports and imports in Eastern Europe in 1989 and 1990 indicates that large changes are possible in the context of systemic reforms and foreign economic liberalization (see Tab. D4). Poland's hard currency exports in 1990 increased by almost 40 percent while imports increased by only 2.7 percent. However, this does not indicate a sustaining improvement in international competitiveness since at least part of the Polish export boom is explained by the firms' strategy to dissolve hoarded factor inputs which were a system-specific trait of socialist economies; moreover, the collapse of domestic demand and - as we will see below - the removal of export restrictions in combination with monopolies in industry can explain the export boom. Hungary also recorded a double digit increase in exports in 1990. It is certainly true that the end of the CMEA encouraged a regional reorientation of trade in all East European economies. Hungary, Romania and the CSFR recorded double digit growth rates of imports. Bulgaria which faced external illiquidity in 1990 sharply had to reduce hard currency imports. This points to the general fact that East-West trade can only expand if foreign debt remains manageable. It is uncertain whether debt reduction increases the inflow of foreign capital. Mexico's experience after 1985 suggests such a possible link but the situation in Eastern Europe differs in many respects from the situation in developing countries (the BRADY plan helped to reduce the foreign debt-GDP ratio from 60% to 25 % in 1991, GATT membership reduced tariffs very much in 1986, investment inflows increased from $ 2.6 bill. in 1988 to about $ 10 bill. in 1991, capital flight was reversed, inflation fell sharply - down to 12 % in 1991 - and the number of state firms reduced from 1100 in 1982 to some 150 in early 1992 when the stock market index stood at 450, up from a $-based index value of 5 in 1982).

Tab. D4: Eastern European Convertible Currency Trade

	exports[a]		imports[a]		trade balance	
	1989	1990	1989	1990	1989	1990
USSR [b]	5.5	7.6	22.3	5.8	-1.536	-.854
CSFR[b]	8.5	8.4	1.3	21.1	.287	-.368
Romania	-4.2	-43.5	24.4	45.1	2.604	1.661
Bulgaria[b]	-14.3	-4.8	-2.5	-25.4	-1.445	-.594
Poland	2.7	39.4	6.4	4.2	.766	3.798
Hungary	2.4	16.9	2.4	11.7	.554	.935

a) = changes in US dollar; b) trade with non-socialist countries
Source: UN (1991), Economic Survey of Europe in 1990-1991, New York 1991, p. 101.

2.1 Import Competition

Theoretical Aspects of Foreign Economic Liberalization

Foreign economic liberalization in socialist economies offers a host of problems. There is a limited range of liberalization models and policy experiences which can be considered as useful.[3] Developing country experience can provide some useful insights, however, one cannot overlook various system-specific problems. Price distortions in socialist economies are much stronger, the role of currency substitution often greater and the problem of big state monopolies more widespread than in most developing countries. McKINNON (1991) emphasized early on the problem of negative value-added evaluated at world market prices, and HARE and HUGHES (1991) provide empirical evidence for this phenomenon in Hungary, Poland and the CSFR. The required microeconomic reorganization and the scope of structural adjustment in the economy at large can thus be considerable, and it certainly is time-consuming. With import liberalization the window of opportunities for international outsourcing will increase and to the extent that the export sector can successfully expand, the efficiency of the whole economic production process will gain from a better integration into the international division of labor and know-how. Not only imports from Western Europe could rapidly increase but also those from many NICs which provide cheaper products of similar quality than many suppliers from the OECD countries.

To reap the benefits from an effective international division of labor a new approach to foreign trade will be required in Eastern Europe where often autarkic ideas are still widespread; it should be obvious that even a country a big as Russia is small relative to the huge world

---

[3] See KÖVES, A. and MARER, P., eds. (1991) for a collection of different views. For an analysis of traditional trade organization in the CMEA see WOLF, T.A. (1988), Foreign Trade in the Centrally Planned Economy, New York: Harwood.

economy. In socialist command economies exports and imports were controlled by the state which effectively enforced a quota system on the economy. Exports were mainly undertaken in order to obtain imports necessary for achieving planning goals. Relative price structures among CMEA countries differed and there was no link to relative world market prices. The consequence were considerable distortions and negative welfare effects.

If East European economies are to switch to a market economy they need to create private industry and to establish competition in the first place. Privatization of existing industry takes time and so does the creation of new business establishments. Therefore the argument is made that import liberalization should increase competitive pressure, especially as long as the host of monopoly firms owned by the state have not been dissolved. This is one argument for Western Europe and the U.S. to call for a unilateral reduction of import barriers. However, one may doubt whether this alone could stimulate efficiency and growth and hence East-West trade. High foreign indebtedness in Eastern Europe implies that the expansion of exports from the former CMEA countries must accompany rising imports of Eastern Europe. Moreover, whether or not foreign suppliers prefer a high price policy - at least transitorily - and thus follow the price leadership of domestic monopolies is an open question.

Products for which after-sales services are important are particularly suited for international price discrimination. E.g. regionally defined warranty conditions rule out that price arbitrage is as effective in Eastern Europe as it will be in the EC after 1992. It seems clear that regional economic integration could provide some extra benefit in the context of price discrimination. If the minimum optimum plant size is such that only big markets allow a greater diversity of products which increase competition via a greater assortment of available near-substitutes, one can expect lower price-cost margins in larger economic areas; spatial price discrimination will follow the inverse elasticity rule, i.e. the mark-up price ratio $(p-k')/p$ will be equal to the inverse of the demand elasticity. This elasticity is raised by a greater range of substitutes such that economic integration should translate into lower mark-up price ratios of foreign suppliers and thereby improve the terms of trade of the integration area.

Some Aspects of Tariffs

Let us now take a look at an import market and analyze what impact one should expect from privatization and foreign direct investment. We take as a typical initial situation the case where imports are controlled by tariffs (rate t) or by quantitative restrictions. In Fig. D3 the domestic supply curve is SS_0, the world supply curve without tariffs is S^* and with tariffs S^{*+t}. Domestic demand is DD_0. An import quota of IH in Fig. D3 is equivalent to the tariff rate t, so that the price is p^{*+t}.

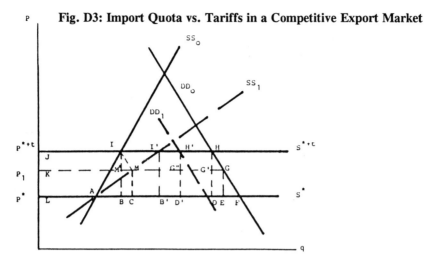

Fig. D3: Import Quota vs. Tariffs in a Competitive Export Market

One basic rationale of privatization (in socialist countries and in Western countries) and of FDI is to make the supply curve more elastic - the supply curve in Fig. D3 rotates downward. With competition among private producers the pressure increases to quickly realize minimum optimum plant sizes and thus to produce in the minimum of the average cost curve instead of staying on the steeper short-term marginal cost curve.

If the supply curve is more elastic (SS_1) a given import quota yields a smaller price increase than before. The price would be P_1. With a tariff t the tariff revenue will reduce from the area BIHD to I'B'HD. This clearly is a problem in countries in which tax revenues represent a significant share of overall government revenues (above all in the USSR). The producer rent increases by the area AII'. Government could appropriate part of this residual income via taxes. However, in the case of foreign ownership and high capital mobility government is unlikely to be successful in effectively imposing taxes on capital income without weakening the incentive for sustaining investment inflows and reinvestment. The reduction in tariff revenue will accentuate if rising unemployment reduces aggregate demand, thus implying a shift of the demand schedule towards the origin. As regards the aggregate fiscal result of reducing tariffs, however, one must not overlook that lower tariffs for imported intermediate products and capital goods will reduce costs in many industries such that aggregate production is likely to increase which in turn implies higher tax revenues in the medium term. As regards the alternative of import quota versus tariffs one should always prefer tariffs which distort trade and allocation less than quotas.

In Fig. D4 we show a well-known effect (see e.g. LINDERT, 1986, App. F) of imposing a quota for the case that there is only one domestic producer. If the initial world market price is P_0 a tariff of t_1 would lead to the higher price P_1, but the domestic firm would still be a price taker; if a quota is imposed the welfare loss will be much higher since now the domestic demand curve becomes a kinked demand curve such that the firm will act as a monopolist and maximize profits by equating marginal revenue to marginal costs. The welfare loss increases by the monopoly loss ABC minus the triangle a which is higher than the welfare loss under a tariff, namely the triangle b+d.

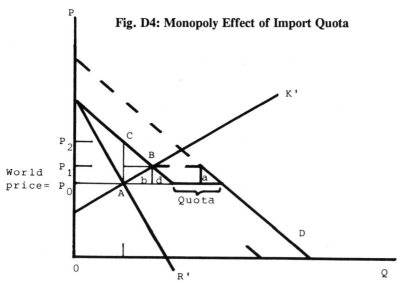

Fig. D4: Monopoly Effect of Import Quota

Tariffs as Government Revenues

In 1986 tariff revenues amounted to 0.7, 2.8, 3.5 and 7.2 percent of GNP the CSFR, Poland, Hungary and the USSR.[4] With a ratio of government expenditures to GNP of roughly 50 percent in most Eastern European economies, tariff revenues significantly contribute to government receipts, although the significance is lower than in many developing countries. In the short term it still holds true that for fiscal reasons governments might become reluctant to combine vigorous privatization and a comprehensive competition policy. In all East European governments there is a natural fear that a rising budget deficit stemming from reduced tariff revenues (still 12 percent of the Soviet budget receipts in 1989) and privatization proceeds could accelerate inflationary anticipations or topple agreements and adjustment programs fixed with the IMF.

---

[4] See TANZI, V. (1991), Tax Reform and the Move to a Market Economy: Overview of the Issues, in: OECD, The Role of Tax Reform in Central and Eastern European Economies, Paris: OECD.

2.2 Export Liberalization

With the envisaged external liberalization a host of new problems will be faced by East European economies. We will take a look at two major problems: (i) the liberalization of export markets; and (ii) the implications of liberalization for economic policy.

Fig. D5 shows the problem of monopoly pricing cum export liberalization. We assume that domestic demand is given by D^h and that output in the socialist command economy is Oq_1. Output produced is allocated - at the state-administered price p^a in a preferential way such that demanders M to R (out of a total of A-Z) will obtain the good. In contrast to a market economy the demand is not served "from above", i.e. not necessarily those people with the highest willingness to pay obtain the good in the official economy. An example from Poland illustrates the point: in 1989 180,000 cars were produced of which 130,000 were allocated in a preferential "assygnata system" in favor of influential groups (coal miners, state bureaucracy, taxi drivers etc.). In 1988 the average price of a Polish car in the official economy was 1.3 Mill. Zloty which was 2.4 times the average annual income of 535,800; however, evaluated at black market exchange rates the unofficial car price in early 1989 was only 434 US \$;[5] this was about 10 percent of its export or world market price.

If in a market economy the same output Oq_1 were produced, the output is q1; for simplicity we have assumed here that this is exactly the output at which domestic marginal revenue R'^h=marginal costs K' which implies - under profit maximizing behavior - the monopoly price p^h. We disregard here the dishoarding effect which can be expected in the transition to a market economy with competing suppliers of intermediate products - inventories in the firm will come down to a normal level, where the stock-adjustment process leads to a transitory increase in output and sales (in domestic or foreign markets). The switch from the low state-administered price p^a to the monopoly price p^h is considerable. It must be emphasized that the regime switch to market clearing implies a once-and-for-all price increase, and this increase will be particularly high if monopoly pricing is prevailing.

If the country liberalizes exports the monopoly situation in the domestic market is likely to lead to additional price increases as a consequence of opening up the economy. This paradox result is easily explained. Each monopoly faces a given world market price p* which represents marginal revenue abroad. Profit maximization behavior requires that marginal revenue at home must be equal to the marginal revenue abroad. Hence the interception of the world price line p* with the R'^h schedule (point J) is realized such that the new Cournot point I and the increased monopoly price p'^h will hold. Profits of the monopoly will exceed that of

---

[5] See WORLD BANK (1990), Poland: Economic Management for a New Era, Washington, D.C.

an industry with perfect competition by the rectangle P*JIP$^{'h}$. If domestic or foreign investors can acquire a monopoly they will be willing to pay more than otherwise, and this could reduce the incentive for government to implement competition. An open question - neglected here - is whether or not the marginal cost curve in a competitive setting would not shift downwards and hence represent faster technological progress than in the monopoly case.

Fig. D5: Monopoly and Export Liberalization

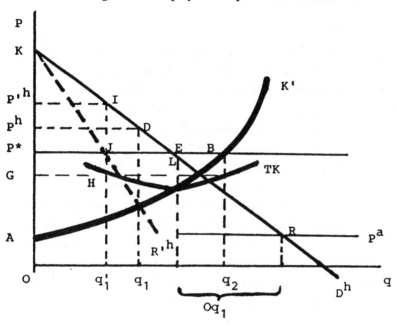

Monopoly output is q_2 and is determined by the intersection of the marginal cost curve K' with the world market price line P*; q'_1 is sold at home (which is less than q_1), and the difference between output q_2 and q'_1 is exported. Hence exports will be equivalent to the distance JB which is greater than EB, the exports under perfect competition.

From the theoretical analysis it follows that export liberalization in the presence of domestic monopoly leads to price increases that are higher than in the case of market-clearing prices under perfect competition; furthermore, exports - at least in the short run - will be higher under monopoly conditions than under competition. This might explain some puzzling observations in the first stage of the Polish transformation process when - in 1990 - the inflation rate was about 150 percentage points above the growth rate of the money supply and when hard currency exports boomed at an annual growth rate of 40 percent in real terms. However, it is clear that privatization and foreign direct investment as well as competition policy will reduce these anomalies in the medium term, and with Poland's imports rapidly rising in 1991 and exports growing slowly one can already foresee new balance of payments problems. Part of the problem is, of course, related to the misalignment that results when fixed exchange rates are realized while inflation continues at double digit annual or even monthly rates.

2.3 Sequencing and Foreign Direct Investment

Selected Sequencing Issues

From the theoretical analysis it seems clear that at least a comprehensive scenario for privatization cum competition is required at the beginning of designing a macroeconomic stabilization and liberalization plan in formerly socialist command economies. The experience with trade liberalization in developing countries suggest (PAPAGEORGIOU et al., 1990) that a critical minimum momentum is needed to successfully implement liberalization programs. A similar reasoning holds in a more general sense for Eastern Europe. Only if in the initial stage of transformation a comprehensive package of internal and external liberalization measures are adopted can one expect a sustaining transformation process. Without increasing the responsiveness of the supply side by means of privatization, competition and FDI there is also limited scope for stimulating net exports via a real devaluation - this reasoning applies in particular if there is an initial trade balance deficit. In the case of a small country the ROBBINSON condition for an improving balance of payments in foreign currency can be written as $X(1+\sigma) > X^* (1+\alpha)$, where X and X* represent exports and imports, respectively, while σ and α stand for the supply elasticity of exports and the demand elasticity of imports.

2.3.1 Demonopolization

Applying some general considerations of TIROLE (1988, ch. 2) to the case of socialist economies in transition one can provide a strong argument why privatization and competition policy should play an important role in an early stage of the reform process. Otherwise, there is a risk that economic distortions increase over time, namely as the elasticity of demand is increasing in many markets; and, there is the risk that foreign investors which acquire a monopolistic producer, appropriate a gradually increasing share of the potential consumer rent under competition. The reasoning is straightforward. If we assume (for simplicity) constant marginal costs c and an isoelastic demand function of the type $q = p^{-\epsilon}$ ($\epsilon > 1$), one can show (TIROLE, 1988) that the welfare loss from a monopoly is the difference between welfare under competition (W^c) and welfare in the monopoly case (W^m), namely such that the welfare loss L is a positive function of the elasticity ϵ.

$$L = W^C - W^m = [c^{1-\epsilon}/\epsilon - 1] \left[1 - \frac{(2\epsilon-1)(\epsilon)^{-\epsilon}}{(\epsilon-1)(\epsilon-1)^{-\epsilon}} \right] > 0$$

For our analysis a particularly relevant case is that of a relatively high elasticity of demand. In the transition to a market economy, a more diversified assortment of products will become available such that over time the increasing availability of substitutes will raise the demand elasticity; a more varied supply could ultimately erode monopoly positions unless the original monopoly itself engages in product differentiation. Furthermore, one may assume that - at least in many cases - the elasticity of demand will increase with higher real income such that the switch to a market economy and greater prosperity brings about more elastic demand in markets for standard products. Technically, we will treat in the following analysis demand elasticity as given, but we are interested in the question as to which way consumer surplus or social welfare (as the sum of consumer and producer surplus) behaves as ϵ changes.

In a socialist economy the switch to more producers typically will go along with an increasing product variety and hence a move towards monopolistic competition. In consumer markets one may assume as a long term result an increasing variety such that for each commodity there will be a rising number of close substitutes which makes individual demand curves increasingly elastic.

With a switch from competition to monopoly the relative welfare transfer that occurs between consumers and producers is given by $Z^m/W^c = \epsilon^{-\epsilon}/(\epsilon-1)^{-\epsilon}$ so that the right-hand side is an increasing function of ϵ. The share of the potential consumer rent that is appropriated by a domestic monopoly - possibly acquired by a foreign investor - is an increasing function of the elasticity of demand.[6] It is clear that with heavy FDI in monopolistic industries there could be an international welfare transfer to the disadvantage of the host country. This negative wealth

---

[6] With $\epsilon=2$ the monopoly gain in the sense of increased profits from switching from competition to monopoly is about 2/3 of consumer welfare W^c. This is particularly important for savings and investment. If one assumes that capital owners have a higher propensity (s_1) to save than workers (s_2) a monopoly might raise aggregate savings in the short term. The medium effects are ambiguous since private savings $S = s_1 Y(..) + s_2 Y(..)$, where it is doubtful that Y will grow faster in an economy with monopolies than in a competitive economy. In the case that foreign ownership of capital plays a role the transfer of welfare or wealth between consumers and producers is also important. The consumer surplus that can be captured by foreign monopoly owners implies a currency devaluation and thereby raises the value of any existing foreign debt of the host country. Since all former CMEA countries, except for the CSFR, are heavily indebted it seems sensible that competition be established first and only then are foreign owners to be actively invited to take part in the privatization process. There is indeed a conflict of interest for the government which seeks to maximize revenues from privatization. However, it should be clear that long term revenue maximization should focus on the tax base Y and hence stimulate economic growth. A value-added tax could hence play a crucial role in East European tax systems.

effect could compensate the positive welfare effect that is expected from trade liberalization (unless there is a case of immiserizing growth).

The normative conclusions for Eastern Europe are straightforward: If transformation programs do not realize a proper sequencing and in particular join adequate internal supply-oriented measures with external liberalization there is a risk that the transformation process is interrupted as soon as negative net welfare effects of foreign economic liberalization become apparent. One may add that only if a critical minimum growth rate for Eastern Europe can be generated after an initial unavoidable fall of output as a consequence of adjusting to relative world market prices, can sustaining economic reforms be expected.

The traditional sequencing debate which used to focus on the problem of whether to liberalize the trade account or the capital account first is somewhat neglected here.[7] We take for granted that Eastern Europe is in such a critical economic and political state that the removal of capital import controls is highly unlikely to bring about massive inflows which might then induce a real appreciation of the currency such that the growth of exports is impaired.[8]

2.3.2 Strategic Role of FDI

Given the need for modernization, economic growth and competition in Eastern Europe one cannot neglect the important contribution which FDI could make to the responsiveness and structure of output, employment and exports. In 1990 only Hungary recorded a significant FDI inflow of $ 1 bill., whereas Poland recorded only $ 350 mill. With inflows of about $ 3 bill. the whole former CMEA group (disregarding the GDR) recorded just 1.5 percent of worldwide flows of FDI. As may be concluded from the experience of developing countries where 4 countries account for 50 percent of all FDI inflows in the 1980s - Taiwan, China/Hong Kong, Brazil and Mexico - there will likewise be regional concentration

---

[7] A good summary of key arguments is found in SELL (1988, 1989, 1990). CORDEN (1987) also treats basic problems of economic liberalization. An interesting analysis of the Latin American experience - with a strong emphasis on wage adjustment problems - is given by EDWARDS (1988a, 1988b, 1990). *Korea, Taiwan and Chile favored "trade liberalization first" - with positive economic effects; Argentina and Uruguay begann foreign liberalization with the capital account in the 1970s; since domestic capital markets were quite distorted capital flight was encouraged and liberalization was not sustainable.*

[8] The liberalization of capital outflows is a more critical issue in Eastern Europe because ongoing macroeconomic instability, slow growth and political instability could lead to large outflows of capital which would trigger a strong devaluation. This is a critical problem in Eastern Europe because of widespread currency substitution. The overall money supply in this case is given by $M + eM^*$ (with e=exchange rate; M and M* representing the domestic money stock and the amount of foreign money used by domestic residents, respectively). This leads to the suggestion that the trade account definitely be liberalized first and only later the capital account - namely after monetary stabilization has worked and foreign money balances are primarily used as a store of value within the overall portfolio and no longer for transaction purposes.

tendencies in FDI flows to Eastern Europe provided that sufficient FDI for this area is mobilized at all. Attracting a critical minimum of FDI yields positive multiplier effects in the sense that a major motive of FDI is found to be follow-up investments that are combined with existing production facilities.[9] Hence it is important to mobilize a critical mass of foreign capital already in the first stages of systemic reforms and approach the problem of monetary stabilization with resolve and prudent institution building.[10]

Germany plays a key role in East European FDI for two reasons. Before World War I Germany was a leading investor in this region and given geographical proximity and the sustaining interest in avoiding excessive migration pressures from Eastern Europe one may expect that the German government will actively encourage German firms to invest in Eastern Europe. However, from the perspective of most host countries in Eastern Europe, there is caveat with respect to German FDI flows. Whenever Germany is dominating, the whole issue of FDI - sometimes that of privatization, too - becomes a political issue in which history mingles with fear of German economic dominance. In mid-1991 Germany's share in Poland's FDI was still 27 percent, followed by the U.S., the Netherlands, Sweden, the U.K., Austria, Italy and France with 9.7, 8.1, 6.9, 6.7, 6.2, 5.6 and 5.3 %. Compared to its leading position in global FDI flows the virtual absence of Japanese investors in Eastern Europe is a paradox. The U.S. and the U.K. which are, measured by their shares in FDI stock values, the world's leading FDI countries are represented both in Poland and in Hungary with a relatively small share. German investment is also dominant in the CSFR, where claims of former German expellees stir no less political unrest than in the Polish case. German investors and Austrian investors - the latter also with a strong position in FDI in Eastern Europe - are often perceived together as part of a new German threat (especially after the merger of the two Germanies) since the delicate interwar history and the memory of World War II are still alive in many part of Eastern Europe. In the interwar period part of German industry was not devoted to an open multilateral trade system but supported the idea of a German economic bloc in Central and Eastern Europe which would counterbalance British, French and US regional spheres of dominance. German cartels - legal at this time which is in sharp contrast to the FRG's post-World War II history - played a strong role in promoting the idea of regional bloc building and protectionism (after 1933 the Nazi government implemented this strategy aggressively and against the small remaining camp of "multilateralists" in German industry, e.g. Siemens). The new German assertiveness shown in 1991 by the German government and, less so, by German industry is very critically received in Eastern Europe. However, the lack of feasible alternatives with respect to major foreign investors is indeed likely to lead to a dominant position of Germany in central Europe.

---

[9] See on this dominating motive for FDI - along with the motive of direct access to local markets - GROUP OF THIRTY (1987), Foreign Direct Investment, 1973-87, New York.
[10] For an analysis of stabilization in a period of opening up see BRUNO (1988).

The developments in Russia, Belarus and the Ukraine are still uncertain; however, German investors can be expected to play a relatively strong role together with Canadian, U.S. and some West European investors. Scandinavian investors could play an important role in the new Baltic states which are economically in a very difficult situation. It remains doubtful that the absolute amount of FDI inflows into the CIS will be significant in the early 1990s. Where expectations of foreign investors have to be influenced favorably by successful reorganization and restructuring first, it seems crucial that expectations of domestic consumers and voters not be raised too fast since otherwise the disappointment will be extreme and political extremism could spread.

Foreign direct investment could be attracted not only by Eastern Europe, but at least some OECD countries could actively promote FDI flows to this region as well. The European Energy Charter proposed by the Dutch Prime Minister Lubbers could e.g. be a starting point for the EC to encourage private investment flows into the modernization of energy generation in Eastern Europe. The Lubbers plan envisages combining the potential energy surplus countries in Eastern Europe with the energy-hungry countries in Western Europe. Since the introduction of a market economy in Eastern Europe should help to drastically improve the energy efficiency of production one may indeed anticipate that Eastern Europe could become a main exporter of energy in the future. However, even in the EC trade in energy is not free; instead a system of regional power monopolies exists where free trade is blocked because firms producing energy also own the transportation network. Only if the existing system would be changed and if Eastern Europe itself would not imitate the West European system of public power monopolies could one hope for considerable FDI flows to Eastern Europe which could in turn increase its exports of energy to Western Europe.

In addition to the role foreign investors play in capital formation and technology transfer, it is well known from Western economies that they also contribute in the long term to the provision of the international `public good' free trade. Multinational companies have an active interest in maintaining free trade because this is a prerequisite to optimally making use of an international production network in which trade flows are as much within companies as between companies. Moreover, effective lobbying pressure for reducing import barriers in the EC, the U.S. and Japan cannot be expected if no foreign subsidiaries from Western Europe, the U.S. and Japan are present with a critical minimum engagement. Only then are the parent companies likely to support reducing import barriers vis-à-vis Eastern Europe. The fact that FDI tends to occur in regional clusters - often fueled by oligopolistic interdependence of rival investors and recent network tendencies in industry - implies the risk that only some of the former CMEA countries will enjoy in the long term the benefits of Western FDI, including lobbying pressure for reducing import barriers in the OECD countries.

One way to spread benefits from trade and investment more evenly in Eastern Europe would be to set up an East European free trade union or to set up a wider Baltic Free Trade Area (on BAFTA see WELFENS, 1990b); another way would be to adopt common rules and regulations for FDI. The expansion of East-West trade cannot be an aim in itself but should go along with increasing regional trade in Eastern Europe itself. A negative example of one-sided trade expansion is found in America: Trade in America has increased between North America and Latin America, however, Latin American countries have been very slow to recognize the opportunities of regional trade, and only in the late 1980s have new efforts been undertaken to foster intra-Latin American trade.

One may doubt that an enlargement of the EFTA is a politically feasible alternative for more free trade in Eastern Europe although the proposal itself has some intellectual charm (KOSTRZEWA and SCHMIEDING, 1989). A major problem lies in the fact that several EFTA member countries have applied for EC membership which raises doubts about the viability of the EFTA in the long term. As the example of the Asean member countries shows, in which a free trade zone proposal was discussed in 1991, even developing countries have become more self-confident to embark upon free trade arrangements; both trade and foreign investment can be expected to increase in a larger free trade area.

2.4 Links between Trade Liberalization and Foreign Direct Investment

The socialist East European countries had most of their trade among themselves. One might argue that this is in line with trading patterns in Western Europe.[11] Even in the smaller countries export-GNP ratios were in the range of 20-30 percent - low when compared to Spain, the Netherlands or Belgium with ratios of 22, 60 and 65 % (or Korea with 40 %) in the late 1980s.

Moreover, in centrally planned economies with rigid quantitative targets along industry lines world market impulses could not affect via substitution effects or complementary goods the whole array of tradables and nontradables; and there were no multinational companies (MNCs) which account in Western market economies for about 30 % of all international trade. Not allowing foreign direct investment implied not only foregoing multinationals' intra-firm trade and hence having a different trading pattern and a lower trade level than otherwise; it also implied that international technology transfers were low which in the OECD countries mostly go through the network of MNCs or cross-licensing arrangements between MNCs.

---

[11] In the CMEA there was bilateralism as opposed to multilateral trade relations in the EC; there was almost no intra-industry trade but monopolistic specialization among CMEA countries, and all countries were relatively less open than their Western counterparts. See CSABA (1990).

Most East European countries are heavily indebted and require the inflow of foreign capital for modernization needs such that high (net) export growth is vital for these economies. Only if the production potential can be modernized and the tradables sector enlarged can one expect sustaining economic growth.

With foreign capital inflows the switch from low state-administered interest rates to market-clearing rates will, of course, be less severe than otherwise. This is not only important for firms but also for governments whose budget financing so far benefits from interest rates on deposits and treasury bills that are below competitive market clearing levels (Fig. D6). In panel c) we show the supply of savings in Eastern Europe, where $S^*=s(r)Y$; a similar functional relationship will hold in the rest of the world, namely that savings S are a positive function of the real interest rate r and real national income Y. The demand for loans D (see the demand schedule D in Fig. D6 c) is proportional to investment dK/dt ($=I$) such that $D = a(r,E,E')dK/dt$; a similar reasoning holds for D^* in the rest of the world (panel a) where the proportionality factor a also depends on the real interest rate r^* and the expected profitability of investing at home E^* and abroad $E^{*'}$, respectively. Panel b) shows the world loan market in the sense that it shows the regional net excess demand from Eastern Europe and the net excess supply from the rest of the world; the intersection of the two curves determines the real interest rate worldwide (we assume full capital mobility) so that different national real interest rates prevail no longer.

From a strict theoretical perspective it is clear that the loan market represents on the supply side and the demand side stock variables, not savings and financing needs for investment as assumed for simplicity in Fig. D6. The ratio S/D can be written in the case of a linear homogeneous production function $Y=Y_KK + Y_LL$ (Y_K,Y_L =marginal product of capital and labor, respectively) as $[s(..)/a(..)][(\beta/j) + Y_L/(I/L)]$. A similar expression holds for S^*/D^* in the rest of the world; hence the excess supply of savings from the rest of the world (ROW) which is available for financing needs in Eastern Europe rises if s^*/a^* increases or if the investment-output ratio j^* or the per capita investment I^*/L^* is reducing.

If profit expectations improve in the rest of the world relative to Eastern Europe, this mainly would raise the demand for loans in the rest of the world, which would lead via higher international real interest rates to a lower demand for loans, lower investments and reduced output growth in Eastern Europe. A supply-augmented macro model (Appendix D2) suggests that monetary policy - and fiscal policy - might have different effects than suggested by the traditional IS-LM model.

Fig. D6: Effects of Capital Flow Liberalization

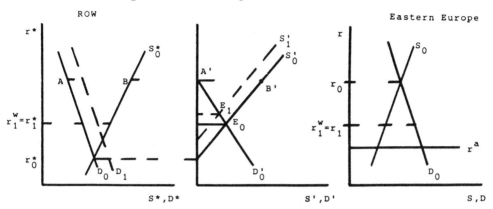

A decisive part of liberalization will concern foreign direct investment (FDI). Greenfield investments will increase the capital stock of East European host countries, and the acquisition of existing firms - e.g. in the course of the privatization of industry - will increase the foreign exchange reserves and contribute to restructuring the industry.

Foreign investors can support trade liberalization, but they might also impair it. In the medium term they are likely to contribute to higher import tariffs which help to achieve a greater amount of profitable investment. Host countries, eager to attract foreign investors and to rather rely on FDI inflows than on portfolio investment - raising foreign indebtedness - are likely to concede rising tariffs. Samsung with its local TV production in Hungary, Fiat with its investment in Poland, where automobile tariffs were raised, as well as Mercedes Benz' demands vis-à-vis the CSFR's government point to such a problem; in early 1992 Mercedes Benz was willing to take over two of the CSFR's truck producers but asked for higher tariffs on newly produced trucks and for an import quota on the import of used trucks. In the long term one may assume that foreign investors will have built up a relatively strong local customer loyalty and high market shares such that the demand for import protection will reduce. Moreover, the interest in exports to the parent's company market or third country markets will increase. Since target export countries will reduce import barriers only if the exporting country is in turn reducing its tariffs (or maintaining low ones) the "demand for protection" from foreign investors should decline over time in Eastern Europe. Finally, with a critical mass of foreign investors present in an East European economy the country might well hope that its political calls for improved foreign market access are supported by the parent companies of MNCs and their worldwide network of firms abroad.

As regards FDI in Eastern Europe there are four critical issues:

- (1) Given the fact that FDI in developing countries is heavily concentrated in a few countries one must raise the question how strong the regional concentration of FDI in Eastern Europe could be; improving the infrastructure in the region could contribute even further to regional concentration effects.

- (2) Can FDI significantly contribute to capital formation at all? So far only in Hungary where FDI in 1990 and 1991 accounted for 10 and 15 percent of new capital formation, respectively, was there a case of significant FDI (for comparison: Taiwan had a sustaining share of FDI in total investment of 10 % in the 1960s). While Hungary recorded inflows of $1 bill. and $ 1.5 bill in 1990 and 1991, Poland had insignificant inflows of around $ 500 mill. which looks even worse in a comparison on a per capita basis. In 1991/92 the CSFR was in a position almost as favorable as Hungary and there are positive expectations for the early 1990s, too. However, with worldwide FDI flows of some $ 200 bill., the inflow of $ 3 bill. in 1991 into Eastern Europe is not at all impressive. This holds especially if one takes into account the low basis of FDI in Eastern Europe; one may take note that - as an extreme case for comparison - in Belgium 45 percent of manufacturing industry is owned by foreign investors.

- (3) Whether FDI can be attracted to a sufficient degree depends upon the host countries' locational advantages to which stable economic policies, improved infrastructure as well as a competitive domestic supplier industry can contribute. The latter depends much on rapid progress in the privatization of industry and the formation of new firms. A factor determining the acceptable amount is the regional distribution of source countries. For most countries in Eastern Europe a dominating share of German FDI is difficult to accept in the medium term (this might change in the long run), both because of fear of economic dominance by the new Germany and for historical reasons. Only in Hungary and Bulgaria are German investors not at the top of the list. A diversified FDI basis would be important for Eastern Europe. This points to the necessity to involve the world's three main sources of FDI, namely the U.S., the U.K. and Japan. British and even more so Japanese investments play no significant role in Eastern Europe so far. If from a source country perspective one considers FDI outflows to Eastern Europe as an investment into the formation of market economies one might consider as useful some "managed international capital" flows in the sense of urging Japanese firms to assume a fair share of FDI as part of international burden sharing.

- (4) The relative share of benefits from FDI will be critical for organizing a sustaining and significant share of foreign investment in Eastern Europe. Given long established East European resistance to FDI and the transitorily growing distributional conflicts in the reforming economies, this issue seems to be of particular importance. The traditional analysis (in the MacDougall diagram) suggests that in the capital importing country capital income will fall and workers' income will increase. This conclusion is typically drawn within the framework of a one sector analysis. However, a two-sector model with a nontradables sector and a tradables sector in a simple two-country model with Eastern Europe (country 1) and the rest of the world ("ROW"= country 2) suggests a different analysis if we assume that the presence of foreign investors brings positive spill-over effects for the nontradables sector. Foreign investors which typically first engage in the tradables sector would then affect the nontradables sector indirectly. The basic idea is that with FDI in the tradables sector the marginal product of capital will increase in the nontradables sector, too. This holds mainly because modern modes of organizing production and distribution will be imitated by the nontradables sector. For the whole economy the traditional conclusion that capital income will reduce in the capital importing country is then not necessarily valid. Moreover, if FDI allows a backtransfer of generally applicable know-how, labor income in the source country could increase, e.g. in the N-sector the marginal product could shift upwards (see the dashed line in panel a, Fig. C5), and indeed FDI could lead in the medium term to higher real interest rates worldwide - not lower ones as suggested by standard approaches. The development of capital income, although no longer heavily taxed in Eastern Europe, is important among other things for the public deficit; actually, apart from workers and capital owners government - guided by its revenue interests - could work in favor or against FDI. There can be, of course, foreign investment in the nontradables sector, too. If not all industries can be privatized and opened up for foreign investors at the same time one may raise the question which industries should be turned to private domestic or foreign investors first. From the perspective of welfare theory there seems to be a clear-cut answer with respect to sequencing in this respect. One should demonopolize industries with a high elasticity of demand first and one should open the same industries to foreign investors first, if one is interested in realizing a high ratio of consumer rent to producer rent (see appendix).

Fig. D7 shows a downward-sloping standard demand schedule D_0 and an upward-sloping supply curve S which represents the aggregate marginal cost curves of the industry's firms. That is, demand reduces as the price increases and the supply will rise as the price is increasing. Under competition the intersection of the two curves determines the market-clearing equilibrium price at which each firm will sell its output and at which each consumer will buy. However, as indicated by the demand curve most consumers had been willing to pay more than the market price, and the triangle F_1 is an indicator of this extra benefit from market allocation: the consumer surplus triangle. A similar reasoning holds with respect to producers; as indicated by the supply curve it holds that at least some producers had been willing to supply even at prices lower than the actual market-clearing price - the triangle F2 indicates the so-called producer surplus which is a true residual income. In the long term when firms can realize the optimum plant size (or choose the optimal amount of the fixed factor), the aggregate supply curve will be less steep which is crucial in the context of FDI. If one can assume that foreign investors can transfer internationally their experience in choosing the optimal plant size and thereby switching to an output at the minimum of the total cost curve the conclusion can be drawn that the supply curve of the respective industry will become more elastic than in the presence of - inexperienced - domestic producers only. This is crucial for the relative share of benefits from FDI in the nontradables sector (a generalized analysis is possible). To stay as simple as possible one may assume that the whole industry is owned by foreign investors such that the producer surplus fully goes to them. The ratio of the consumer surplus F1 to the producer surplus F2 is given by the relation of the slope of the demand curve (b) and that of the supply curve (g). Eastern European countries would like to have as much consumer surplus relative to the producer surplus as possible, and therefore they should open up for FDI up industries with a low demand elasticity (high value of b, relative to the slope of the supply curve, g). R&D policies and competition policies that encourage product innovation would help to raise b over time, and, possibly, to reduce g - until process innovations raise g again. Taking into account the modified TIROLE analysis presented before, one could argue that import liberalization and domestic competition for eliminating monopolies are particularly important in industries with a high elasticity of demand, while FDI liberalization should occur in industries with a high ratio of b/g.

Fig. D7: Welfare Effects with Foreign Direct Investments in Industry

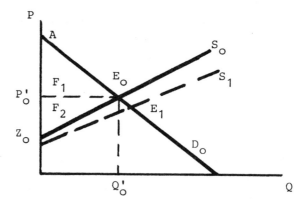

A similar reasoning holds if FDI occurs in the tradables industry. One only has to take into account the broken supply curve S_1 in Fig. D7.[12] If FDI makes supply more elastic the amount of goods exported will be higher than in the case of domestic ownership only. A different question, however, is the rate of technological progress in the case of no foreign ownership vs. full (or strong) foreign ownership of an industry. Diffusion effects and process will change - as discussion in the previous chapter - the slope of the supply curve.

Fig. D8: Welfare Effects of Tariffs in the Presence of FDI

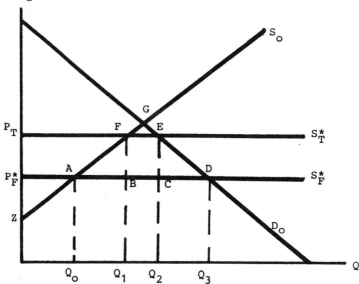

By all we know from the literature it seems to be clear for the technically non-leading East European economies that technology transfer would be accelerated by FDI and hence the static supply improvement (in the sense of a higher supply elasticity) be reinforced over time. It is true, however, that in the first stage of FDI there may be some balance of payments problems. The case of the Republic of Korea shows that in the late 1970s MNCs accounted for a higher share on the goods import side than on the goods export side; with a negative trade balance the conclusion was clearly that MNCs reinforced trade balance problems, but a decade later the position on the import side and the export side had switched such that MNCs contributed to a trade balance surplus.[13]

---

[12] With g declining, the international conflicts over gains from FDI - in the sense of the ration F1/F2 - would reduce provided that workers/voters dislike profits accruing to foreign capital owners not much more than in the case of domestic ownership.

[13] See INOTAI, A. (1991), Liberalization and Foreign Direct Investment, in: KÖVES, A. and MARER, P., eds., Foreign Economic Liberalization, 99-112. *The historical experience suggests that high tariff rates do not promote economic development. In 1902 (LITTLE et al., 1970) the nominal tariff levels for manufacturing amounted to 131 percent in Russia, to 73 in the U.S. (1912: 41 %), 34, 27 and 25 percent in France, Italy and*

One may raise the question whether foreign investors have an interest in tariff reduction. The standard analysis applied to Eastern Europe (Fig. D9) suggests no in the case of a typical import market. If the free trade price is P^*_F a tariff increases the price to P_T such that domestic output will rise from Q_0 to Q_1 and imports from Q_3-Q_0 fall to the difference between domestic demand - now at the higher price being only Q_2 - and domestic output, namely Q_1. The producer surplus in a situation with an import tariff is given by the area $FAP^*_FP_T$. Foreign as well as domestic producers in the industry will clearly oppose the removal of tariffs and they might actually call for even higher tariffs. The worst that could be accepted by the host government is to impose quantitative import restrictions (prevalent in the former socialist system) which effectively would allow a single producer to act as a monopolist. This could be a problem in those cases where the industry in the respective East European economy is still a private - domestically or foreign owned - monopoly.

3. Liberalization and Economic Integration

Given the increasing role of intra-company trade and international technology flows as well as the surge in international R&D cooperation in the 1980s (UNCTC, 1988; KLEIN and WELFENS, 1990) one may also emphasize that foreign direct investment is an engine of economic growth. MURRELL (1990) argued that the absence of FDI largely explains the distorted trade patterns and slow economic growth in socialist economies. If one adopts this view the conclusion is that Eastern Europe needs not only institutional liberalization, but positive incentives for exports and FDI. Given the positive experience of the EC where up to half of a percentage point of economic growth is accounted for by integration effects (COE and KRUGER, 1990) one may also raise the question whether or not regional economic integration could not play a distinct role in Eastern Europe. A secondary effect of regional integration and higher economic growth would be expanding East-West trade. Higher economic growth in Western Europe would stimulate imports from Eastern Europe and thereby help these countries maintain convertibility, cope with foreign indebtedness and expand the export sector. This in turn would stimulate growth in Eastern Europe where part of the then rising import demand would fall on Western Europe.

Germany; and to 9, 7 and 3 percent in Japan, Switzerland and the Netherlands, respectively. The weighted post-Tokyo tariff level in the US in 1980 was around 5 percent. The GATT organization paved, of course, the way to tariff reduction: From the pre-Geneva level (index =100) the nominal rate came down 4/5 in 1980, however, non-tariff barriers increased; see BHAGWATI (1988).

3.1 The Role of the EC

With the disintegration of the CMEA, the emergence of new countries in Eastern Europe and the systemic transformation in the formerly socialist CMEA countries, the existing international trade and investment relations will change. The changes will also affect the international economic order as shaped by the IMF and the World Bank, the GATT, the WIPO (World Intellectual Property Organization) and the Bank of International Settlements in Basle. All Eastern European countries are now members of the three main international organizations, the GATT, the IMF and the BIS. The Bank of International Settlements - founded in 1930 to organize German reparations payments for World War I - is a relatively silent, but increasingly influential player in the coordination of monetary policy in Europe. Moreover, since the foundation of the Cooke Committee in 1974 it is engaged in the international harmonization of prudential supervision. This field is becoming increasingly important for Eastern Europe as new two-tier commercial banking systems are developed within the transformation process. A functional monetary system and efficient financial markets in turn are quite important for achieving monetary stability, full convertibility and economic growth in Eastern Europe - all being indispensable if Eastern Europe is to attract an increasing share of foreign direct investment and is to develop growing international trade. Internal financial instability and speculative attacks on the East European currencies endanger a functional international trade and investment system as much as misalignment. In the 1920s Eastern Europe could not achieve significant capital inflows because protectionism, misalignment and politico-economic instability made it unattractive for U.S. and West European investors to engage in investment projects.

In 1990 EC imports increased by only 5 percent after an increase of 15 percent in 1989. East European economies could correspondingly increase their exports to the Community by about 5 percent, where Poland, Hungary and Bulgaria could raise agricultural exports in particular. However, the association talks between Poland, Hungary and the CSFR were difficult because France as a major EC agricultural producer/exporter found it unacceptable to liberalize agricultural imports vis-à-vis Eastern Europe. The EC is more inclined to largely liberalize imports of textiles and steel into the Community in the very long run.

It is surprising to see how difficult Western Europe finds it to liberalize imports from Eastern Europe. This region accounts for just 3 percent of all European imports (see Tab. D5). What is worrying Western Europe and the EC in particular is that factor endowments and historical traditions make Eastern Europe a natural exporter of agricultural products (except for the CSFR between 15 and 25 percent of the labor force is still in agriculture). The GATT Uruguay Round has already faced repeated difficulties with respect to liberalizing agricultural trade.

With the systemic transformation in Eastern Europe the problem has become even more urgent and delicate - it seems indeed strange that the U.S. and the EC not only want to be net exporters of industrial goods but are the world's leading net exporters of agricultural products, too. The well-organized and well-motivated minority of farmers in the EC and the U.S. are overproportionately influential in politics, and prospects for liberalization are therefore bleak.

Tab. D5: East European Exports to Western Europe

	1980-84	1985-87	1988	1989		1990 IV.Q.
	as % share of Western Europe's total imports					
USSR	2.5	1.9	1.6	1.4	1.6	1.6
other East Europ. Ec.	1.5	1.4	1.3	1.3	1.3	1.3
CSFR	0.32	0.30	0.28	0.28	0.27	0.28
Poland	0.43	0.40	0.41	0.41	0.48	0.53
Hungary	0.28	0.28	0.29	0.29	0.31	0.33
Bulgaria	0.10	0.07	0.05	0.05	0.06	0.05
Romania	0.32	0.30	0.25	0.24	0.14	0.13
Yugoslavia	0.4	0.6	0.6	0.7	0.7	0.6

Note: Western Europe = European OECD-countries (except for Finland which has a special relationsship with the USSR).
Source: OECD/BIS (1991)

Tab. D6: Imports and Exports from the USSR and Central Europe in 1989 (bill. US $)

	World	USSR	Bulgaria	CFSR	GDR	Hungary	Poland	Romania
			Imports from					
Western Europe	1,361	21.3	.7	3.7	2.6	3.9	5.4	3.0
EC	1,165	16.5	.6	2.8	1.8	2.9	4.3	2.8
US	493	.8	.07	0.1	0.2	0.4	0.4	0.09
Japan	211	3.0	.05	0.1	0.1	0.1	0.1	0.2
			Exports to					
Western Europe	1,317	19.0	2.0	3.4	2.8	4.4	5.3	0.8
EC	1,130	13.6	1.6	2.6	1.8	3.3	4.3	0.8
US	364	4.3	0.2	0.05	0.09	0.1	0.4	0.2
Japan	275	3.1	0.2	0.06	0.02	0.1	0.2	0.05

Note: Trade between the FRG and the GDR is not included; for the GDR Western Germany was the most important trading partner, representing a share of roughly 30 percent, followed by the USSR with 24 percent.
Source: GATT (1990), International Trade 1989-90, Geneva, Appendix Tab. 1.

With regard to the economic relations between Western Europe and Central Europe, there is a clear conflict of EC deepening versus EC widening. Given the principles of EC 1992, namely the free flow of capital, labor, goods and services, Eastern European countries that are considering EC membership would face the problem of fully accepting foreign capital inflows - there are still reservations against German inflows in most East European economies. The EC countries would have to accept labor mobility and migration to an extent that might not be politically feasible. Hence the seemingly easiest way to increase East West trade within Europe, namely an EC enlargement, is hardly a realistic medium-term option. Too early an EC enlargement could also weaken the political and economic cohesion of the existing community in the trade and monetary sphere (WELFENS, 1991c, 1992d).

There is the risk that similar to the 1920s - when misalignment and protectionism prevented significant foreign investment in Eastern Europe (DRABEK, 1985) - investment flows from Western Europe remain small. The conclusion to be drawn for Eastern European exchange rate regimes would be that fixed exchange rates are inappropriate, especially because systemic transformation implies monetary and real adjustments which should be reflected in a changing nominal and real exchange rate. The desired economic growth requires maintaining the policy instrument of nominal exchange rate changes. As observed by KRAVIS and LIPSEY (1988), the relative price of nontradables to tradables is increasing with rising per capita incomes. While the latter is an explicit goal of transformation and foreign economic liberalization in Eastern Europe, a weakening price incentive for exports is not desirable over time.

Eastern Europe is still facing the move towards a service economy. The service sector has been much neglected in socialist command economies because of their alleged non-productivity (in terms of Marx' theory). While the share of services in value-added in OECD countries and in some NICs reaches 50 percent or more, the former CMEA countries recorded shares of only about 35 % (Hungary: 49 %; see Tab. D7). This backlog in the move to a service economy, the increasing mobility of service users and service providers as well as attempts in the GATT Uruguay Round to reduce barriers to trade in services could contribute to rising East-West trade in services. Services so far account only for about 20 percent of global merchandise trade. However, deregulation and privatization on the one hand, and, on the other hand, an enlarged GATT code that would encompass the services industry could contribute to rising exports of services from the West to Eastern Europe. A corollary of this development would be that Eastern Europe would specialize more in manufacturing industrial and agricultural exports to Western Europe.

Tab. D7: Income Disparities in Europe and Service Sector Share in GNP

ICP-estimate for GDP per capita (US =100) 1985		year	Lowest 20 %	Second Quintile	Highest 40%/20%	Highest 10 %	Service -Share in GNP %
Malaysia	–	1987	4.6	9.3	73.4/51.2	34.8	47
Turkey	20**	1985	4.4	8.5	73.4/51.9	35.8	46
Korea	24.1		–	–	–	–	
Poland	*24.5*	*1987*	*9.7*	*14.2*	*58.1/35.2*	*21.0*	*35*
Hungary	*31.2*	*1983*	*10.9*	*15.3*	*55.2/32.4*	*18.7*	*49*
CSSR	*–*						*33*
USSR	*–*						*35*
Italy	65.6	1986	6.8	12.0	64.5/41.0	25.2	56
Austria	66.1		–	–	–	–	51
Germany(W)	73.8	1984	6.8	12.7	62.8/38.7	23.4	47
France	69.3	1979	6.3	12.1	64.3/40.8	25.5	60**
Sweden	76.9	1981	8.0	13.2	61.4/36.9	20.8	54
Japan	71.5	1979	8.7	13.2	60.6/37.5	22.4	57
U.S.	100.0	1985	4.7	11.0	65.9/41.9	25.0	65

Note: ICP refers to the UN International Comparative Program; data are preliminary Phase V results.
* Share of services (for 1988, except for Malaysia: 1965) in total value-added.

Sources: World Bank (1990), World Development Report, Table 3 und Table 30; OECD (1990a), Services in Central and Eastern European Countries, Paris 1991.

Another impact of the shift to the services industry - and to the market economy in general - will be that the income distribution in Eastern Europe will become more uneven. The so far relatively privileged poor income groups will suffer a decline in their relative income share. In Poland and Hungary the lowest quintile recorded income shares that were more than double those in the U.S. and 3 percentage points higher than in Western European countries. Highly qualified personnel in the services industry and the liberal professions whose salaries in market economies are high will reinforce income disparities in Eastern Europe where workers' wages were relatively high so far. Therefore it is clear that especially among the lower income groups would be potential migrant workers looking for employment and income opportunities in Western Europe in the 1990s. East-West income gaps evaluated at median incomes are certainly even higher than the average per capita income figures (on a purchasing power basis) as suggested in Tab. D7.

3.2 West European Integration and Eastern Europe

Economic liberalization is often sustainable only on a two-way basis. If Eastern Europe is to liberalize its trade Western Europe should liberalize its trade, too. The EC is Eastern Europe's most important trading partner. With the EC's signing of association treaties in late 1991, free trade for most goods has been granted to the reform trio CSFR, Poland and Hungary; however, the EC will (transitorily) maintain quotas in the trade of textiles, steel and coal as well as in the whole area of agricultural trade. Agricultural trade liberalization ranked high on the agenda of the Uruguay Round but it seems clear that the round will be concluded without significant reductions of tariffs in agricultural trade. During the Uruguay Round many new voluntary export restraint agreements have been adopted both in agricultural and industrial trade which certainly does not testify to a global liberalization drive.

Regional economic integration schemes are dominating in the 1990s, and even the Asean countries have decided to form a free trade area by the year 2007 at the latest. In Europe the EC is a powerful regional integration scheme whose attractiveness has increased after the collapse of the East-West antagonism and the reduced attractiveness of political neutrality. EC trade with Eastern Europe has increased in 1990/91, especially in the case of Hungary and Poland (see Tab. D8).

Tab. D8: Trade between the EC and Eastern Europe, 1986-90 (Mill. ECU)

	imports from				exports to				trade balance	
	1987	1988	1989	1990	1987	1988	1989	1990	1988	1990
land	2907	3360	3857	5156	2332	2755	3944	4393	-604	-763
change	-1.4	15.6	14.8	33.7	-2.3	18.1	43.2	11.4		
FR	2055	2211	2557	2690	2078	2170	2384	2608	-41	-82
change	-2.5	7.6	15.6	5.2	6.9	4.4	9.9	9.4		
ngary	1996	2158	2587	2934	2372	2354	2988	2875	197	-59
change	5.7	8.1	19.9	13.4	-3.2	-0.8	26.9	-3.8		
mania	2429	2234	2548	1604	651	614	689	1227	-1620	-377
change	-2.2	-8.0	14.1	-37.0	-34.0	-1.6	12.2	78.1		
lgaria	517	462	531	583	1453	1406	1477	9005	945	318
change	-5.8	-10.6	14.9	9.8	-12.9	3.2	5.0	-39.1		
SR	13128	12988	12166	16167	9189	10113	12603	11184	-2875	-4983
change	-0.2	-1.1	-6.3	32.9	-6.9	10.1	24.6	-11.3		
R	1390	1401	1644	1166	1086	1264	1661	925	-136	-242
change	-14.5	7.9	17.3	-29.1	13.1	16.4	31.4	-44.3		
lbania)	56	72	100	81	56	67	121	118	-5	37
hange	-55.2	28.6	38.9	-19.0	-13.8	19.6	80.6	-2.5		
tal	24478	24884	28991	30381	19217	20745	25867	24230	-4139	-6151
change	-1.6	1.7	16.5	4.8	-5.1	8.0	24.7	6.3		

Source: EUROSTAT, Comext data base, own calculations

EC exports towards Eastern Europe can be expected to rise in the 1990s provided that Western banks can come up with flexible financing schemes and that state guaranty export schemes can cope with rising transitory risks in the former CMEA area. It is clear that the EC has a manifest interest in promoting trade and growth in Eastern Europe because too wide an intra-European income gap could lead to strong westward migration flows.

Austria probably will be the next EC member and some other European countries could follow in the late 1990s. At a time when the southward enlargement of the EC has not been completed yet - there are transition periods for Spain/Portugal until 1993 - the eastward enlargement of the Community has already begun. The former GDR became a silent member of the EC via German unification and the preamble of the association treaties with the reform trio explicitly mention the future possibility of EC membership. Bulgaria, Romania and the former USSR are suffering from trade displacement effects from the association treaties which gives free access to EC producers in the late 1990s and thereby relatively discriminates against former suppliers from the ex-CMEA countries.

A similar discrimination - this time vis-à-vis all East European countries - is caused by the creation of a European economic area comprised of the EC and the EFTA countries; the new enhanced free trade agreement will also bring free trade in services as well as free movement of capital and labor in the whole of Western Europe. The displacement effect is easily understood from Fig. D9.

If the EC concludes a free trade agreement with a West European *-country (say, an EFTA country), while an East European country offers the lowest supply price under free trade (P^{**}_F), the tariff which initially was equally high for both the **-country and the *-country will reduce to zero for *-countries.

Consequently, the East European **-country will not deliver goods at P^{**}_T - namely according to the difference between Q_5-Q_4, but Q_3-Q_0 will be imported from the *-country at the price P^*_F. The import supply curve is no longer given by P^*_T but by the price line P^*_F (this is under Eastern Europe's supply price plus tariff: P^{**}_T). From the EC perspective there will be a negative welfare effect equivalent to the surface B'BC'C - the loss of tariff revenues; but there will also be a positive welfare effect, namely the equivalent of the two triangles ABF plus CDE (Fig. D9). The net effect can be evaluated only empirically.

Fig. D9: Trade Diversion as a Consequence of West European Economic Integration

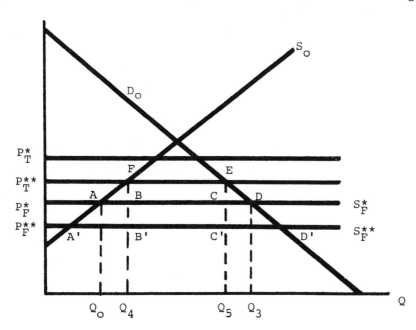

An interesting view about trade liberalization problems - expressed even by East European negotiators - is that quotas maintained by the EC are insignificant because so far export quantities have not exhausted these limits. This idea neglects the links between FDI and trade; it is at best misleading. One should take into account the effects on capital flows. Foreign direct investment into industries which are subject to import quotas abroad will be lower than otherwise. Lack of FDI in certain industries could have negative spill-over effects to other sectors. If infrastructure investment in certain areas requires a critical mass of foreign investors the collective good infrastructure might not be supplied at all.

One might argue that joint economic liberalization in Eastern Europe could be useful. It has already been emphasized that the modernization needs mainly require the import of capital goods with medium or advanced technologies such that the traditional CMEA specialization in the field of low technologies of engineering goods does not support the case of East European regional integration directly. However, one may argue from a more general perspective and advocate free trade in Eastern Europe or the whole of Europe or some other form of functional integration. A free trade agreement among Eastern European countries is not necessarily a reasonable way towards progressive trade liberalization. It may well be that a customs union would have less displacement effects than a free trade zone - at least the case of the Americas suggests that careful analysis is needed if trade diversion is not to exceed trade creation on the one hand, and, if on the other hand, induced protectionism on the global level is not to impair the growth of trade and international investment.

The analysis of Latin American free trade agreements (FTAs) has raised doubts whether free trade agreements that encompass an advanced region - North America - and an economically backward region - South America and Latin America - are optimal in generating benefits from regional trade liberalization. According to a recent study of the World Bank[14] 90 percent of the benefits for the non-US countries would concern Mexico and Brazil, and there would be serious trade distorting effects. Even if only Mexico was to be included in a North American FTA, there would be serious displacement effects. Trade diverting effects would amount to $0.44 bill. of which countries other than Latin America would be mostly concerned; displacement effects for Latin America would be only $ 28 mill. One may always be skeptical with static analyses of free trade; however, it is an open question whether or not a customs union would be superior to a free trade agreement. These and other considerations lead to more general questions of international liberalization. The only major long term advantage of Eastern European transformations is that all major countries in Europe will be members of the multilateral trade organizations and the IMF. By raising the number of players in these institutions and by offering new opportunities for the formation of various coalitions, the problem of consensus building could, however, become more difficult to solve in the 1990s than before. Moreover, one should not disregard the fact that the collapse of socialism in Eastern Europe and the disintegration of the USSR silently eliminates a catalyst factor for Western economic and political cohesion.

4. Role of a New Marshall Plan

There is a real danger for the sustaining economic growth and stability in Germany and the whole of Europe - the risk lies in a rising intra-European income gap coupled with increasing migration in a situation in which the mood in many EC countries is already characterized by the feeling: The boat is full. Indeed, there is the risk that successful economic development in Eastern Germany could become the basis for the destruction of this very new prosperity. Namely, this could occur if a rising intra-European economic divide would trigger increasing westward migration pressure in Poland, the USSR and other countries whose attempts at market-oriented reforms yield too slow an economic growth rate to reduce the East-West income gap. If we take into account that real GNP in Poland fell in 1990 by about 12 percent and is expected to reduce by another 5 % in 1991/92, whereas Eastern Germany might record

---

[14] See WORLD BANK (1991), Free Trade Agreements with the US: What's in it for Latin America?, Washington D.C.

a growth rate of 10 %, it is clear that rising incomes in the former GDR will intensify the public pressure on the Polish government to generate visible and considerable economic progress. What holds from the German perspective with respect to Poland, holds mutatis mutandis for the Polish-Soviet economic divide. Economic stagnation in the USSR coupled with high economic growth in Poland is bound to generate high migration pressures in the USSR - a heavy influx of Soviet people into Poland could in turn destabilize the still fragile Polish politico-economic system and ultimately endanger a first economic success of reforms in Poland. Hence, a German policy concept which wants to ensure prosperity and stability in Eastern Germany and the whole of Germany must take into account Polish and Soviet economic developments.

In Eastern Europe and the USSR there are high hopes that the move to a market economy will improve the economic situation within a few years. Compared to Eastern Germany expectations are certainly more modest as regards the speed of catching up with the West. However, there is little doubt that systemic reforms cannot be maintained politically if a critical minimum economic growth rate is not achieved. There are, however, some prospects for increasing East-West trade (VAN BERGEIJK and OLDERSMA, 1990) and there is a gradual internal transformation in the sense of privatization, developing functional market institutions and achieving monetary stability in Hungary, Poland and the CSFR. Their reform attempts in combination with the East German experience could point the way to sustainable reforms in other parts of Eastern Europe, too.

One crucial problem in Eastern Europe is the lack of foreign direct investment which would not only contribute to capital formation, but - at least as important - bring access to advanced technologies that typically are traded on an intra-company basis. Due to the imperfections in the markets for technologies and innovations, even a very prudent policy of technology imports through licenses would imply a considerable time-lag in the transfer of advanced technologies.

The former GDR enjoys the benefits of West German firms moving in and investing quickly, often driven by the oligopolistic rivalry for market shares in the united German market. It is an open question whether Eastern Europe can attract the amount of foreign direct investment that would be necessary to reach sustaining economic growth.

One important question for economic growth and trade creation concerns the exchange rate regime in Eastern Europe. It seems clear that a fixed exchange rate regime is not reasonable. However, a fully flexible exchange rate system would not be conducive to trade expansion either. Speculative capital flows, overshooting and undershooting as well as a high variance of the real exchange rate could distort the allocation process and trade in particular. If nominal exchange rates were to change according to some credible rules (every year or so), the problem of misalignment as well as that of exchange rate volatility could be avoided. As regards the interest of foreign investors in predictable exchange rates and freedom to repatriate profits one might consider an internationally financed guarantee fund for the whole of Eastern Europe. The purpose of such a fund to which FDI host countries would have to contribute most, would be to help prevent real exchange rates for profit transfers from changing by more than 10-15 percent annually. This approach to reducing profit uncertainty should contribute to raising the overall amount of FDI for Eastern Europe. However, no significant capital inflows can be expected if political stability cannot be established by the host countries on the one hand. On the other hand, without external support that helps to achieve convertibility and to overcome bottlenecks in public and private infrastructure, economic growth and trade creation would be limited. From a European perspective this holds all the more since the U.S. will be primarily concerned with East Asia and Latin America, and, of course, Western Europe, while Japan's focus could be mainly on Asia, North America and the EC. From a global perspective, the development of savings ratios and economic growth are additional elements that have to be taken into account in Eastern Europe.

Which Type of Support for Eastern Europe?

There is little doubt that without external support Eastern Europe cannot successfully manage the transition to a market-based system and integrate itself into the world economy. However, the question is how a resource transfer could be organized and what goals could realistically be achieved by this. Given the problems in Eastern Europe the main goals of a Western support program could be debt relief, support for privatization, investment and trade expansion. The greater the trade and investment stakes of OECD countries in Eastern Europe already are, the more directly one can expect positive feed-back effects from a concerted aid program. Unfortunately, the share of Eastern Europe in U.S. trade is around 1 percent, and for Western Europe it is not higher than 2 percent. U.S. and West European foreign direct investment in Eastern Europe is small so far and Japan is almost absent. This creates specific problems, namely that donor countries will find it difficult to perceive quick positive feedback effects of major aid programs which otherwise might not be feasible in the domestic political arena.

In contrast to the U.S. Marshall plan for Western Europe after 1945, the receiving countries in Eastern Europe are not yet functional market economies such that a resource transfer program for Eastern Europe would yield less direct and short term benefits than the Marshall plan. For over four years the U.S. devoted about 1 % of its GNP to a resource transfer program which specifically helped to finance investment in Europe and pay for U.S. exports to Europe. Since the U.S. industry at this time was well positioned to increase investment abroad the U.S. could also hope to reap indirect benefits from renewed prosperity in Western Europe and expanding markets in the U.K. and on the continent.

Marshall funds received in 1948-52 amounted in European receiving countries to between 2 and 14 percent of their respective GNPs. 16 countries organized in the OEEC (the predecessor of the OECD) received aid of $ 12.4 bill., where about 90 % of this amount was in the form of grants. The European Payments Union (1950-1959) which supported trade creation in Western Europe also benefitted from Marshall funds as did two intra-European Payments Agreements of 1948/49 and 1949/50. Marshall funds thus helped to promote trade in Western Europe and to achieve currency convertibility in most countries by 1959.[15] At 1989 prices the $ 12.4 billion allocated under the Marshall plan would be equivalent to $ 65.4 bill.

If Eastern Europe (including the USSR) were to receive 2 % of its GNP as a resource transfer and given an estimated GNP of the former CMEA countries (without the GDR, Cuba and Mongolia) of between $ 600 and 700 bill., $ 12-14 bill. would have to be financed by Western Europe and the U.S annually. If one takes into account that pessimistic estimates (e.g. of the Group of Thirty) put the necessary debt financing needs for Eastern Europe at some $ 50 bill. over five years - without any net resource transfer - it is clear that no considerable resource transfer could be achieved without allocating at least $ 100 bill. to Eastern Europe. If we assume a capital output coefficient of 2.5 for Eastern Europe $ 330 bill. annually over 10 years would be necessary to totally renew its capital stock; but if one assumes a domestic savings ratio of 15 percent and assumes that only 50 percent of the capital stock is obsolete, a net resource transfer of $ 75 bill. would be necessary. If we add to this about $ 50 bill. necessary for alleviating external debt problems the annual required transfers would be in the range of $ 125 bill. annually. This is slightly more than 1 % of the OECD GNP in 1991. The resource transfer could come from reduced military expenditures in the OECD countries which would have to reduce military budgets by about 1 percentage point of GNP. In the case of Japan this would have to be less, since Japan only devotes 1 % of GNP for defence; however, the EC countries spend between 2 and 4 percent of GNP on defence, while the United States spends 5-6 percent of its national output.

Since it takes time for East European economies to implement market-oriented institutions and to liberalize the economy a Western program for Economic Support for Private Restructuring, Investment and Technology Transfer ("ESPRIT") could start with relatively low amounts of aid in the initial stage and increase financial support as soon as a critical minimum of systemic reform and external liberalization has been undertaken. Given the distortions of the socialist

---

[15] For the figures indicated see BRABANT, J. (1990), p. 107-108. West Germany received some $ 1.6 bill. under the Marshall plan and about the same amount under the GARIOA program of the U.S.

systems and the long established dominance of the state and state industry it would be useful to focus technical and financial support on privatization, foreign direct investment and the formation of new business establishments. All three reform elements promise only gradual and long term benefits in the form of sustaining growth of output, investment and trade, but given the legacy of the command economy only a long term oriented program promises success. In contrast to the Marshall program an ESPRIT program would have to focus on a time span of about a decade, not just a few years.

A major difficulty on the side of the donor countries would be precisely the long term nature of the benefits to be expected since all politicians in Western democracies are subject to short-term reelection pressures. Moreover, the introduction of political competition and pluralism in Eastern Europe implies that pressure for quick and visible success of systemic transformation and economic reforms is also considerable. Finally, a major problem is that in contrast to the Marshall plan which was launched by a far-sighted U.S. administration an OECD-organized ESPRIT program would be much more complex to administer since the 24 member organization itself consists of heterogeneous member countries with conflicting interests.

References

AMPOFO-TUFFUOR, E. et. al. (1991), The Nature, Significance, and Cost of Rent Seeking in Ghana, Kyklos, Vol. 44, 537-559.

BALASSA, B. (1978), Exports and Economic Growth: Further Evidence, Journal of Development Economics, 181-189.

BHAGWATI, J.N. (1982), Shifting Comparative Advantage, Protectionist Demands and Policy Response, in: BHAGWATI, J.N., ed., Import Competition and Response, Chicago: University of Chicago Press.

BHAGWATI, J.N. (1988), Protectionism, Cambridge: MIT Press.

BIS (Bank of Internatioal Settlements, 1991), 61st Annual Report, Basel.

BRABANT, J, M. van (1990), Remaking Eastern Europe - On the Political Economy of Transition, Boston: Kluwer.

BRUNO, M. (1988), Opening Up: Liberalization with Stabilization, in: Dornbusch, Rudiger and F. Leslie C.H. Helmers, eds., The Open Economy Tools for Policymakers in Developing Countries, New York: Oxford University Press/The World Bank, 223-248.

CHAPONNIERE, J.R. (1992), The Newly Industrialising Economies of Asia, STI Review, No. 9, 65-131.

COE, D.T. and KRUGER, T. (1990), Wage Determination, the Natural Rate of Unemployment, and Potential Output, in: LIPSCHITZ, L. and McDONALD, D., German Unification. Economic Issues, Occasional Paper No. 75, Washington, D.C., 115-129.

COLLINS, S.M. and RODRICK, D. (1991), Eastern Europe and the Soviet Union in the World Economy, Washington D.C.: Institute for International Economics.

CORDEN, W. M. (1987), Protection and Liberalization: A Review of Analytical Issues, IMF Occasional Paper No. 54, Washington, DC.

CSABA, L. (1990), Eastern Europe in the World Economy, Cambridge: Cambridge University Press.

DINOPOULOS, E. and LANE, T.D. (1991), Market Liberalization Policies in a Reforming Socialist Economy, IMF working paper, WP 91/119, Washington DC.

DRABEK, Z. (1985), Foreign Trade Performance and Policy, in: KASER, M.C. and RADICE, E.A., eds., Economic Structure and Performance between the two Wars, Vol. 1 of the Economic History of Eastern Europe 1919-75, Oxford: Oxford University Press.

EDWARDS, S. (1989a), On the Sequencing of Structural Reforms, NBER Working Paper No. 3138, Cambridge, MA.

EDWARDS, S. (1989b), Tariffs, Capital Controls, and Equilibrium Real Exchange Rates, Canadian Journal of Economics, Vol. 22, 79-92.

EDWARDS, S. (1990), Stabilization and Liberalization Policies in Eastern Europe: Lessons from Latin America, paper presented at the American Economic Association Annual Meetings, Washington, DC, Dec. 27-30, 1990.

EDWARDS, S. and WIJNBERGEN, S. VAN (1986), The Welfare Effects of Trade and Capital Market Liberalization, International Economic Review, Vol. 27, 141-148.

GATT (1990), International Trade 1989-90, Geneva.

GREENE, J. and ISARD, P. (1991), Currency Convertibility and the Transformation of Centrally Planned Economies, IMF Occasional Paper No. 81, Washington D.C.

GRENBERG, G.M. and HELPMAN, E. (1990),Trade, Innovation and Growth, American Economic Review, P&P, Vol. 80, 86-91.

GROUP OF THIRTY (1989), Foreign Direct Investment, 1973-87, New York.

HARE, P. und HUGHES, G. (1991), Competitiveness and Industrial Restructuring in Czechoslovakia, Hungary and Poland, London: CEPR Discussion Paper No. 543.

HAVRYLYSHYN, O. and TARR, D. (1991), Trade Liberalization, in: MARER, P. and ZECCHINI, S., eds., The Transition to a Market Economy, Vols. 1/2, Paris.

HESTON, A. and SUMMERS, R. (1988), A New Set of International Comparisons of Real Product and Price Level: Estimates for 130 Countries, Review of Income and Wealth, Vol. 34, 1-25.

IMF (1990), Directions of Trade Statistics, Yearbook 1990.

INOTAI, A. (1991), Liberalization and Foreign Direct Investment, in: KÖVES, A. and MARER, P., eds., Foreign Economic Liberalization, 99-112.

KENEN, P.B. (1991), Transitional Arrangements for Trade and Payments Among the CMEA Countries, IMF Staff Papers, Vol. 38, 235-267.

KLEIN, M. und WELFENS, P.J.J., eds., Multinationals in the New Europe and Global Trade, Heidelberg: Springer.

KOSTRZEWA, W. and SCHMIEDING, H. (1989), The EFTA Option for Eastern Europe: Towards an Economic Reunification of the Divided Continent, Institute fuer Weltwirtschaft, Kiel Working Papers, 297, October 1989.

KÖVES, A. and MARER, P., eds. (1991), Foreign Economic Liberalization, Boulder, Co.: Westview.

KRAVIS, I. and LIPSEY, R. (1988), National Price Levels and the Prices of Tradables and Nontradables, American Economic Review, P&P, Vol. 78, 474-478.

KRUEGER, A.O. (1990), Asian Trade and Growth Lessons, American Economic Review, P&P, Vol. 80, 108-112.

LINDERT, P. H. (1986), International Economics, 8th ed., Homewood, Ill.: Irwin.

LITTLE, A; SCITCOVSKY, T. and SCOTT, M. (1970), Industry and Trade in Some Developing Countries, London: Oxford University Press.

LUCAS, R. E., Jr. (1990), Why Doesn't Capital Flow from Rich to Poor Countries, American Economic Review, P&P, Vol. 80, 92-96.

McKINNON, R. (1991), Liberalizing Foreign Trade in a Socialist Economy: The Problem of Negative Value Added, in: WILLIAMSON, J., ed. (1991), 96-115.

MOHAMMAD, S. and WHALLEY, J. (1984), `Rent Seeking in India: Its Cost and Policy Significance, Kyklos, Vol. 37, 387-413.

MURRELL, P. (1990), The Nature of Socialist Economies, Princeton: Princeton University Press.

MURRELL, P. (1991), Evolution in Economics and in the Economic Reform of the Centrally Planned Economies, University of Maryland, mimeo, May 1991.

OECD (1991a), Financial Market Trends, No. 48, Paris.

OECD (1991b), Services in Central and Eastern European Countries, Paris.

OECD (1992), Reforming the Economies of Central and Eastern Europe, Paris 1992.

PAPAGEORGIOU, D., CHOSKI, A.M. und MICHAELY, M. (1990), Liberalizing Foreign Trade in Developing Countries, Washington, D.C.: The World Bank.

PINDYCK, R.S. (1991), Irreversibility, Uncertainty, and Investment, Journal of Economic Literature, Vol. 29, 1110-1148.

POZNANSKI, K. (1987), Technology, Competition and the Soviet Bloc in the World Market, Berkeley: Institute of International Studies.

RIEBER, W.J. and ISLAM, I. (1991), Trade Liberalization in Asian Newly Industrialized Countries, The International Trade Journal, vol. V, 471-490.

RIEDEL, J. (1990), The State of Debate on Trade and Industrialization in Developing Countries, in: Pearson, C. and Riedel, J., eds., The Direction of Trade Policy, London: Basil Blackwell, 130-149.

RIEDEL, J. (1990), The State of Debate on Trade and Industrialization in Developing Countries, in Pearson, Charles and Riedel, James, eds., The Direction of Trade Policy, London: Basil Blackwell, 130-149.

ROMER, P. (1990), Are Nonconvexities Important for Understanding Growth?, American Economic Review, P&P, Vol. 80, 1110-1148.

ROSATI, D. K. (1991), Institutional and Policy Framework for Foreign Economic Liberalization, in: UN COMMISSION FOR EUROPE (1991b), Economic Survey for Europe 1990-1991, New York, 21-31.

SCHRENK, M. (1990), The CMEA System of Trade and Payments: Today and Tomorrow, SPR Discussion Paper No. 5, January 1990.

SELL, F.L. (1988), "True Exposure": The Analysis of Trade Liberalization in a General Equilibrium Framework, Weltwirtschaftliches Archiv, Vol. 124, 635-652.

SELL, F.L. (1989), Die Rolle ökonomischer Verhaltensweisen für "Timing" und "Sequencing" handelspolitischer Liberalisierungsprogramme, Zeitschrift für Wirtschafts- und Sozialwissenschaften, Vol. 109, 449-466.

SELL, F.L. (1990), "True Financial Opening Up": The Analysis of Capital Account Liberalization in a General Equilibrium Framework, Universität Giessen, Discussion Papers in Development Economics, No. 9, mimeo.

SENGUPTA, J.K. (1991), Rapid Growth in the NICs in Asia: Test of the New Growth Theory for Korea, Kyklos, Vol. 44, 561-580.

STEHN, J. and SCHMIEDING, H. (1990), Spezialisierungsmuster und Wettbewerbsfähigkeit: Eine Bestandsaufnahme des DDR-Außenhandels, Die Weltwirtschaft, H. 1.

TIROLE, J. (1988), The Theory of Industrial Organization, Cambridge, Ma.: MIT Press.

UNCTC (1988), Transnational Corporations in World Development, New York 1988.

VAN BERGEIJK, P.A.G. and OLDERSMA, H. (1990), Détente, Market-oriented Reform and German Unification: Potential Consequences for the World Trade System, Kyklos, Vol. 43, 599-610.

WELFENS, P.J.J. (1988), The Economics of Military and Peacekeeping, Jahrbuch für Sozialwissenschaft, Vol. 40, 358-385.

WELFENS, P.J.J. (1990a), Internationalisierung von Wirtschaft und Wirtschaftspolitik/Internationalization of the Economy and Economic Policies, Heidelberg: Springer.

WELFENS, P.J.J. (1990b), Economic Reforms in Eastern Europe: Problems, Options and Opportunities, paper prepared for testimony before U.S. Senate, Small Business Committee, March 23, 1990, revised draft in: INTERECONOMICS, 1991/5.

WELFENS, P.J.J. (1991), EC Integration and Economic Reforms in CMEA Countries: A United Germany as a Bridge Between East and West?, in: Welfens, Paul J.J., ed., Economic Aspects of German Unification, Heidelberg und New York: Springer 1992, 9-42.

WILLIAMSON, J., ed. (1991), Currency Convertibility in Eastern Europe, Washington, D.C.: Institute for International Economics.

WOLF, T.A. (1988), Foreign Trade in the Centrally Planned Economy, New York: Harwood.

WORLD BANK (1990a), Poland: Economic Management for a New Era, Washington, D.C.

WORLD BANK (1990b), World Development Report 1990, New York.

WORLD BANK (1991), Free Trade Agreements with the US: What's in it for Latin America?, Washington D.C.

Appendix D1: Ratio of Consumer Surplus to Producer Surplus

We assume standard functions for economic demand and supply, and to stay as simple as possible we assume linear functions with parameters a, b, f and g (all >0). The implicit demand curve that relates the quantity demanded (q^d) and the price p of the respective good is given by $p = a - bq$; the supply curve which represents in the medium term the short term marginal costs curves of the industry's firms is implicitly given by $p = f + gq$ so that firms' output is the lower the greater fixed costs are (related to f) and the greater the higher the price is (the responsiveness depends upon the parameter g). The point of intersection of the demand schedule and the supply schedule as defined by equations (1) and (2), respectively, is obtained from $a-bq = f + gq$, that is the market-clearing quantity $q*$ is:

$$q* = (a-f)/(b+g); \text{ and therefore}$$

$$p* = a - \frac{b(a-f)}{b+g}$$

The social surplus is equal to the triangle $AE_oZ_o= 0.5 (a-f)q*$ and is comprised of the consumer surplus triangle F_1 and the producer surplus F_2.

$$F_1 = 0.5 (a-p*)q* = 0.5\frac{b(a-f) \ (a-f)}{(b+g) \ (b+g)} = 0.5 \ b[(a-f)/(b+g)]^2$$

$$F_2=AE_oZ_o-F_1= 0.5(a-f)q* -0.5[(a-p*)q*] =0.5[(a-f)- \frac{b(a-f)}{b+g}]q*=$$

$$= 0.5[(a-f)[(b+g)-b]]/(b+g))q*$$

Hence $F_2 = 0.5 (a-f)^2 [g/(b+g)^2]$ which implies that $F_1/F_2 = b/g$

The price elasticity of demand is, of course, equal to $p/(a-p)$, but in the text we refer to a demand curve as elastic if b is relatively low.

$F_2/p*q*$ is the profit rate of the industry. If the industry considered is the investment goods industry, the profit rate should be equal to the real interest rate r.

$$F_2/p*q* = 0.5g(a-f)/(ag+bf)$$

Profit maximization requires that the following equilibrium condition will hold:
$0.5g(a-f)/(ag+bf) = r$, so that r would be endogenously derived. If r is exogenous one may use the approach presented to derive the optimum technology - firms would pursue innovations that lead to such a slope g (for a given f) that profits are maximized. With given parameters f and g, firm could pursue product innovation - process innovations for the consumer industry - that would help increasing the slope of the demand curve.

Appendix D2: A New Supply-augmented IS-LM Model

It always has been a theoretical challenge to refine the MUNDELL-FLEMING modell, and this is done here by integrating the supply-side into the IS-LM(-ZZ) approach - but we neglect the capacity effect of investment I so that the new model is still a Keynesian one. Assuming a linear homogenous production function real output $Y(K,L) = Y_K K + Y_L L$; taking a Cobb-Doublas function $Y = K^\beta L^{(1-\beta)}$ and assuming profit maximization real interest rate r $= Y_K$ ($\delta Y/\delta K$ is Y_K: the marginal product of capital; $Y_L =$ marginal product of labor), the equilibrium condition for the goods market can be written - using a conventional consumption (investment) function $C(I)$ - as equation (1):

(1) $rK + (1-\beta)Y = c(1-t)Y + I(r) + G$ (ISK curve; case of a closed economy)

(2) $M/P = m(i,Y)$ (LM curve; according to FISHER $i = r + \pi$)

Equation (2) is the equilibrium condition for the money market, where we assume that the real demand for money depends on the nominal interest rate i and real income Y. The slope of the ISK curve can be positive or negative, depending on the tax rate t and ß. We differentiate equation (1), assuming that K employed is constant; hence $Kdr + (1-\beta)dY = c(1-t)dY + I_r dr$. Here Kdr is the supply-side effect of an increasing real interest rate which, ceteris paribus, implies that capital income - being a mirror of rising output - will increase along with r; this holds for domestic and foreign capital owners (one might modify the model by assuming that ß depends on r or the unemployment rate u: from here one could integrate the PHILLIPS curve). We neglect here the long term adjustment in the optimum K that one can expect as a result of a permanent change of r. We focus on the medium term. The slope of the ISK curve is $dr/dY = (1-c(1-t)-\beta)/(-K+I_r)$; if the slope is negative - as in the standard IS-LM model - the ISK curve is less steep than suggested by the standard model - or the very short run perspective; as an extreme case one might assume that the initial (profitable) capital stock is very low which indeed might be relevant in Eastern Europe. Interesting modifications could be to consider the role of G in the production function (or the share devoted to public investment; or one could consider G as an intermediate good as could be done with imports X*), and one might also consider the case that the savings ratio s is equal to ß which would imply a classical world in which only capitalists save.

In our simple supply-augmented macro model ("SAMM", see Fig. D10a) we find that the sign of the system determinant DET depends on the income tax rate t, where the crucial equation is: $t^2 - (2-s)t - (1-\beta) = 0$; fiscal policy is counterproductive, that is $dY/dG < 0$ if DET< 0 unless we include G in the production function and assume that $\delta Y/\delta G > 1$ (!). Now let us integrate the equilibrium condition for the foreign exchange market (ZZ curve; equation 3) which requires that net capital exports Q are equal to the trade balance $X(Y^*,q)-qX^*(q,Y)=Z$; $q=eP^*/P$ (terms of trade; e= exchange rate): (1') $rK + (1-\beta)Y = C(Y,t,A) + I(r,r^*,q) + G + Z(Y^*,q,Y)$; (2) $M/P = m(i,Y)$; (3) $Q(i,i^*,a,q) = Z(Y^*,q,Y)$.

These three equations determine the equilibrium values of r, Y, e and, via the difference between i and r, we also find the inflation rate π which, of course, in a stationary model is given by the growth rate of the money supply g_M. Note that we have modified the consumption function C to include effects from real wealth $A = M/P + eF/P + B/P + K$, where F is the stock of short-term foreign bonds and B is the stock of short-term domestic bonds. In Fig. D10 a) we show an IS(K)-LM-ZZ system under high capital mobility in a flexible exchange regime. An expansionary monetary policy shifts the LM curve to the right and by lowering r (point F) induces a devaluation and an improving trade balance: there is a shift to IS_1. To stay as simple as possible: The interest parity $i = i^*+a$ implies that the ZZ curve shifts downward because i falls in the short run - via the liquidity effect - which implies for a given i* that a<0. But i will rise in the medium term as a result of an anticipated inflation rate $\pi>0$, and this implies a>0. However, in the medium term also purchasing power is assumed to hold, that is a= $\pi-\pi^*$ which implies that real interest parity will hold (or $Q=Q(r,r^*,q)$), so that we move back to ZZ_0 whose intersection with the IS curve determines r and Y. With $\pi>0$ (and a=π if $\pi^*=0$), there will be a jump in the price level until (see panel b) real money balances have reduced from m_0 to m_1 (if Y increases the m curve will shift to the right). This implies that A reduces, so that the IS curve moves leftwards unless a rise of e raises an already existing net creditor position vis-à-vis the rest of the world - this is assumed in Fig. 10a) so that IS_1 is the final position of the IS curve whose intersection with ZZ_0 determines r; the LM curve shifts leftwards as P rises via an increase of e. The nominal interest rate is i_1, and the real interest rate increased to r_1. The vertical distance between point E_1 and the LM curve (point G) represents the inflation rate. If the "final" ZZ curve had shifted downwards, r could be below r_0 so that inflation would have reduced r - e.g. if the ZZ curve would pass through the intersection of LM_1/IS_1.

Fig. D10a) Supply-augmented Macro Model   **Fig. D10b) Money Demand Function**

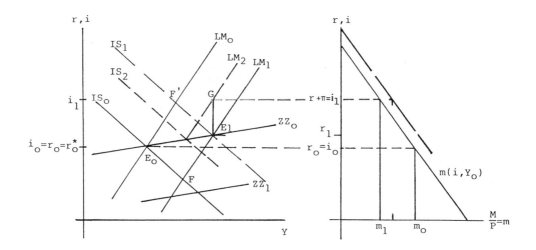

Appendix D3: Tab. D9: Exports to European CMEA Partners as a Percentage of Total Exports*

	Soviet Union	Other Eastern Europe	of which						Yugo-slavia**
			Bulga-ria	CSFR	GDR	Hun-gary	Po-land	Roma-nia	
non-convertible trade valued at national rouble/dollar cross rate									
Rub/$ rate	0.63	–	0.65	1.51	1.74	2.09	2.96	0.96	–
Soviet Union	–	32	66	31	24	25	21	23	22
GDR	10	5	6	7	–	5	4	5	2
Other east. E.	36	15	12	17	18	10	10	10	11
non-convertible trade valued at 2 roubles to the dollar									
Soviet Union	–	28	49	27	22	26	25	14	–
GDR	5	4	4	6	–	5	4	3	–
Other east. E.	17	13	9	14	17	11	12	6	–

* Data refer to 1989.   ** Yugoslavia's non-convertible trade with the Soviet Union is not denominated in transferable roubles.

Sources: CMEA. UN Economic Commission for Europe and national data/BIS, Annual Report, Basel 1991.

E: East-West Problems in Europe and North-South Conflicts

1. The New Europe

A new Europe is emerging after the politico-economic collapse of socialism in Eastern Europe. The smaller countries of the former Council of Mutual Economic Assistance (CMEA) have split into two groups: on the one hand, the group of fast reforming economies Poland, Hungary and the CSFR - possibly enlarged by Croatia and Slovenia -, and the slowly changing countries Romania and Bulgaria in which former communists exert no less influence than in Yugoslavia's core Serbia. The former USSR has disintegrated into several countries, most of which are forming the Commonwealth of Independent States. The CIS and the future countries that might finally emerge from it - with separate currencies and new customs duties that impair trade - face much more difficult problems in systemic transformation than the smaller ex-CMEA countries. Without a functional memory of the market economy and a stabilizing middle class and saddled with ethnic minority problems in a period of new nationalism as well as so many new economic problems, the former USSR will face a difficult adjustment path.

Russia has reemerged as a political entity, more eager than ever to look West, but also with less geographic overlap with Western Europe than ever. Territorial claims are raised in many East European countries. The existence of many ethnic minorities as well as the emergence of new states is bound to constitute the potential for economic and political conflicts in the region. The amassed military power - especially the resources of the former USSR - has to some extent lost significance for global power politics, but at the same time the very existence of military resources in a regional conflict-prone setting increases the risk that politico-economic conflicts could turn into regional military conflicts: civil wars or international wars. While it seems that the US-Soviet antagonism has collapsed there is a growing fear of regional conflicts in Europe and the Middle East. Yugoslavia already demonstrated the explosive mixture of ethnic, economic and political conflicts, and it testifies to the negative political fall-out that conflicts can create in peripheral European areas for the whole of Europe. Moreover, several regions of the former USSR offer new opportunities for neighboring Islamic countries to upgrade their conventional and military arsenal and know-how, respectively. With new countries emerging, inexperienced leaders facing tremendous economic challenges and rising potential conflicts over income positions, minority rights, migration problems and contested territories the world is not necessarily becoming safer. The collapse of socialism has renewed nationalist tendencies not only in Eastern Europe's new or reestablished states, but elsewhere, too; in many countries religious forces show a dramatic revival, e.g. in Algeria, Iran and several countries of the Middle East. There the Gulf war showed a new dimension of international war, followed by a civil war in defeated Iraq. Statistics show that the risk of casualties is higher for civilians than for the military personnel in most wars (Tab. E1; E2).

Tab. E1: European Wars in Modern History

Wars	period	countries involved	intensity*	casual- ties**
Dutch War of Independence	1585-1609	3/5	1 060	190 000
30 Years War	1618-1648	6/7	20 000	2000 000
Dutch Wars of Louis IV	1672-1678	6/7	3 600	300 000
Wars of the Augsburg League	1688-1697	5/7	6 900	700 000
Spanish War of Succession	1701-1713	5/6	12 500	1300 000
Austrian Wars of Succ.	1739-1748	6/6	3 400	400 000
Seven Years War	1755-1763	6/6	9 100	1000 000
French Revolution Wars/Na- poleonic Wars	1792-1815	6/6	21 000	2500 000
World War I	1914-1918	8/8	58 000	7700 000
World War II	1939-1945	7/7	125 000	19000 000

* casualties per mill. inhabitants in Europe
** only casualities from warfare included

Sources: LEVY, JACK S. (1985), Theories of General War, in: World Politics, Vol. 37, 344-371; SIVARD, RUTH L. (1988), World Military and Social Expenditures, 12th ed., Washington, D.C.: World Priorities.

Tab. E2: International Wars and Civil Wars 1900-89

	NUMBER OF WARS		casualties(1000)			casual.in civ.wars		TOTAL
	civil wars	intern. wars	civi- lians	military personnel	$\frac{B1}{B2}$	civi- lians	military personnel	in % of the world popul.
	(A)	(B)	(B1)	(B2)		(A1)	(A2)	(C)
1900-09	10	6	230	12	19.17	25	139	0.02
1910-19	15	9	7045	13470	0.52	1140	139	1.13
1920-29	11	8	21	42	0.50	39	111	0.02
1930-39	11	8	933	838	1.11	646	1109	0.17
1940-49	13	7	20176	19110	1.06	1007	5	1.70
1950-59	20	5	1073	1926	0.56	1571	253	0.17
1960-69	12	9	622	605	1.03	1827	1222	0.13
1970-79	18	7	639	606	1.05	3543	1236	0.16
1980-89	29	6	702	931	0.75	1899	179	0.08
1900-89	141	63	31440	37539	0.84	11697	4393	0.43*

* arithmetic average of decade figures

Source: SIVARD, RUTH L. (1988, 1989), World Military and Social Expenditures, 12th ed./13th ed., Washington, D.C.: World Priorities; own calculations

Economic analysis suggests that strong mutual trade links reinforce the interest in peaceful conflict resolution (e.g. SAY, 1834; POLACHEK, 1980). The economic ties among East European countries are weakening in the immediate aftermath of the systemic transition and political disruptions of the early 1990s. Moreover, economists have argued (BECKER, 1957; BRETON, 1964 and JOHNSON, 1965) that nationalism generates a kind of psychological utility or quasi-income for individuals in relatively young states with a weak historical identity; nationalism is often combined with aggressive attitudes and strategies vis-à-vis other nations.[1] As war mostly starts as a military conflict between neighboring countries, the emergence of young nations in Eastern Europe contains an element of risk. Whether Poland, the Ukraine, Russia, and Georgia (and Iran, Turkey and other countries) will be able to define institutional arrangements and establish economic links that foster regional and global peace is an open question. This is particularly so because new political regimes have emerged whose rules of the game are not firmly rooted, whose legitimacy is not strong, whose institutions enjoy low reputation and whose leaders have very limited experience. To control the new economic and political dynamics while channelling "unfocussed energies" upon productive and peaceful development is a major challenge in Eastern Europe.

The new Europe will consist of more countries and will face a transitorily increasing East-West income gap as the East European economies go through the first stage of systemic transition. There will be rising migration pressure that will gradually emerge from a combination of improved information and communication in the whole of Europe and greater international income disparities. With more countries and more conflicts there are reduced prospects of achieving political consensus in European affairs. This could seriously weaken the economic dynamics of the Old World. Only in the case that Eastern Europe could define functional federalist models of government in each country as well as adopt growth-oriented transformation strategies and if in Western Europe policies were pursued which actively stabilize and nurture the market-oriented transformations in Eastern Europe could one expect that political conflicts in the former CMEA area remain manageable.

The socialist model is no longer attractive to many developing countries now that it has visibly failed in Eastern Europe. In Eastern Europe and in the developing countries the immediate impact of losing a guiding role model is disorientation. Whether countries and regions in the

---

[1] For economic analyses of conflicts see HIRSHLEIFER, J. (1986), The Economic Approach to Conflict, in: RADNITZKY, G. and BERNHOLZ, P., eds., Economic Imperialism, New York: 335-364; SCHELLING, T. (1966), Arms and Influence, New Haven: Yale University Press. For a broader survey on the economics of peacekeeping and elements of theoretical analysis see WELFENS, P. (1989b), The Economics of Military and Peacekeeping: An Emerging Field, Jahrbuch für Sozialwissenschaft, Vol. 40, 358-385; ISARD, W. et al. (1989), Arms Races, Arms Control, and Conflict Analysis, Cambridge: Cambridge University Press. Publications that explain economists' perceptions of military problems are KENNEDY, G. (1975), The Economics of Defence, London: Macmillan; SCHMIDT, C., ed. (1987), The Economics of Military Expenditures: Military Expenditures, Growth and Fluctuations, Hampshire: McMillan.

Third World will be able to generate novel ways to ensure political stability, economic prosperity and peaceful cooperation is an open question. To the extent that the military represents in some socialist countries one of the very few institutions that are characterized by functional hierarchies, a positive image and strong modernization attitudes, the military could become more influential in some developing countries in a renewed period of generally increasing uncertainty, lack of identity and pressure for modernization. If this happens in countries with established conflict fields - say in India and Pakistan - the result could be intensified regional armament races and actual military warfare. A rapidly expanding military industry in the Third World that targets its product development more towards regional conflicts with advanced military hardware could directly lead to a greater intensity of Third World conflicts in a new global environment that will reduce the classical superpower emphasis on "high technology armament".[2] Moreover, with the U.S.-Soviet antagonism collapsing, both the U.S. and the CIS will exert less control over former client governments in the Third World. Developing countries' increased autonomy could result in more spontaneous military conflicts - e.g. from disputes over natural resources or minority rights.

Global economic disparities have widened. A report by the UN Development Programme shows that by 1990 the richest 20 percent of the world's population had incomes 60 times greater than the poorest 20 percent, whereas in 1960 this was only 30 times. These figures are based on the distribution between rich and poor countries. Comparing the richest income groups in OECD countries with the income position of the poorest quintile in developing countries would show much stronger discrepancies. The report suggests that the industrial countries should devote part of the "peace dividend" to increasing development assistance and also should support environmentally sustainable development by a 1-$-per barrel oil consumption tax, an equivalent coal tax and revenues from introducing rationing certificates for CO_2 emissions.[3]

2. Economic Aspects of Instability and Conflict in Europe

Problems of Conversion and Structural Adjustment
Eastern European economies face enormous economic problems in the various stages of systemic transformation. Except for the former GDR with its favorable fate of receiving massive Western German resource transfers, no East European economy can hope for a quick

---

[2] See on some problems of armaments production and military dynamics in the developing countries and industrial countries e.g. BROZKA, M. (1986), Arms Production in the Third World, London: Taylor; DEGER, S. and SMITH, R. (1990), Military Expenditure: The Political Economy of National Security, Oxford: Oxford University Press.
[3] See UN Development Programme (1992), Human Development Report 1992, Oxford: Oxford UP. On increasing international income differentials see also KRELLE (1989).

economic recovery or even an economic miracle. With the economic pie shrinking, political authorities weakened and restricted capabilities to create a new political consensus there are few reasons to assume that within a few years after the collapse of socialism economic prosperity and political stability will govern Eastern Europe. This holds especially if it is true that innovativeness and hence a major basis of economic growth is based on accumulated experience and know-how. If the old skills and economic structures become largely obsolete in Eastern Europe, while the new required knowledge and modern skills have to be acquired first, structural adjustment and rising per capita incomes will take at least a decade to achieve in the ex-USSR. It lacks established trade and investment links with the West upon which countries like Hungary, Poland and the CSFR can build.

Western support for the reforming countries will remain limited at first since there is a need for a time-consuming political adjustment in the context of necessary and possible reductions in military expenditures. There are only two OECD countries which enjoy the benefit of having solved this problem already and can enjoy the advantage of not spending more than 1 to 2 percent of GNP in the 1990s:

- Japan's rule - following the wisdom of U.S. political pressure after World War II - to limit its defence expenditures to 1 percent of GNP certainly has left the country with a smaller tax burden than in the U.S. with 5-7 percent of GNP spent on defence; moreover, it helped to focus R&D resources on civilian output and tradable goods. (After the end of the cold war the U.S. could finally "Japanize" its own R&D strategy by reducing the share of military R&D in total R&D expenditures from over 50 % under the Reagan Administration to the roughly 5 percent share of Japan as well as by scaling down the defence industry[4]).

- Germany is about to reduce military spending to below 2 percent in the 1990s, where the main impulse stems from German unification. Eager to obtain Soviet consent for German unification in 1990, the Federal Republic of Germany accepted as part of a deal with the USSR a significant reduction of its all-German forces, so that Germany might spend one percentage point less on the military in the 1990s than in the 1980s. The problems of military expenditure reduction and conversion policies will be faced in a much more complex way in France, the U.K. - with defence accounting for 3-4 percent of GNP -, the U.S. and Eastern Europe with its increased number of political entities.

---

[4] On some problems and traits of the U.S. military sector see especially BURNETT, W.B. and SCHERER, F.M. (1990), The Weapons Industry, in: ADAMS, W., ed., The Structure of American Industry, 8th ed., London: Macmillan, 289-317.

With a ratio of military expenditure to GNP in the range of about 15 percent the former USSR and its republics now face a huge conversion problem.[5] While many defence contractors in OECD countries have a long tradition of producing civilian goods under conditions of international competition, East European military producers with their very strong specialization on military output will face a much more difficult conversion process than their Western counterparts. Conversion problems could seriously destabilize the CIS. Moreover, eager to survive under new systemic conditions many of these military producers could become major exporters to Third World countries with their high potential of instability. There new military conflicts are then likely to create additional human suffering and hardship to which Western countries would react with rising development assistance or humanitarian aid. It would make more sense to actively subsidize military conversion in the first transformation stage in Eastern Europe - e.g. by setting up a multilateral fund for launching new business enterprises, establishing retraining centers and subsidizing the switch to civilian production - rather than to pay later additional financial aid to developing countries devastated by wars, burdened by high military expenditures and facing stagnation along with a growing inability to service their foreign debt.

For the average taxpayers in the OECD creditor nations debt reduction or outright default nearly always means higher taxes, mostly because banks that permanently write off their claims against developing countries will pay lower taxes on their reduced profits. If 10 % of the outstanding total external debt of $ 1,300 bill. cannot be collected by Western creditors, this would mean a loss of $ 130 bill. for the Western world (and some Arab states). Total Western aid and support for East European transformations was less than $ 3 bill. in 1991.

Systemic transition to a market economy will not only imply enormous structural adjustment needs, high unemployment, greater income disparities and slow economic growth; there will also be a comprehensive need to reallocate resources so far employed for military purposes. There are historical examples of rapid economic conversion, especially in the U.S. (see Tab. E3) and Western Europe after World War II; but there were functional market economic structures with an expanding civilian industry that could absorb resources from a shrinking military sector. There is no historical precedence for rapidly reducing military expenditures while going through a stage of systemic transformation at the same time.[6]

---

[5] See on the case of the (ex-)USSR: CHECINSKI, M. (1989), The Legacy of the Soviet War-Economy and Implications for Gorbachev's Perestroika, The Journal of Soviet Military Studies, Vol. 2, 206-240. The U.S.-Soviet dynamics are addressed in BYERS, J.D. and PEEL, D. (1989), The Determinants of Arms Expenditures of NATO and the Warsaw Pact: Some Further Evidence, Journal of Peace Research, 26 (1989), 69-77. On the Soviet expenditures see STEINBERG, D. (1990), Trends in Soviet Military Expenditure, Soviet Studies, Vol. 42, 675-699.

[6] Military conversion is a complex field that not only creates structural adjustment problems but may require substantial regional changes, too. See GORDON, S., McFADDEN, D., Ed.(1984), Economic Conversion,

Tab. E3: Effects of Demobilization and Disarmament Options of the U.S.

former reductions of military exp.	reduction of expenditures in $bill.**	average reduction of M(percentage points)	reduction of military ratio M (%-points)	reduction of military person.(1000)
after *World War II* (1945-48)	121	44	11.5 1944/47: 41%/4%*	3 559 p.a.
Korea War (1952-54)	83	23	1.4***	250 p.a.
Vietnam War (1968-1973)	17	6	0.7	260 p.a.
Future Reductions				
Option I (1991-95)	11	4	0.3	77 p.a.
Option II (1991-95)	18	7	0.4	126 p.a.
Option III (1991-95)	25	10	0.5	190 p.a.

* The reduction of the military ratio (military expenditures relative to gross national product) from 44 % to 4 % within four years went along with a minor recession; ** in prices of 1990; *** annual average reduction in the period 1953-56.
Note: In early 1992 the Bush administration proposed to cut defense expenditures by $ 50 bill over 5 years.

Sources: Department of Defense Budget and CBP Projections, quoted from DEUTSCHE BANK (1991), The Peace-Dividend - How to Pin it Down?, Frankfurt/M., p. 30. Council of Economic Advisers (1991), Economic Report of the President 1991, Washington D.C.

Military specialists who see their income and prestiges fall rapidly (while politico-economic uncertainty is spreading) could join former communists in an attempt to establish a right-wing authoritarian regime. Moreover, there is an intensified risk of international proliferation of nuclear and military know-how since many oil rich countries - some of them in the Arab world - are eager to attract military specialists from the former USSR. Military conversion is not the only supply shock to affect the former CMEA countries. Systemic transformation has one specific aspect that is related to price liberalization and adjustment to world market prices. There will be a supply-side shock akin to the oil price shocks of the 1970s in the OECD

Cambridge; PAUKERT, L. and RICHARD, P. (1991), Defence Expenditure, Industrial Conversion and Local Employment, Geneva: ILO.

countries which all suffered from stagnation and inflation in the 1970s - but had a market-system and functional firms in place that were able to absorb a large part of the external shocks. With the switch from low energy prices to much higher world market prices a large part of the ex-USSR's capital stock will become obsolete. This energy price shock will also concern the other former members of the CMEA. With restricted adjustment capabilities and high marginal costs of structural change - especially in the case of existing firms - there is a strong case for gradual and preannounced adjustment steps.

EC Problems

While prospects for regional economic growth are modest in the medium term in Eastern Europe, Western Europe seems better positioned for sustained economic growth. The EC has established a wider economic circle in Western Europe, namely the European Economic Space in which the EFTA countries are linked to the project EC 1992. The single market project will create a unified EC market as of 1993. Whether the EC will indeed maintain its present political cohesion is doubtful to some extent, especially since German unification has changed the balance of power in the Community.

France has to redefine its role in Europe since its nuclear Force de Frappe no longer is a strong asset for improving its European political bargaining situation. French industry seems not likely to become a real counterweight against German economic influences in Eastern Europe, but in any case a series of so-called defeats of the French business community in East European projects in which German firms are rival bidders could shift the public attitudes in France towards less support for Franco-German political cooperation. Moreover, if German monetary and fiscal policy continues to cause economic problems in France via higher real interest rates, diverging national interests in France and Germany could once again play a greater role. Germany would be absorbed by the challenge of economic unification while French interests would emphasize the goals of full employment and growth in France.[7] Finally, it will be difficult to maintain traditional French political strategies to use the EC institutions as an additional and specifically French basis for political power in Europe. Both a greater British role in the EC after the end of the THATCHER-era and a growing role of Germany will reduce the traditional French power basis in the EC. Whether an expansion of the EC encompassing Eastern Europe would strengthen the French position may also be doubted.

The EC has established closer links with three reforming former CMEA countries, namely Poland, Hungary and the CSFR with which association treaties were concluded in late 1991.

---

[7] On major national and international economic problems associated with German unity see WELFENS, P.J.J., ed. (1992), Economic Aspects of German Unification, Heidelberg and New York: Springer.

These treaties mention the long term possibility of an EC membership and hence one may argue that the East European enlargement of the Community has begun in a silent manner - indeed before the full incorporation of Spain and Portugal has been completed at all (there are transition periods until 1993). As a matter of fact German unification already brought an eastward expansion of the dynamic EC. However, as strong as its medium-term prospects for economic growth might be, the EC faces various political problems that will affect both its internal coherence and its capability to organize peaceful economic and political cooperation in the whole of Europe. Although the Maastricht EC summit of late 1991 has shown the ability of the Community to find compromises in the fields of EC monetary integration (WELFENS, 1991) and common foreign economic policy, the Yugoslavian crisis and the unsuccessul role of the EC raise doubts about the political power of the economic giant EC. Germany's quick and somehow surprising drive to acknowledge an independent Croatia has even raised the question whether German unification - which naturally strengthens in the political German arena the emphasis on self-determination - would change the internal balance of power in the Community.

With the U.S. standing on the political sidelines in the Yugoslavian crisis - Washington's focus was centered on Japan, the USSR, the Middle East and domestic politics - the new Germany's position became more articulate and influential in Western Europe than it otherwise would have been. It is an open question whether German unification reinforces the cohesion of the EC in the medium term and to which extent problems of EC deepening and EC widening are affected by this. Germany's assertiveness emerges in a period in which the U.S. is deliberately reducing its military presence in Western Europe and in which U.S. military forces yield less political leverage than in the Cold War. In addition to this the U.S. is weakened by a permanent Japanese challenge, high budget deficits, a fragile financial system and military expenditures that in 1991 still amounted to some $ 250 bill. or 5 percent of GNP (with the federal deficit reaching 3.5 % of GNP or, if social security funds are excluded, 4.5 %). The political system in Germany is largely absorbed by problems of the reconstruction of the former GDR, but after the turn of the century a consolidated Germany is likely to focus more on its external relations again and might show a stronger profile in a politically fragmented Eastern Europe.

2.1 Is Europe Returning to the Interwar Period?

The emergence of new states is not new for Europe in the 20th century as the creation of Czechoslovakia, Yugoslavia and Hungary as well as the resurrection of Poland in 1918 shows. Europe seems to be returning to a post-World War I scenery in which trade was reduced with its newly emerging political boundaries and in which investment and growth rates were low in many countries. Eastern Europe's fragile economies, misalignment and protectionism made the region suffer overproportionately from the world depression 1929-38, when per capita imports decreased by 2/3. In 1938 exports expressed as a percentage of GNP reached 13.9, 12.1 and 10.8 % in Bulgaria, Hungary and Slovakia, while Poland and Romania recorded even lower ratios, namely 6.8 and 6.2 %, respectively (WEBER, 1971; BRIEFS, 1950). There was insufficient international political cooperation and on the part of the respective national business communities there were strong tendencies for regional bloc building and protectionism. In contrast to the interwar period the 1990s can build upon preceeding decades of multilateralism, experience in international cooperation via institutions and organizations as well as "competitive multilateralism" on the part of industry. Influential national or international cartels that contributed so much in the interwar period to economic bloc building and political rivalry on the international level play no role in Western Europe.

Two countries which had lost their previous ideological identity decisively contributed to international conflicts in the period between 1919 and 1939: A weak Germany and a weak Russia were elements of the unstable interwar period which led to the Great Depression, then economic chaos in Latin America (debt default, loss of currency convertibility etc.) and a considerable push for totalitarian forces in Germany and Russia. German unification is unlikely to seriously weaken Germany, but Russia could be unstable in economic and political terms again. Socialist Eastern Europe - headed by the Soviet Union - has lost the economic race of the systems; moreover, its political identity and its established elites have lost their traditional rank and power. The dismemberment of the USSR in Minsk in late 1991 was a political *fait accompli*, but it was also a shock for Eastern Europe's old elites, and, finally, together with the Alma Ata declaration to form a new Commonwealth of Independent States it was the funeral for the USSR's existing institutions. The socialist economies of Eastern Europe face a complex systemic transformation towards some kind of market economy. However, functional institutions to run such a system and competent actors for a competitive market-based system are lacking. Functional institutions are important to provide a basis for consistent individual expectations and thereby facilitate in a decentralized economic system economic coordination which in turn is important for economic efficiency and growth. Switching from a centralized command economy towards a decentralized market economy naturally adds to the significance of functional institutions (or the lack of them).

A New Weimar Syndrome?

Eastern Europe looks to some extent like the first democracy established in Germany after it had lost World War I. The so-called Weimar Republic (named after the birthplace of the first democratic constitution in Germany) was a democracy without convicted and experienced democrats; moreover, democratic policies were not successful in economic terms and thereby never gained legitimacy via sustained success of politics. The new Weimar system faced the problems of intensified social conflicts, shattered dreams of global dominance, weak political institutions and strong external economic pressure. In the 1990s the newly created market economies in Eastern Europe look like market economies without entrepreneurs, and there is some doubt that there will be a significant number of successful and influential entrepreneurs that could generate Schumpeterian innovation dynamics and at the same time contribute to general prosperity. Whether Eastern European societies can stand a strongly rising inequality of incomes which will also become more visible in the more open societies is a delicate question if one considers the decades of socialist emphasis on the goal of small economic disparities in society. Finally, it is unclear, how the management bottleneck could be quickly overcome (especially since creating new universities and business schools is a slow process).

There are parallel risks between Weimar and Minsk/St. Petersburg, too. Every economic failure and the difficult economic legacy might be blamed on the new democratic system (of Weimar or CIS, respectively). There is little reason not to believe that many or even most people in Eastern Europe will not blame unavoidable and accidental economic failures as well as the difficult legacy of distorted centrally planned economies on the new democratic systems and governments. Post-Versailles Germany and the new CIS share some traumatic experiences on the part of the established political and military elite on the one hand; on the other hand, there is no proven mechanism of bringing a new generation of leaders into top positions and thereby guaranteeing economic prosperity and political stability under a new set of rules of the game. Another common feature concerns the disillusionment and disappointment of the leaders as well as the disorientation of large strata of society. The credibility of established institutions is shattered; there is a feeling of effectively having lost the quest for global supremacy and the last war, respectively; and there is the lack of experience of the new rulers which makes it difficult to generate consensus and to develop a new accepted course of politics and policy. Finally, there is a large group of former supporters of the ancien régime which have much to lose and whose members might try to discredit and hinder new policies.

Relevant Time Span
If one takes the period from the Versailles Treaty in 1919 to 1933 as a relevant time span for a negative dynamics in Germany - that might have developed more favorably if at certain points of time better policy measures than those actually taken had been adopted - one may suggest the following: not so much the short term impacts of the collapse of the USSR and socialism in Eastern Europe are decisive but a longer time span of 10-15 years will determine the questions of the external impact of the collapse of the USSR and socialism in Eastern Europe.

If the relevant time horizon for systemic transformation - for successful completion or definite failure - is one or two decades rather than a few years, it seems decisive from a Western perspective not only to focus on the short term problems of systemic transformations in Eastern Europe but to develop long term schemes for stabilizing Eastern Europe. The focus should be on integrating it firmly into the world economy and into international burden sharing and political cooperation. This could also mean actively encouraging East European countries (as well as developing countries in Asia, Africa or Latin America) to develop new regional institutions that would contribute to new regional political links and provide an opportunity to learn the task of regional consensus building. The global organizations cannot serve this purpose well since they are both dominated by the OECD countries and because their global focus leaves little room for specifically coordinating policies of particular regions.

Public choice theory suggests that the time horizon of politicians is relatively short in Western democracies. Hence long term benefits of short-term political actions (e.g. support for systemic transformation in Eastern Europe) will be heavily discounted. The long term nature of systemic transformation, however, also has the advantage that consensus building among rival parties in OECD countries is easier compared to issues with high short term costs and benefits that would become natural fields for developing political profiles via disagreement. In Eastern Europe "short-termism" of the new democratic systems is not likely to encourage adjustment trajectories with high short term costs counter-weighted by very high future benefits. Feasible trajectories (adjustment paths) have to yield short term tangible benefits.

If one takes the case of Germany and World War I and World War II, respectively, one fundamental lesson certainly is that one should avoid undertaking anything that only after another global military conflict enough willingness for international cooperation and multilateral institution building is created. Functional multilateral institutions can effectively help to organize a peaceful world. After World War II Western economies laid international institutional foundations to systematically strengthen cooperation and peaceful conflict-resolution. The Bretton Woods institutions International Monetary Fund and World Bank, respectively, the General Agreement on Trade and Tariffs as well as the UN were elements of a system of multilateral institutions which had no parallel in the interwar period - except for the UN's predecessor, the League of Nations which, however, was not a functional organization. The only international institution of the interwar period was the Bank of International Settlements whose initial task was to organize German reparation payments after World War I. The BIS never served this purpose well, but the existing institutional platform of the BIS was later almost ideal to deal with problems that constituted its major fields of activity after 1934. Nowadays the BIS monitors from its seat in Basle international financial markets, harmonizes national prudential supervision schemes and helps to coordinate monetary policies of the industrial market economies.

There is one other important institution for the international policy dialogue, namely the OECD which grew out of the OEEC founded in 1949 to administer the Marshall plan aid. At present Mexico is being considered for membership in the OECD. If it is considered as useful to integrate a major newly industrializing country into the OECD club of nations willing to coordinate economic policies one should certainly consider inviting for at least an associated status (which Yugoslavia has) all important countries of Eastern Europe, including the CIS.

At the beginning of the 1990s we have a new OECD sub-entity, namely the "Centre for Co-operation with European Economies in Transition" (CCEET) which could become the nucleus of an OECD enlargement. However, getting policy advice given from this new OECD center is not the same as including the new market economies of Eastern Europe in the deliberations of the various committees of the OECD; thereby Eastern European decision-makers could learn about future tendencies of OECD policies early on and they could acquire valuable experience on how to organize international policy cooperation on a routine basis.

A late child of the OECD is the International Energy Agency in Paris. For this Agency a similar reasoning holds with respect to membership of East European economies (including CIS). Finally, a very influential club of policy-makers is the G-7 (initially the G-5) group of leading OECD countries which since 1975 regularly focuses on important topics and issues of economic policy.

One may well consider including Poland, the Ukraine and Russia in a separate G-10 group which could regularly meet and serve not only the function of exchanging political information but help to firmly root Eastern European core countries in the West's established set of multilateral institutions and thereby contribute to world peace.

While growing world trade was the engine of economic growth in the OECD countries in the 1960s and the 1970s, a rising two-way flow of foreign direct investment became a major force of growth in the 1980s. In the second half of the 1980s foreign direct investment flows grew at twice the pace of world trade, and Japan - becoming No. 1 in foreign investment flows in 1989 - reinforced the links among the major OECD countries. Japan's natural interest in improving politico-economic relations with China has been weakened only to a minor extent by the East European systemic transformations which renewed its hopes for a deal with Russia on the Kurile Islands.

2.2 Replacing Coercion with Positive Economic Interdependence

In the first four decades after the end of World War II political stability in Eastern Europe has been largely achieved by Soviet political and military dominance as represented in the Warsaw Treaty Organization. This was further achieved by a dependency model of economic integration, namely the CMEA in which the USSR mainly supplied raw material and energy at costs below the world market while importing machinery and equipment at relatively high prices from specialized state monopolies in the smaller CMEA countries.

The political climate gradually changed in Europe only in the 1970s. Germany was keen to improve its political and economic relations with Eastern Europe. At the same time it sustained its role in Western Europe, namely to provide new impulses for the EC in a preferred partnership with France and to support the U.S. position in NATO and elsewhere. At this time the Soviet interest was clearly to drive a wedge between the U.S. and its European NATO allies. It also hoped that communist parties in Italy, France, Spain and Portugal as well as in Scandinavia would gain political influence over time.

The Double Significance of Alliances

Economists usually emphasize the uneven spread of benefits and costs among alliance members (OLSON and ZECKHAUSER, 1966). In the context of the East European transformation a different aspect is more interesting. Military alliances serve several purposes: one concerns creating internal cohesion; another one, of course, providing a common defence or deterrent (external aspect).[8] The dynamics of the international armaments race typically poses certain risks and might entail extreme international external effects. But as long as a balance of power exists internationally and as long as political and military leaders follow some rational decision rules one may hope for the provision of the collective international good peace.

---

[8] On problems of the armaments race see DEGER, S. and SMITH, R. (1990); dynamic arms race models were developed e.g. by BRITO, D.L. (1972), A Dynamic Model of an Armaments Race, International Economic Journal, Vol. 13, 359-375. See DUMAS for a variant of the duopoly model: DUMAS, L.J. (1979), Armament, Disarmament and National Security: A Theoretical Duopoly Model of the Arms Race, Journal of Economic Studies, Vol. 6, 1-38; BRITO, D.L. and INTRILIGATOR, M.D. (1981), Strategic Arms Limitations Treaties and Innovations in Weapon Technology, Public Choice, Vol. 3, 41-59. On game theory and theoretical developments of as well as empirical evidence for Richardson-type international arms race dynamics see BRAMS, S.J. (1985), Superpower Games: Applying Game Theory to Superpower Conflicts, New Haven; McMILLAN, J. (1986) and RICHARDSON, L.F. (1960), RICHARDSON, L.F. (1960), Arms and Insecurity, Chicago: University of Chicago Press; SIMAAN, M. and CRUZ, J.B., Jr. (1975), Formulation of Richardson's Model of the Arms Race from a Differential Game Viewpoint, Review of Economic Studies, Vol. 42, 67-77; empirical evidence is presented by McGUIRE, M.C. (1977), A Quantitative Study of the Strategic Arms Race in the Missile Age, Review of Economics and Statistics, Vol. 59, 328-339. Political and economic aspects of armament races in the nuclear age are analyzed in SIPRI (1988, 1991 and before), SIPRI Yearbook 1988, Oxford: Oxford University Press. For historical efforts of arms control see THEE, M., ed.(1981), Armaments, Arms Control and Disarmament, Paris: Unesco.

However, there are internal effects of alliances, too, and these were important in the first four decades after World War II. NATO has served both the purpose of preventing a military conflict with the Warsaw Treaty Organization and of generating political cohesion among the industrialized market economies. The presence of U.S. troops in Western Europe was perceived by several NATO countries as a guarantee against West German "Sonderwege", neutralism and political experiments. NATO helped to avoid military conflicts between its allies - above all in the case of Greece and Turkey. Moreover, NATO has been based upon shared values and a deliberate free choice to join forces to provide common security.

In Eastern Europe, the formation of the Warsaw Treaty Alliance has also served both an external and an internal purpose. Except for the USSR there are, however, doubts to which extent member countries were free to choose between membership and non-membership or to determine much of the design of WTO policies. The external purpose of the WTO was to defend the socialist system against the capitalist US and West European powers. At the same time regional cohesion was developed internally.

Fear of the Soviet Union's military force and influences was one major element of cohesion in Eastern Europe. Another important impulse has been - at least in some countries - fear of Western Germany. Poland as well as the CSFR perceived their Western borders as highly uncertain in the 1950s and the 1960s, and the political leadership as well as the population were well aware that the alliance with the USSR probably was the only means to maintain these borders. Yugoslavia, although neither a member of the CMEA nor of the WTO, was also held together by fear of Soviet interference (and, of course, the charismatic leadership of Tito).

Exhibit E1 shows the type of cohesion that characterized Eastern Europe in the 1950s and the 1960s. The smaller countries a,b,c,d,e,f followed the economic and political role model of the dominating (great) power G. Fear of interference on the side of G limited the degree of freedom in politics in the smaller countries.

Fear of losing power and weakening their own position would induce governments of the smaller countries to forbid themselves to openly discuss potential areas of bilateral conflicts which would have created a political risk - that Soviet power would be used either in the role of an external arbiter or as the decisive impulse in favor of one major political faction in each country, thereby determining the domestic political game. The repressive framework established by G (the Soviet Union) collapsed in the late 1980s.

Exhibit E1: Cohesion by a) External Threat in a Hegemonic Regime vs. Cohesion from b) Positive Economic Interdependence

a)

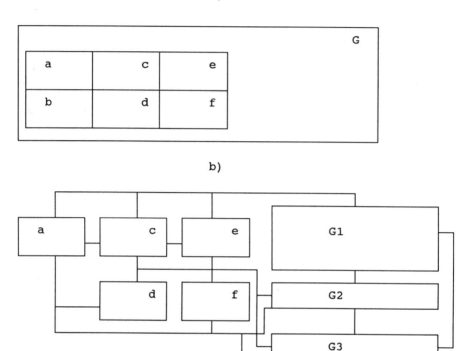

b)

Countries whose trade relations and political relations were hegemonically structured by the Soviet socialist system before decided to switch to a new "economic grammar" - the market economy - and to leave the hegemonic institutions CMEA and WTO. The smaller ex-CMEA countries became individual players with a new economic system (only the GDR went under). There are new political systems in which competition will play a decisive role and in which parties are eager to develop a profile by emphasizing internally or externally relevant issues. The "glue of Soviet power" that held together the smaller CMEA countries for so long is gone, and no alternative links of regional cohesion have been developed so far. Positive interdependencies will take much time to develop and whether indirect links - e.g. via rising trade with the EC - could provide a common anchor that could substitute for indigenous regional links is quite doubtful. From this perspective and in view of the fragility of the CIS an East European payments union could make sense as would common infrastructure projects. If competing long-distance telecom services of private firms are possible in North America (ignoring US-Canadian political borders), why shouldn't several East European countries or states join to set up regions big enough to accommodate competing private domestic or foreign telecommunication companies? Why should one not consider encouraging the formation of multinational Eastern European companies that some day could become viable competitors in world markets, too?

As regards Eastern Europe one can be certain: In any case it will take longer to establish new multilateral structures of positive interdependence than the two years in which the hegemonic ancièn régime collapsed. Therefore there is a dangerous period of transition which could bring instability to the whole of Europe. This could endanger the development of traditional Western forms of regional cohesion in Eastern Europe: two-way trade and two-way investment flows as well as common institutions for regional and international cooperation as well as regional institutions.

Economic growth in country a stimulates imports from countries b-G whose rising exports in turn raise national incomes which stimulate imports from a. National and regional economic growth makes the countries concerned more attractive for foreign investors, which in turn stimulates the international transfer of technology - being conducive to further growth. However, if regional trade reduces and growth thereby is reduced there will be negative regional multiplier effects via contracting trade volumes and slower capital formation.

Domestic firms in particular would benefit from sustained growth, not least because it allows an easier exploitation of static and dynamic economies of scale which enhance international competitiveness and trade and further contribute to economic growth. One could thereby create a virtuous circle which, however, could also be easily interrupted as soon as foreign investors' confidence collapses - because of political uncertainties or because national protectionism is spreading and leading to an international tariff race. This would indeed lead to a vicious circle, in which politicians from now more independent nations could try to compensate lack of domestic economic success via brinkmanship in foreign policy.

The whole problem set could be quite complex since the former hegemonic power, the USSR, has disintegrated into several countries. Finally, one must keep in mind that the introduction of political competition in the form of pluralistic democracy generally raises the incentive to explore a more diversified and possibly more extreme menu of policies in the short term and the medium term. This holds especially since the new parties of the new democracies will exhibit the natural tendency of parties for policy innovations as part of the pluralistic competition game in which they all have yet to develop their own profile. Only in the long run when a limited number of parties has survived the sharp initial competition among many parties could one expect more middle of the road policies.

Extreme and volatile foreign policies can be avoided from the outset a) by prudent constitutional restrictions - which are unlikely to be agreed upon in the delicate situation of the 1990s -, b) by restricting national policy options via membership in institutional organizations and c) by Western economies' systemic incentives for adopting specific policies. There are few reasons to believe that these options will be used to successfully control political dynamics.

2.3 Politico-economic Aspects of the East European Transformations

Uncertainty, Regional Disintegration and Opening up

The systemic transformation means considerable uncertainty for individuals, groups and institutions in Eastern Europe. As old elites and hierarchies are no longer recognized and established institutions have collapsed, there is a widespread disorientation in the former CMEA countries, above all in Russia. The Washington conference of January 1992 and the Münster conference of May 1992 have dealt with some needs of the Commonwealth of Independent States; trade ministers and economics ministers from the G-7 group defined actions needed to increase foreign direct investment in Eastern Europe - legal protection of foreign investment and private property, functional banking systems and well-defined contract laws. But the Münster meeting did not indicate special actions to be prepared by OECD countries to liberalize market access for Eastern European economies, to encourage the formation of regional institutions or to directly support retraining programs and initiatives for improving human capital formation in Eastern Europe. There was no positive strategy of modernization and economic opening up that would both stabilize the economic situation, improve the prospects for renewed growth and stimulate trade dynamics in Eastern Europe (EC protectionism is not declining). There seem to be considerable illusions on both sides: Western governments overestimate the capability of Eastern Europe to quickly switch to a market economy and overcome economic stagnation. Eastern European governments hold the wrong expectation that Western investors would naturally be eager to quickly undertake major investments in the region. Given the political uncertainty and economic stagnation in Eastern Europe investors will be initially quite reluctant to finance major investments. Moreover, the example of successful Asian economies shows that even under favorable circumstances not more than 10 percent of new capital formation could come from foreign investors. Moreover, in the 1980s FDI flows from OECD countries were concentrated more strongly than before on the industrial world, while the relative share of flows going to developing countries decreased. Japanese FDI flows have become a major additional source of global FDI flows in the 1980s. However, Japan's focus is on the U.S. and Western Europe as well as some Asian NICs. Japanese FDI in 1991 increased only slightly from $ 120.8 bill. to $ 121.9 bill., while depressed Japanese stock markets stimulated a very strong rise of capital inflows - mainly from firms and investment funds in other OECD countries -, namely from $ 77.2 bill. in 1990 to

158.5 bill. in 1991. In a period of high real interest rates and increased global capital mobility, Eastern Europe could find it extremely difficult to attract significant FDI inflows into major countries of the region.

Political Economy of Liberalization

Politicians will face some particular problems in the opening up of Eastern Europe. Some result from the diverging benefits of free trade in the short run and the long run. A standard result of the Heckscher-Ohlin theory suggests - assuming in country X the price of wheat (to be exported in return for textiles) will rise with opening up the economy - the following assignment of winner and loser positions for owners of land and workers will hold. In the short run when factors cannot move between sectors (wheat production and textile production) the positions will be as follows (see e.g. LINDERT,1986, p.70):

Exhibit E2: Effects of Free Trade in the Short Run (the Long Run)

	in country X		rest of the world	
	landowners	workers	landowners	workers
in wheat	+(+)	+(-)	-(-)	-(+)
in textiles	-(+)	-(-)	+(-)	+(+)

note: the macroeconomic consistency requirement is that $S(Y_{workers}, Y_{landowners}) + (T-G) - I(r,r^*) = [X(..) - qX^*(..)]$. With a flexible exchange rate e, the squared bracket which represents real net exports must be equal to $(d(eF)/dt)/P$ which is the increase in the stock of claims on the rest of the world ("abroad" or *)

In the above exhibit only four out of eight cells show the same sign for the short term impact and the long term impact in the liberalizing country X and the rest of the world. Hence the length of the capitalization horizon and the discount factor will play a role for those actors which face different impact signs in the short term and the long term. Moreover, one might consider a series of alternative coalitions between the factors labor and domestic and foreign landowners (or capital owner in a modified model). For multilateral liberalization the non-standard case becomes even more interesting: The case with foreign direct investment, that is foreigners could buy land - while labor is still assumed to be immobile. In reality complicating effects could furthermore stem from external effects from trade or foreign direct investment on the one hand, and, on the other hand, from changing savings and investment rates as a consequence of changing output structures or changes in absolute and relative income positions. Short term resistances could prevent the expected long term benefits from being realized at all.

Moreover, it is clear that lack of infrastructure, housing shortages, subsidies and other impediments from the inherited socialist Pandora box can lead to an adjustment trajectory in which even the long run is always composed of a series of short term adjustments in which the "analytical long term" of full factor mobility is never reached within each country. Finally, there is the problem whether compensation schemes can be developed that would allow long term winners to compensate long term losers and cover short term losses.

The EC will play a crucial role for Eastern Europe. It is, however, unlikely that the EC will be as open for firms from Eastern Europe in the 1990s as the U.S. has been for the Asian Newly Industrializing Countries and some Latin American economies in the 1970s and the 1980s. The U.S. is not likely to directly play a decisive role for Eastern Europe's integration into the world economy. U.S. politicians cannot gain much at the ballot box if they support a strong U.S. economic engagement in Eastern Europe. An enlarged American free trade zone would have trade-diverting effects for (Eastern) European countries (WORLD BANK, 1992). Moreover, the high U.S. budget deficit and the still considerable current account deficit make the U.S. neither conducive to initiate a Marshall plan-like G-7 scheme nor to generally advocate free trade in the world economy. Finally, U.S. investors play a major role in Eastern Europe only in Hungary. They could play a decisive role in the former USSR in the long term, too. U.S. support for the East European transformation will mainly be channeled through the international organizations which could provide some effective framework in stabilizing East European economies. This holds true, however, only if one systematically learns from individual country experiences and develops some concepts that would address common adjustment problems of several East European countries. Finally, one would have to adopt a pragmatic approach in accepting transitional violations of free enterprise principles, provided that well-defined measures of state interference increase the ultimately achievable degree of economic freedom and compliance with international regulations governing trade and investment in the OECD countries. If - as expected - Mexico is to become an OECD member in the 1990s one may well consider accepting applications of East European economies with similar per capita incomes and state interference. Membership in the OECD could become a condition for generous Western financial and economic support in the difficult transformation stage. An enlarged OECD could indeed become the platform for a new type of Marshall plan for Eastern Europe, such that aid would be effectively coordinated.

2.4 The Role of the New Germany

The New Germany will play a decisive role in Western Europe and in Eastern Europe in the 1990s. Germany's postwar trade orientation as well as the focus of its foreign direct investment outflows could become partly diverted to Eastern Europe. Whether Germany can economically dominate major parts of Eastern Europe - and this could reduce the capacity for consensus-building in the whole of Europe - depends on the question how dynamic the economies of France, the U.K. and the U.S. will be in the 1990s and how strong their foreign direct investment focus on Eastern Europe will be.

From a political perspective and in terms of balance of power considerations in Europe, it would be highly desirable that French, British and American foreign direct investment counterbalance high German capital exports to Eastern Europe. However, this is unlikely at least in the British and the U.S. case because traditional regional emphasis of investment and trade is not in Eastern Europe. Government-business community relationships in both countries do not lead one to expect that governments would systematically encourage, coordinate or even subsidize investment outflows into the former CMEA area. Germany and France are different in this respect, and the same holds - although Japan so far is almost absent as an investor in Eastern Europe - for "Nippon Inc.". Although French global FDI flows were higher than Germany's in 1989, the weak growth record of France in the early 1990s raises doubts that French firms will continue to outpace German firms in FDI. Moreover, as various competitive biddings in Eastern Europe have shown so far, French firms are not very successful in outbidding German enterprises in Eastern Europe. Since financial capital flows and trade largely follow accumulated foreign direct investment one may expect that Germany's capital exports as well as its exports and imports of goods and services will continuously increase in Eastern Europe in the 1990s. It is, however, unlikely that Germany's regional trade orientation would become strongly centered on Eastern Europe as it was in a time when Europe was last comprised only of market economies: in 1913 (Tab. E4).

Tab. E4: German Trade Orientations in 1913 and 1989*
(shares for merchandise trade with selected countries)

	Country Share in German Imports		Country Share in German Exports	
	1913	*1989*	*1913*	*1989*
USA	*15.9*	7.6	*7.1*	7.3
Russia**	*13.2*	1.7	*8.7*	1.8
(Poland)		0.7		0.7
Great Britain	*8.1*	6.8	*14.2*	9.3
Austria-		(A)4.1		(A)5.5
Hungary***	*7.7*	(H)0.5	*10.9*	(H)0.6
(CSFR)		0.5		0.4
France	*5.4*	11.9	*7.8*	13.2
Italy	*3.0*	8.9	*3.9*	9.3
China****	*0.7*	1.1	*1.2*	0.7
(Taiwan)		1.1		0.6
Romania	*0.7*	0.3	*1.4*	0.1
Serbia*****	*0.1*	1.3	*0.5*	1.1
Japan	*0.4*	6.3	*1.2*	2.4
Bulgaria	*<0.1*	0.1	*0.3*	0.2

* figures for 1989 are for West Germany; ** figures for 1989 refer to the Soviet Union. *** figures for 1989 are comprised of the country shares of Austria, Hungary and the CSSR. **** figures for 1989 refer to the PR China; ***** figures for 1989 are for Yugoslavia.

Source: WELFENS, P.J.J. (1992a), p.27.

Tab. E4 shows that on the import side Russia (to which part of Poland belonged at the time) was then No. 2 and on the export side it was No. 3 with trade shares of 13.2 and 8.7 percent, respectively. This is in marked contrast to the less than 2 percentage points in the late 1980s for the USSR.

The emergence of Japan and the Asian NICs as global trading powers implies that there is no prospect for restoring Eastern Europe's high regional trade shares in the case of Germany. There is certainly room to expand the trade between Germany and the former CMEA countries whose rapidly rising Western exports in 1990/91 already contributed to rising trade links with Germany. However, East European firms have to gain market shares in OECD countries against very strong competition from strong local firms, a new brand of "Euronationals" - stimulated by the EC 1992 project - and aggressive and experienced competitors from NICs and Japan.

Germany's role for Eastern Europe will be important in various ways. One aspect is German unification which, of course, creates a rising demand for German imports (partially falling on Eastern Europe) and contributes to transitorily higher real interest rates worldwide. If the reconstruction and revival of Eastern Germany could be completed by the late 1990s this would strongly inspire East European economies to emulate some form of Germany's social market economy model. If institutional settings and rules of the game in Eastern Europe were similar to those at home, Germany's industry would gain most by saving on information costs. In this respect the rising role of EC laws, regulations and institutions tend to reduce the otherwise strong advantage of German industry. The united Germany will in any case not only maintain its role as the most important export country for East European economies - except, maybe, for Bulgaria - but it is likely to remain together with the U.S. the most important investor in Eastern Europe.

3. North-South Conflicts and Global Aspects

The demise of socialism in Eastern Europe has spill-over effects to the Third World, where market-oriented reforms already have become increasingly popular as a consequence of visible economic success of outward-oriented (world market oriented) NICs. Naturally, it will take time for new elites and new economic and political models to drive out old regimes and concepts. The transition period promises internal conflicts, possibly civil war and regional politico-economic disruptions. All this will happen in poor countries with a high net reproduction rate such that economic hardship, demographic pressure and political chaos could join their destabilizing impulses in a conflict-prone way. New international institutions and new policy initiatives from the West are required in such a situation in order to set up some intellectual and political lighthouses that can refocus lose political energies and ideas as well as encourage market-oriented forces in the Third World to develop their own national and international initiatives.

Intraregional trade in Latin America, Africa and Asia (with regional exceptions) is relatively small so far, especially if compared to international trade with the U.S., the EC and Japan, respectively. With many market economies in the same regions of the Third World there might be some long term regional spill-over effects via increasing trade and investment flows. The tendency of a rising share of intra-OECD trade in world trade - rising from about 40 % in 1953 to more than 60 % in the 1980s - could thereby be reversed in the long run. The East European experience of rapidly declining regional trade in the first stage of systemic transformation suggests, however, that the medium term impact of market-oriented reform could be increasing North-South trade rather than South-South trade.

One certainly would like to avoid the transition of some socialist problem regions in Africa to Latin American-type problem regions in which feudalism, militarization of industries, some islands of competitive capitalism and authoritarian regimes represent a systemic synthesis that cannot generate prosperity and stability.

Instead we see economic stagnation and lack of regional economic integration. There is more trade with the US than among Latin American countries - and recurrent foreign debt problems combined with high inflation and unemployment. Argentina's generals gave an example of how the lack of internal economic success can translate into military adventurism abroad in the Falklands War. One certainly would not like to see similar developments in Eastern Europe. Successful developments of Asian Newly Industrializing Countries certainly come closer to the desired state of affairs in Eastern Europe.

If Eastern Europe were successful in attracting high capital inflows, developing countries might suffer, especially those with high foreign indebtedness.[9] Traditional patterns of North-South conflicts could thereby change. A second-worst scenario could be a global allocation of capital in which neither Eastern Europe nor the Third World would be able to attract enough capital and generate sufficient domestic savings to enter an economic take-off stage.

---

[9] This East-South trade-off with respect to the flow of international capital is briefly discussed in COLLINS, S.M. and RODRIK, D. (1991), Eastern Europe and the Soviet Union in the World Economy, Washington D.C.: Institute for International Economics.

3.1 "De-socialization" of Developing Countries: Changing North-South Conflicts

With the collapse of socialism in Eastern Europe the socialist model of economic development in the Third World is on the demise. However, there is no natural and easy way from socialism to a market economy - either combined with pluralistic democracy or an authoritarian regime. Developments in Iran, Algeria and some other developing countries show that the various brands of Western or Asian capitalism are not the most attractive alternative to an economically disastrous command economy. Diverse traditions and cultures in the Third World provide incentives to look for different models that are often founded upon religious principles. Religion is not a problem in itself as the role of Calvinism for economic prosperity and capitalism shows. However, if religious zeal goes so far as to suppress competition of ideas and institutions so that intolerance and intellectual infertility develop, stagnation and political conflicts will emerge which in turn can translate into outward-oriented aggressiveness.

From an economic point of view no economic system can succeed which is not based upon open competition, individual freedom and multinational corporate organization. A revival of rigid religious traditions could lead in parts of the developing country group to the spread of new collectivist systems in which governments will rely on propaganda, illusory promises and the military. As the economic disaster of socialism has testified human beings' (restricted) intelligence may well follow dead-end-strategies of economic development for several decades. These strategies are bound to fail in economic terms as long as the aspiration level of people is influenced by the performance of OECD countries or the Asian NICs economic performance. As non-market systems in the Third World will periodically face situations of political discontent and economic crisis the respective governments may well be inclined to distract opposition movements by engaging in military adventures.

There are empirical economic studies which clearly show that monopolistic power regimes and poor developing economies in general tend to spend more on the military - relative to GNP - than industrial market economies (Tab. E5).[10] One can conclude from this that economic catching up and pluralistic democracy are still valuable ingredients for improving regional and global security in developing countries. To a large extent these countries need - especially in the transition period to a functional market economy (and basically only then and in emergency situations) - active economic support from the OECD countries. The main avenue of support would be open access to OECD markets which, however, is not the case at present. Even during the Uruguay GATT round the number of voluntary export restraints and other forms of non-tariff barriers was increasing. Moreover, the lack of liberalization on the side of the EC in

---

[10] See the studies of HEWITT, D.P. (1991a), Military Expenditure: International Comparisons of Trends, IMF Staff Working Paper, Washington D.C.; HEWITT, D.P. (1991b), Military Expenditure: Econometric Testing of Economic and Political Influences, IMF Staff Working Paper, Washington D.C.

Tab. E5: Military Expenditures in Federal Spending, Government Expenditure Ratios and Military Ratios in Selected Countries

R= military expenditures relative to federal government expenditures, Q= federal government expenditures relative to GNP, M = military expenditures relative to GNP), countries ranked in the order of per capita income

	1972 (R)	1989 (R)	1972 (Q)	1989 (Q)	1972 M=RQ	1989 M=RQ
Countries with low income						
Nigeria	40.2	2.8	8.3	28.1	3.3	0.8
India	26.2	17.2	10.5	17.7	2.8	3.0
Kenya	6.0	12.2	21.0	28.0	1.3	3.4
Pakistan	39.9	–	16.9	21.5	6.7	–
Countries with medium income						
Egypt	–	14.4	40.2	–	–	–
Philippines	10.9	13.0	13.4	15.7	1.5	2.0
Morocco	12.3	15.1	22.8	29.1	2.8	4.4
Thailand	20.2	17.8	13.1	14.6	2.6	2.6
Turkey	15.5	11.6	22.7	23.7	3.5	2.7
Jordan	33.5	25.9	–	38.4	–	9,9
Brazil	8.3	4.3	29.1	30.6	2.4	1.3
Poland	–	–	–	ca. 50.0	–	–
USSR	–	20–30*	–	ca. 60.0	–	12–18
Yugoslavia	16.7	53.4	21.1	5.3	3.5	2.8
Korea, Rep. of	25.8	24.9	18.0	16.9	4.6	4.2
countries with high income						
Spain	6.5	6.5	19.6	34.3	1.3	2.2
Israel	42.9	26.1	43.9	49.1	18.8	12.8
Australia	14.2	8.9	20.2	27.0	2.9	2.4
U.K.	16.7	12.5	31.8	34.6	5.3	4.3
Italy	6.3	3.6	29.5	37.9	1.9	1.4
Netherlands	6.8	5.0	41.0	54.5	2.8	2.7
Austria	3.3	2.7	29.6	39.3	1.0	1.1
France	–	6.1	32.3	42.6	–	2.6
Canada	7.6	7.3	20.1	23.1	1.5	1.7
Germany (W.)	12.4	8.7	24.2	29.0	3.0	2.5
USA	32.2	24.6	19.1	23.0	6.2	5.7
Sweden	12.5	6.1	27.9	40.6	3.5	2.5
Japan	7.9*	6.1*	12.7	16.5	1.0	1.0

* own estimate; *Source: WORLD BANK (1991), World Development Report 1991, New York; own calculations*

the fields of textiles, steel, coal and agricultural trade vis-à-vis Poland, Hungary and the CSFR suggests if problems cannot successfully be solved even in Europe, they will be impossible to solve on a global scale.

The PR of China used to be considered in some parts of the Third World as a distinct model of a socialist economy. As long as China's poor economic record is not fully recognized worldwide and the socialist system there is not changing China may still sustain some hopes in the Third World about a revival of socialism. The Chinese regime will try hard to maintain its power, not least because they are afraid of Yugoslavian-type or USSR-like disintegration in the context of economic and political reform. A similar reasoning could explain continuing socialist policies in some developing countries. As long as there is no successful example of a rapid systemic transformation in Eastern Europe, regimes in the Third World are not actively encouraged to envisage systemic transformation, and opposition parties are naturally weakened by the systematic warning of chaos and stagnation in the course of transformation.

A useful way to encourage the shift to a market system could be to provide regional "institutional anchors" for countries with a firm desire to switch to a market-based development strategy. Successful regional integration schemes such as ASEAN, the North American Free Trade Agreement and the EC are the most promising candidates for such a role; both by accepting additional members and by setting an encouraging example they stimulate common attempts for adopting market allocation and international policy coordination. Only with regional economic integration could one expect a strengthening of regional economic relationships in the form of trade, international investment and regional institution-building. Since economic analysis shows that countries with mutually strong economic links tend to be less inclined to engage in military conflicts it is precisely a more strongly rooted regional economic integration that could reduce tensions in the Third World. Africa is foremost of regions needing to develop positive examples of regional integration.

3.2 New Global Security Structures

The traditional Western structures of military security are not automatically strengthened by the collapse of the Warsaw Treaty Organization and the USSR. NATO was a major and somehow successful pillar of peace in Europe in the four decades after 1945. Regional defense treaties under the lead of the U.S. reinforced the role of America in maintaining world peace (except for the Vietnam War). The threat of communism often helped to encourage host governments in the Third World to seek military cooperation with the U.S. or France and the

U.K. Consequently, with the collapse of communism in Eastern Europe the global defence positions of the three leading Western allies have to be reorganized in accordance with new incentive structures. Economic policy will become more important than traditional military policies. The role of foreign economic policies and multilateral organizations will increase. The international economic position of countries will in many cases become decisive.

In Europe the CSCE has advanced to a forum in which the West and Eastern Europe can meet. 48 countries attended the Prague conference of January 1992 to strengthen the role of the CSCE in resolving conflicts (e.g. by sending a fact-finding mission to the Nagorno-Karabakh enclave in the ex-USSR). The participants of the Prague conference agreed to strengthen its Conflict Prevention Center in Vienna: more rapports missions to international hot points will be sent. The U.S., the U.K. and France are reluctant to accept a greater role of the CSCE in conflict resolution since they consider this as a natural realm of UN activities. Germany launched the idea of "green helmets" which would represent a kind of international environmental defence force.

CSCE rules were changed at the Prague conference by declaring that "gross and uncorrected violations of CSCE commitments" could allow a majority vote of the CSCE to decide upon appropriate actions - even without the consent of the country concerned. This means some weakening of the principle of unanimous decision-making that long characterized the CSCE. Until the Prague conference the strict principle of unanimous decision-making and the great number of actors made the CSCE an organization that could act only in slow motion.

While all major economic powers - except for Japan and China - are members of the CSCE, the UN security council whose role increased after the Gulf War does not include Germany and Japan. Attempts to add these industrial market economies would raise a host of time-consuming problems since countries which are not much less significant (or anticipate to not be so) in terms of GNP than the U.K. or France will raise claims for a permanent seat in the UN security council, too. Brazil, India, Pakistan and Nigeria as well as the Ukraine and some other countries might present such an argument. Hence the inclusion of Germany and Japan into the Council could lead to an increased weight of the developing countries; this may be desirable if they were to increase per capita income considerably and could thus really assume a stronger responsibility for global affairs. The game of power in the Council would thereby become both more complex and more influenced by North-South conflicts. A possible solution for the dilemma might be to include the EC and Japan as permanent council members, where these members would each get four votes and the EC would be represented by Germany, France, the U.K. and one alternating other EC member.

A New Role for NATO

There is presently still a major role for NATO in military security, but one might consider other fields and new policy options, too. NATO could form special units for telecommunications, construction and environmental management which would finally result in commercial spin-offs that offer attractive civilian employment for skilled military personnel facing a high risk of unemployment. These special units could launch joint operations with similar special units from the CIS and help to dramatically improve the infrastructure of Eastern Europe via multilateral projects. This would be much needed to stimulate private enterprise activities. It would demonstrate the advantages of modern market economies in the form of tangible individual benefits ("a telephone for everybody"). Joint brigades of NATO, Polish military and CIS military could be active in international construction projects that would improve transportation in Europe. These projects could be organized on a transitional basis. The know-how and organizational skills of certain military brigades could thereby be directly employed in the nurturing of private industry in central Europe, while indirectly preparing conversion of at least some military capabilities. U.S. and West European private business interests are likely to strongly oppose such ideas. However, the backlog in infrastructure quality and quantity in Eastern Europe is so enormous and the need to refocus skilled military personnel so urgent that one might consider the proposed solution in at least some fields. Moreover, the challenges in Eastern Europe are absolutely unique and although free enterprise could be the long term system desired in parts of Eastern Europe, non-market forces could well play a very positive role in supporting the transformation process. Such a strategy is not without risk since it might result in considerable sustaining state enterprise activities or interventionism. The risk of economic Nirvana approaches is not necessarily smaller.

3.3 Proliferation Problems and the Need for a New Schuman Plan

After World War II a clear-cut international system emerged in which the U.S. and its allies opposed the USSR and its allies; the nonaligned movement defined itself as standing outside the two camps. NATO and the WTO were the pillars of defence and deterrence in the industrialized world.

Developing countries which took a clear position on either side of the two alliances typically could hope for financial, political and military support. Some countries like India, Pakistan, Brazil, Argentina, Israel and several Arab countries plus Iran as well as China pursued their own military and industrial policies, where one emphasis typically was on achieving the status of a nuclear military power.[11] If the U.S. and the CIS really follow the envisaged course of sharply reducing their nuclear arsenals two major problems will emerge: (a) the reduction of nuclear arsenals could create power imbalances between the U.S. and CIS, thereby directly contributing in a paradoxical way to less security in a world of superpower disarmament; (b) reduced nuclear military potentials in the U.S. and the ex-USSR encourage other countries - in particular in the Third World - to build up and expand atomic military capabilities. This is the case because it seems to reinforce regional military threat potentials in a period of missing hegemonic global regimes and because skilled military experts from the superpowers will become more easily available when these powers cut their nuclear programs and offer restricted career opportunities at home. In the USSR about 100,000 people were employed in the military's nuclear programs and about 3000 are believed to be top experts of classified materials. This creates new sources for nuclear proliferation.

Small economic reform steps as well as administrative restrictions to labor mobility cannot be expected to reduce this proliferation risk. Indeed only new comprehensive high-technology projects could provide an industrial nucleus that could be attractive enough to keep engineers and physicists in the country, while at the same time contributing to rising factor productivity and economic growth in the former USSR. While the pure textbook wisdom of Western economists would call for free enterprise and market coordination in Eastern Europe as the adequate strategy of transition, the above mentioned political considerations could support the case for a specific kind of industrial policy in which the former military industrial complex would be gradually turned into competitive private firms. These could be active in technologically dynamic areas such as telecommunications, computer engineering, aircraft industries and software development. With regard to the latter, rising car and railway traffic which needs computerized traffic management is indeed one challenge towards which the intellectual capabilities of missile programmers can be converted. A new innovation policy with a strong emphasis on commercial projects might well refocus part of the former military innovation capabilities of Eastern Europe and actually improve the traditionally weak innovation performance of countries in the ex-CMEA area.[12]

Russia as well as the Ukraine are countries big enough to have competing private providers of telecommunications. Part of the technological military establishment could be encouraged to sign up for newly formed companies launched with the help of the state in an initial period. To establish two or three firms that would become competitive suppliers of civilian aircraft would also provide a focal point for the otherwise "foot-loose" technological intelligence of the

---

[11] On the proliferation problem see DUNN, L.A. (1992), Containing Nuclear Proliferation, IISS Adelphi Papers, Washington D.C.

[12] See on the weak innovation performance of socialist systems BALCEROWICZ, L. and WELFENS, P.J.J., eds. (1988).

military. Setting up several competing high-speed train companies would be another possible field in which activities would also contribute to the much required improvements of the physical infrastructure in Europe; a basis for this which would include technology sharing could be a joint (or better several joint) French-German-Polish-Ukrainian-Russian railway company. Here we have the advantage of still existing public ownership in railway systems in Western Europe, namely that political interests of EC countries can more easily be translated into joint international business activities in Eastern Europe. A joint trans-European chip industry could also be launched with government funds from the EC and East European economies in order to promote technological progress and to establish joint control of a crucial field of dual use technology. In a transitory period of a decade or so these activities could be embedded in public works schemes that could help to reduce unemployment in the former USSR and to prevent economic and political chaos. The basic idea here is to both absorb former military personnel and to contribute to the establishment of new markets and enterprises in Eastern Europe. The Schuman plan of the 1950s which linked Germany and France in a jointly organized coal and steel industry in Western Europe after World War II needs a modern analogy in Eastern Europe.

Investment into functional market economies might have a decent pay-off if one takes into account the costs of economic instability and lack of prosperity - or the hope for achieving it. Subsidizing the creation of positive international economic interdependency in the form of increasing trade and investment links would indirectly amount to a subsidization of disarmament. [13] The peace dividend from the East European changes will not come by itself. It takes time and long term action by many actors in economic policy, industry and the military establishments to organize controlled dynamics towards a less conflict-prone global society.

---

[13] This is in the spirit of a proposal of FREY, B.S. (1974), Subventionierung der Abrüstung: Ein unorthodoxer Vorschlag zur Friedensforschung, Annuaire Suisse de Science Politique, Vol. 14, 57-68.

References:

BALCEROWICZ, L. and WELFENS, P.J.J., eds. (1988), Innovationsdynamik im Systemvergleich. Theorie und Praxis unternehmerischer, gesamtwirtschaftlicher und politischer Neuerung, Heidelberg: Physica/Springer.

BECKER, G.S. (1957), The Economics of Discrimination, Chicago: University of Chicago Press.

BRETON, A. (1964), The Economics of Nationalism, Journal of Political Economy, Vol. 72, 376-386.

BRIEFS, G.E. (1950), Shifting Patterns in Eastern Europe's Foreign Trade 1928-1948, Diss. PH.D.Econ, Harvard University, Cambridge: Mass.

BRITO, D.L. und INTRILIGATOR, M.D. (1981), Strategic Arms Limitations Treaties and Innovations in Weapon Technology, Public Choice, Vol. 3, 41-59.

BROZKA, M. (1986), Arms Production in the Third World, London: Taylor.

BURNETT, W.B. und SCHERER, F.M. (1990), The Weapons Industry, in: ADAMS, WALTER, Ed., The Structure of American Industry, 8th ed., London: Macmillan, 289-317.

BYERS, J.D. und PEEL, D. (1989), The Determinants of Arms Expenditures of NATO and the Warsaw Pact: Some Further Evidence, Journal of Peace Research, 26 (1989), 69-77.

CHECINSKI, M. (1989), The Legacy of the Soviet War-Economy and Implications for Gorbachev's Perestroika, The Journal of Soviet Military Studies, Vol. 2, 206-240.

CHECINSKI, M. (1991), The Conversion of the Soviet Arms Industry: Plans, Reality and Prospects, Osteuropa-Wirtschaft, Vol. 36, 15-34.

COLLINS, S.M. and RODRIK, D. (1991), Eastern Europe and the Soviet Union in the World Economy, Washington D.C.: Institute for International Economics.

COUNCIL OF ECONOMIC ADVISERS (1991), Economic Report of the President 1991, Washington D.C.

DEGER, S. und SMITH, R. (1990), Military Expenditure: The Political Economy of National Security, Oxford: Oxford University Press.

DEUTSCHE BANK (1991), The Peace Dividend - How to Pin it Down?, Frankfurt/M.

DUMAS, L.J. (1979), Armament, Disarmament and National Security: A Theoretical Duopoly Model of the Arms Race, Journal of Economic Studies, Vol. 6, 1-38.

DUNN, L.A. (1992), Containing Nuclear Proliferation, IISS Adelphi Papers, Washington D.C.

FREY, B.S. (1974), Subventionierung der Abrüstung: Ein unorthodoxer Vorschlag zur Friedensforschung, Annuaire Suisse de Science Politique, Vol. 14, 57-68.

GORDON, S., McFADDEN, D., Ed.(1984), Economic Conversion, Cambridge.

HEWITT, D.P. (1991a), Military Expenditure: International Comparisons of Trends, IMF Staff Working Paper, Washington D.C.

HEWITT, D.P. (1991b), Military Expenditure: Econometric Testing of Economic and Political Influences, IMF Staff Working Paper, Washington D.C.

HIRSHLEIFER, J. (1986), The Economic Approach to Conflict, in: RADNITZKY, G. und BERNHOLZ, P., Ed., Economic Imperialism, New York, 335-364.

ISARD, W. et al. (1989), Arms Races, Arms Control, and Conflict Analysis, Cambridge: Cambridge University Press.

JOHNSON, H.G. (1965), Nationalism in New and Developing Countries, Political Science Quarterly, Vol. 80, 169-185.

KENNEDY, G. (1975), The Economics of Defence, London: Macmillan.

KRELLE, W. (1989), The Future of the World Economy, Heidelberg and New York: Springer.

LEVY, J.S. (1985), Theories of General War, World Politics, Vol. 37, 344-371

LINDERT, P.H. (1986), International Economics, 8th ed., Homewood, Ill.: Irwin.

McMILLAN, J. (1986), Game Theory in International Economics, Chur: Harwood.

McGUIRE, M.C. (1977), A Quantitative Study of the Strategic Arms Race in the Missile Age, Review of Economics and Statistics, Vol. 59, 328-339.

PAUKERT, L. und RICHARD, P. (1991), Defence Expenditure, Industrial Conversion and Local Employment, Geneva: ILO.

POLACHEK, S.W. (1980), Conflict and Trade, Journal of Conflict Resolution, Vol. 24, 55-78.

RICHARDSON, L.F. (1960), Arms and Insecurity, Chicago: University of Chicago Press.

ROMER, P. (1990), Are Nonconvexities Important for Understanding Growth?, American Economic Review, Vol. 80, P&P, 97-103.

SAY, J.-B. (1834), Catechisme d'économie politique, Paris: Arnaud.

SCHELLING, T.C. (1966), Arms and Influence, New Haven: Yale University Press.

SCHMIDT, C., ed. (1987), The Economics of Military Expenditures: Military Expenditures, Economic Growth and Fluctuations, Hampshire: McMillan.

SIMAAN, M. und CRUZ, J.B., Jr. (1975), Formulation of Richardson's Model of the Arms Race from a Differential Game Viewpoint, Review of Economic Studies, Vol. 42, 67-77.

SIPRI (1988, 1991), SIPRI Yearbook 1988, Oxford: Oxford University Press.

SIVARD, R.L. (1988, 1989), World Military and Social Expenditures, 12th ed., 13th ed., Washington, D.C.: World Priorities.

SMITH, M.R., ed. (1985), Military Enterprise and Technological Change, Cambridge, Ma.: MIT Press.

STEINBERG, D. (1990), Trends in Soviet Military Expenditure, Soviet Studies, Vol. 42, 675-699.

THEE, M., ed. (1981), Armaments, Arms Control and Disarmament, Paris: Unesco.

UN Development Programme (1992), Human Development Report 1992, Oxford: Oxford University Press.

WEBER, E. (1971), Stadien der Außenhandelsverflechtung Ostmittel- und Südosteuropas, Stuttgart: Fischer.

WELFENS, P.J.J. (1989a), The Economics of Military and Peacekeeping: An Emerging Field, Jahrbuch für Sozialwissenschaft, Vol. 40, 358-385.

--- (1989b), Globalization of Markets and Regional Integration, Intereconomics, 1989/12, 273-281.

--- (1991), European Monetary Integration, New York: Springer, 2nd ed. forthcoming.

--- (1992a), Economic Aspects of German Unification, Heidelberg and New York.

WORLD BANK (1991), World Development Report 1991, New York.

WORLD BANK (1992), Free Trade Agreements with the US: What's in it for Latin America?, Washington D.C.

List of Tables, Figures, and Exhibits

TABLES

FIGURES

EXHIBITS

INDEX

Printing: Druckhaus Beltz, Hemsbach
Binding: Buchbinderei Kränkl, Heppenheim

M. W. Klein, Tufts University, Medford, MA; **P. J. J. Welfens,** The John Hopkins University, Washington, DC (Eds.)

Multinationals in the New Europe and Global Trade

1992. XV, 281 pp. 24 figs. 75 tabs. ISBN 3-540-54634-0

The emergence of an integrated European market will provide new opportunities and new challenges to firms operating in the international arena. This volume addresses some timely issues concerning the „new" European market, with a focus on the multinational corporation and foreign direct investment.

The topics addressed in this volume include the multinational corporation and global trade, exchange rate passthrough and the international pattern of production, the macroeconomic determinants of foreign direct investment, the interrelationship between technology and multinationals, foreign direct investment in Eastern Europe, foreign direct investment in Germany, European integration and multinational activity in the European Community, and the behavior of Japanese multinationals in Europe and in the United States.

P. J. J. Welfens, University of Münster

Economic Aspects of German Unification

National and International Perspectives

1992. XI, 402 pp. 19 figs. 67 tabs. ISBN 3-540-55006-2

German unification is changing central Europe, the EC and international economic and political relations. The merger of the two Germanies raises many new questions for Germany itself, Europe, and the whole international community. Will the enlarged Germany become a new economic giant in Europe and can the FRG maintain stability and prosperity? What macroeconomic and structural problems are faced by the new Germany and what are the effects for trade, investment, and growth in Germany's partner countries? Will East Germany catch up with the West and can this process serve as a model for Eastern Europe? What are the views of Poland and the USSR, and what implications arise for Western Europe and the United States? Finally, how is the triangular relationship between the USA, the EC, and Japan affected, and how does this affect the United States' ability to organize economic cooperation with Japan, Germany, and other leading economies?

P. J. J. Welfens, University of Duisburg and The Johns Hopkins University, Washington, D.C. (Ed.)

European Monetary Integration

From German Dominance to an EC Central Bank?

1991. XII, 260 pp. 8 figs. 7 tabs. ISBN 3-540-53790-2

Monetary integration in the EC will continue with the desired hardening of the European Monetary System that is expected to lead to an EC central bank in the 1990s. Why has the European Monetary System been so successful and what role has the Deutsche Bundesbank played in monetary policy and the EMS in Europe?

This book gives an assessment of the EMS developments, analyzes the impact of German monetary unification and shows how financial market liberalization as well as the EC 1992 project affect the process of Economic and Monetary Union.

Springer-Verlag
Berlin
Heidelberg
New York
London
Paris
Tokyo
Hong Kong
Barcelona
Budapest

W. Eucken

The Foundations of Economics

1992. VIII, 358 pp. ISBN 3-540-55189-1

Reprint of the 1st English edition published 1950 by William Hodge and Co. Ltd., London

This is the classic work of German economic literature in the past 60 years. The book was of great importance for the economic order that developed in the Federal Republic of Germany after the Second World War and made Germany the leading economic power in Europe. Walter Eucken places great emphasis on economic reality in his work. Taking everyday observations as his starting point, he attempts to infer complex connections. He provides the reader not only with a comprehensive criticism of classical economics, but also in particular with an analysis of economic systems, economic order, and the course of economic events.
As a consequence of the dramatic changes that have taken place in Eastern Europe, many states now find themselves facing problems similar to those faced by West Germany in its earliest days. Eucken's considerations can be of assistance in the search for the correct concepts.

H. Giersch, Kiel Institute of Worls Economics (Ed.)

Money, Trade and Competition

Essays in Memory of Egon Sohmen

A Publication of the Egon-Sohmen-Foundation

1992. X, 304 pp. 19 figs. 2 tabs. ISBN 3-540-55125-5

This volume examines key aspects of international economic theory and policy. It presents papers from well-known scholars discussing the following topics: historical evidence on free banking, the question whether speculation in foreign exchange markets is stabilizing or destabilizing, the insulation properties of flexible exchange rates, the economics of the Louvre Accord, some basic issues of the German Monetary Union, the merits of financial liberalization in developing countries, the integration of fiscal policy into the theory of international trade, theoretical aspects of international factor flows, the relation between trade restrictions and exchange rates, the recent shift of the United States' trade policy toward agressive unilateralism and the theory and practice of commercial policies since 1945, basic concepts of welfare economies while the other reassesses the vital link between competition and economic growth.

H. Giersch, Kiel Institute of World Economics (Ed.)

Towards a Market Economy in Central and Eastern Europe

1991. IX, 169 pp. 5 figs. 9 tabs. ISBN 3-540-53922-0

The papers in this volume deal with major aspects of the transition in the East, most notably with the causes of the collapse of the old system, the lessons to be drawn from West Germany's successful 1948 reforms and the respective roles and the appropriate timing and sequencing of privatization, macroeconomic stabilization, deregulation and external liberalization.

Springer-Verlag
Berlin
Heidelberg
New York
London
Paris
Tokyo
Hong Kong
Barcelona
Budapest